Popular Mechanics
WORKSHOP

Shelving
& Storage

Hearst Books
A Division of Sterling Publishing Co., Inc.
New York

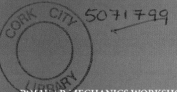
POPULAR MECHANICS WORKSHOP
SHELVING & STORAGE

Copyright © 2004 by Hearst
Communications, Inc.

Produced by Spooky Cheetah Press,
Stamford, CT
Design: Art Gecko Studios

**Library of Congress Cataloging-in-
Publication Data**
Popular mechanics workshop.
   Shelving & storage.
         p. cm.
      Includes index.
      ISBN 1-58816-386-5
      1. Cabinetwork. 2. Shelving (Furniture)
3. Storage in the home. I. Title: Shelving &
storage. II. Popular mechanics (Chicago, Ill.
: 1959)

TT197.P675 2004
684.1'6--dc22

                              2004047504

10 9 8 7 6 5 4 3 2 1

Published by Hearst Books
A Division of Sterling Publishing Co., Inc.
387 Park Avenue South, New York, NY 10016

Popular Mechanics is a trademark owned
by Hearst Magazines Property, Inc., in USA,
and Hearst Communications, Inc., in
Canada. Hearst Books is a trademark
owned by Hearst Communications, Inc.

www.popularmechanics.com

Distributed in Canada by Sterling Publishing
ᶜ/o Canadian Manda Group, One Atlantic
Avenue, Suite 105
Toronto, Ontario, Canada M6K 3E7

Distributed in Australia by Capricorn Link
(Australia) Pty. Ltd.
P.O. Box 704, Windsor, NSW 2756 Australia

Printed in China

ISBN 1-58816-386-5

Contents

Foreword

There's an old saying that a man's home is his castle. But it doesn't take long to fill every available space—right up to the tallest tower—with clothes, toys, electrical equipment, and paperwork. Well if all the "treasures" you've accumulated over the years have got your castle looking more like a dungeon, don't panic. We have just the answer. The editors at *Popular Mechanics* have searched our archives for the best projects to help you get your home in order. You'll see that solutions to your storage dilemma can come in all shapes and sizes: from a modest magazine rack to a spacious three-piece wall unit. And knowing how out of control a workshop can get, we've even included a toolbox for storing the hand tools you'll need to complete these projects. Just because your intentions are practical, doesn't mean you have to sacrifice aesthetics. The projects we've selected—including a reproduction of an antique blanket chest, a five-drawer cherry dresser, and our mahogany office set—are among the most beautiful pieces we've ever featured. Many of our designs are easily modified, so you can customize each piece to suit your individual tastes. (Don't worry, we'll tell you how.) We've given you so many solutions that all you have to do now is decide which room to tackle first—whether it's the living room, home office, or even your child's bedroom.

Joe Oldham
Editor-in-Chief
Popular Mechanics

Bedroom

 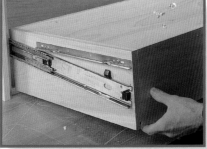 

Lincoln's Chest

First crafted by Abe Lincoln's father, this simple chest makes an appealing reproduction.

I n the early 1840s, when Abraham Lincoln was a newly married young lawyer in Springfield, Ill., his father, Thomas, occupied a farm in the east-central part of the state. It was there that a neighbor helped him cut down a large black walnut tree, saw it into boards, and stack it for seasoning. After curing the lumber, Thomas and his neighbor, Reuben Moore, used it to build two identical blanket chests, one for each of them. Thomas, who had been an outstanding furniture maker for much of his life, designed the chests, using the rich black walnut grain primarily as decoration. Each chest stood 22½ in. high, 37 in. long, and 20½ in. wide.

*Key*POINTS

TIME
Prep Time	4 hours
Shop Time	6 hours
Assembly Time	6 hours

EFFORT
Skill Level	basic

COST / BENEFITS
Expense: **low**
- The chest's elegant look belies its **simple construction.**
- These chests were some of **Thomas' last furniture projects** before his death.

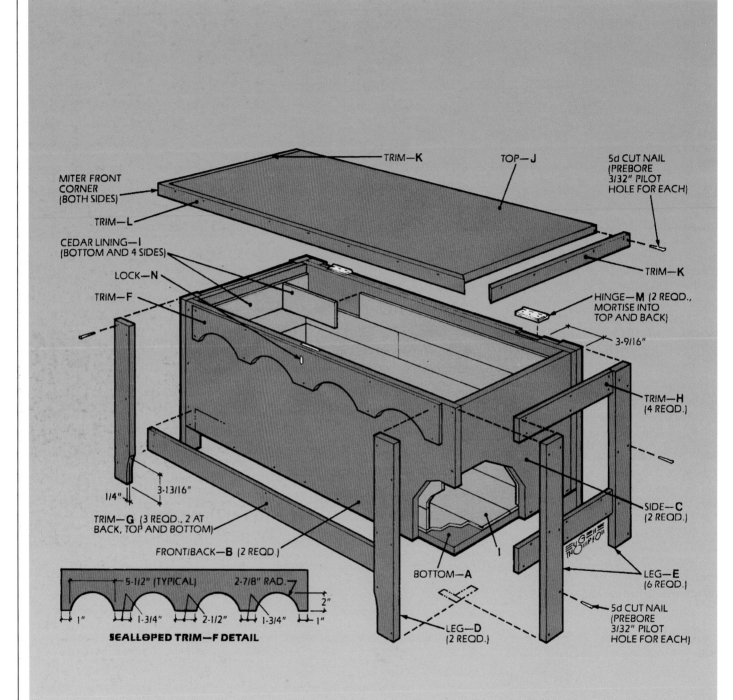

MITER FRONT
CORNER
(BOTH SIDES)

TRIM—K

TOP—J

5d CUT NAIL
(PREBORE
3/32" PILOT
HOLE FOR EACH)

TRIM—L

CEDAR LINING—I
(BOTTOM AND 4 SIDES)

TRIM—K

LOCK—N

TRIM—F

HINGE—M (2 REQD.,
MORTISE INTO
TOP AND BACK)

3-9/16"

TRIM—H
(4 REQD.)

1/4"

3-13/16"

TRIM—G (3 REQD., 2 AT
BACK, TOP AND BOTTOM)

SIDE—C
(2 REQD.)

LEG—E
(6 REQD.)

FRONT/BACK—B (2 REQD.)

BOTTOM—A

1

5d CUT NAIL
(PREBORE
3/32" PILOT
HOLE FOR EACH)

5-1/2" (TYPICAL)

2-7/8" RAD.

2"

1"   1-3/4"   2-1/2"   1-3/4"   1"

LEG—D
(2 REQD.)

SCALLOPED TRIM—F DETAIL

Thomas Lincoln's farm, 8 miles south of Charleston, Ill., is now restored as the Lincoln Log Cabin State Historical Site. One of the two surviving blanket chests is preserved at the site. PM was granted special permission to photograph and measure this easily crafted relic for reproduction.

The blanket chest looks like panel construction, but in fact, it's a simple box nailed together. There are no dovetails or other complex woodworking joints in Thomas' design. Our chest is an exact replica, except that it has been lined with aromatic cedar. It is assembled with cut nails in the manner that Thomas used. However, if you're not concerned with replication, you can avoid the exposed nail heads by simply gluing and clamping the trim and legs in place. If you use this method, mount a triangular 1 x 1-in. glue block in the lower inside corner of each leg.

The chest is built of American black walnut. It pays to shop around for this beautiful but expensive wood. Using the yellow pages, we located a lumber dealer who would sell walnut, milled to $^{13}/_{16}$-in. thickness, at about one-third the usual mail-order cost. Another possible source might be local cabinetmaking shops that buy wholesale.

If you decide to line the chest with cedar, you will need 18 board feet.

Building the Chest

We had to glue up several boards to achieve the widths needed for the six sides of the box. Run the boards through a jointer to achieve flat, square edges (**Fig. 1**). Match color and graining, then edge-glue and clamp the front, bottom, back, sides, and top boards. Alternate the direction of the end growth rings of the boards. Also, alternate clamps from top to bottom, as shown in the photo, so that the glued panels stay flat. Scrape off excess glue with a chisel after it has set for about 30 minutes. When the glue has dried, surface the boards with a belt sander (**Fig. 2**).

Fig. 1 *Straighten the board edges with a jointer, then match them for a pleasing grain. Glue and clamp, alternating clamps top and bottom.*

Fig. 2 *Use a belt sander with 120-grit sandpaper to remove excess glue and level the joints. Sand the entire surface evenly to avoid low spots.*

Materials List

Key	No.	Size and description (use)
A	1	$^{13}/_{16}$ x 17 x 31$^{1}/_{8}$" walnut (bottom)
B	2	$^{13}/_{16}$ x 17$^{7}/_{8}$ x 32$^{3}/_{4}$" walnut (front and back)
C	2	$^{13}/_{16}$ x 17 x 17$^{7}/_{8}$" walnut (sides)
D	2	$^{5}/_{8}$ x 2 x 21$^{11}/_{16}$" walnut (legs)
E	6	$^{5}/_{8}$ x 2 x 21$^{11}/_{16}$" walnut (legs)
F	1	$^{1}/_{2}$ x 4$^{3}/_{4}$ x 30" walnut (scallop trim)
G	3	$^{1}/_{2}$ x 2$^{3}/_{4}$ x 30" walnut (front and back trim)
H	4	$^{1}/_{2}$ x 2$^{3}/_{4}$ x 15$^{1}/_{4}$" walnut (side trim)
I	18	$^{3}/_{8}$" tongue-and-groove cedar plank bd. ft. (lining)
J	1	$^{13}/_{16}$ x 19$^{7}/_{8}$ x 35$^{3}/_{4}$" walnut (top)
K	2	$^{5}/_{8}$ x 1$^{1}/_{2}$ x 20$^{1}/_{2}$" walnut (top side trim)
L	1	$^{5}/_{8}$ x 1$^{1}/_{2}$ x 37" walnut (top front trim)
M	2	2$^{1}/_{2}$ x 2$^{1}/_{2}$" butt hinges (with nonremovable pin)
N	1	brass chest-lid lock

Misc.: 2d, 4d, and 5d common cut nails; 120- and 220-grit sandpaper; orange shellac; boiled linseed oil; 4/0 steel wool.

Cut the back, front, ends, top, and bottom components to the proper sizes given in the materials list (**Fig. 3**). Consider graining in choosing boards. For example, use uninteresting grain or blemished boards for the back and bottom. Use the best for the top and front.

Horizontal and vertical trim strips and legs are thinner material than the boards that form the chest. If these thicknesses are not available from your wood supplier, use a planer to bring stock down to proper thickness, or have these pieces milled to thickness when you purchase the lumber. Rip to width the pieces needed for legs, top trim, and horizontal trim and cut to length.

To make the scallop design, pencil in the pattern on the horizontal trim piece according to the dimensions given in the drawing. Cut the scallop with a band saw or sabre saw, and smooth with a drum sander (**Figs. 4 and 5**). Lay a straightedge across the scallops to check for uniformity. Next, cut out the curved portions in the lower ends of the front legs. Finish sand all surfaces and edges of both chest and trim pieces, first with 120-grit and then 220-grit sandpaper. Then round over the outside corners of the trim slightly with 220-grit sandpaper.

When all the boards have been carefully cut to size, begin assembly (**Fig. 6**). Bore 3/32-in. holes for cut nails as shown in the photo. This will prevent the possibility of splitting the walnut. Then glue and nail the front to sides using 5d cut nails. Join the back in the same way. Finally, nail the bottom in place within the sides, front, and back.

Bore nail holes in trim pieces, and glue and nail each in place with 4d cut nails. Attach the legs first, then mount the horizontal trim. Miter the top trim and glue and nail it to the 13/16-in.-thick walnut top. Set nail heads flush using a nailset.

When the glue has dried, cut tongue-and-groove cedar pieces to lengths required. Line the floor and interior walls of the chest, working from the bottom up, using 2d finishing nails or cut nails (**Fig. 7**). Prebore pilot holes for cut nails.

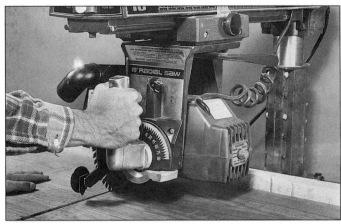

Fig. 3 *Cut the front, back, sides, bottom, and top boards to the widths and lengths in the materials list using a radial-arm or table saw.*

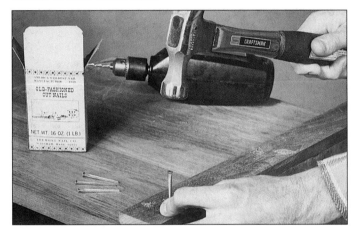

Fig. 6 *Assemble the chest with glue and 5d cut nails; attach the trim with glue and 4d cut nails. Bore 3/32-in. nail holes to avoid splitting the wood.*

SKILL*Builder*

Face It
There's an ancient ritual in woodworking called face and edge. When preparing solid lumber you first start by making one face flat across its width and straight along its length. Here's a quick guide to how it's done.

Face and edge is easily accomplished by pushing the piece over the face of a jointer. It can be done with more sweat by rough planing the piece with a scrub plane and jack plane and then putting the finishing touches on it using a fore or try plane. The result is the same either way.

Next, square one edge to the freshly planed face. The edge must be square and straight along the entire length. To do this on a jointer, run the freshly planed face against the fence, and run the edge you want to square against the cutter. To do this with a hand plane, press a square against the freshly planed face and sight down the edge, then plane off the high spots or anything that is out of square. This should bring the piece to the desired thickness and width.

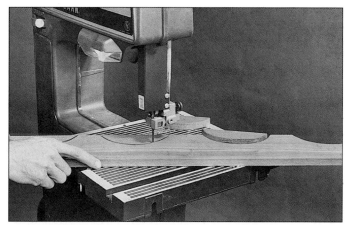

Fig. 4 *Lay out the scallop pattern for the front horizontal trim as shown in the drawing. Cut with a band saw or sabre saw.*

Fig. 5 *Sand the scallop with a 3-in. drum sander installed in a drill press. Use a straightedge to check for uniform valleys in the scallops.*

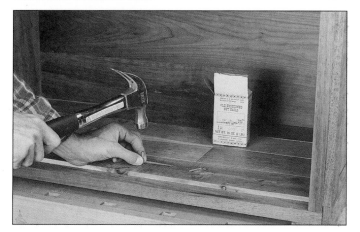

Fig. 7 *Line the interior with tongue-and-groove aromatic cedar, working from the bottom. Use either 2d cut nails or 2d finishing nails.*

Fig. 8 *Mark the locations for the brass butt hinges in both the chest top and the upper back edge. Cut mortises for the hinges using a ¾-in. chisel.*

Carefully measure and mark the locations for the hinges on the top and the upper edge of the back, and use a chisel to mortise to the proper depth (**Fig. 8**). Next, locate and mark the position of the lid lock and catch. Mortise out to proper depth, and bore the keyhole. Do not apply hardware until after finish has been applied.

Finishing

Begin the finishing process by using a diluted walnut stain just to blend in any white sapwood streaks that may be present. Then, using 4/0 steel wool, rub in a boiled linseed oil finish to bring out the rich color typical of walnut (**Fig. 9**). We used three coats, allowing a day between coats for the linseed oil to dry. Then we rubbed on a thoroughly mixed polishing solution of orange shellac lubricated with 10 percent linseed oil. Use 4/0 steel wool and apply the polishing solution with long, even strokes to level out rough spots.

Fig. 9 *Use three coats of linseed oil applied with 4/0 steel wool. Then rub on several coats of shellac mixed with 10 percent linseed oil.*

Cherry Jubilee

This classic five-drawer dresser is as handsome as it is handy.

It seems that these days when you have a storage problem, the solution is usually found in a bigger hard drive or maybe even a new CD burner. Our personal space has come to be defined in megabytes—and when we run short, simply grabbing a nearby empty shoebox is no longer an option. This isn't the case with the more tangible features in our lives. Things can and do get left piled on the sofa or stuffed into an already crowded closet. Our solution doesn't require a plug to play, is guaranteed to work 50 years from now—and is fully compatible with anything you'd care to stow away. It's a classic five-drawer cherry dresser.

*Key*POINTS

TIME
Prep Time .... **8 hours**
Shop Time .... **10 hours**
Assembly Time .... **18 hours**

EFFORT
Skill Level .... **intermediate**

COST / BENEFITS
Expense: **expensive**
• **Traditional design** means this piece will work perfectly in the bedroom, living room, or hallway.

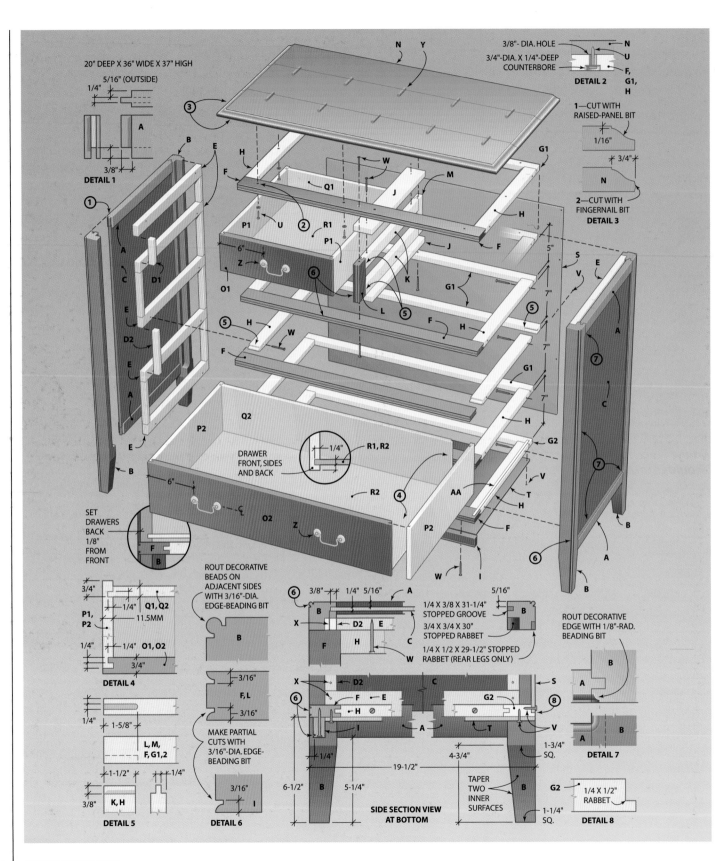

20" DEEP X 36" WIDE X 37" HIGH

5/16" (OUTSIDE)
1/4"
3/8"
A
DETAIL 1

3/8"- DIA. HOLE
3/4"-DIA. X 1/4"-DEEP COUNTERBORE
DETAIL 2

1—CUT WITH RAISED-PANEL BIT
1/16"
3/4"
N
2—CUT WITH FINGERNAIL BIT
DETAIL 3

SET DRAWERS BACK 1/8" FROM FRONT

DRAWER FRONT, SIDES AND BACK
R1, R2

3/4"
1/4" Q1, Q2
P1, P2
11.5MM
1/4" 1/4" O1, O2
3/4"
DETAIL 4

1/4" 1-5/8"
L, M, F, G1,2
1-1/2" 1/4"
3/8" K, H
DETAIL 5

ROUT DECORATIVE BEADS ON ADJACENT SIDES WITH 3/16"-DIA. EDGE-BEADING BIT
B
3/16"
F, L
3/16"
MAKE PARTIAL CUTS WITH 3/16"-DIA. EDGE-BEADING BIT
3/16"
I
DETAIL 6

3/8" 1/4" 5/16" A
B
X D2 E
F H C
1/4 X 3/8 X 31-1/4" STOPPED GROOVE
3/4 X 3/4 X 30" STOPPED RABBET
1/4 X 1/2 X 29-1/2" STOPPED RABBET (REAR LEGS ONLY)
5/16"
B

X D2 C S
F E G2
H I
A T V
6-1/2" B
5-1/4"
1/4"
19-1/2"
4-3/4"
SIDE SECTION VIEW AT BOTTOM
TAPER TWO INNER SURFACES
B
1-3/4" SQ.
1-1/4" SQ.

ROUT DECORATIVE EDGE WITH 1/8"-RAD. BEADING BIT
B
A
DETAIL 7
A B

G2
1/4 X 1/2" RABBET
DETAIL 8

Making the End Panels

Begin construction by cutting $\frac{3}{4}$-in. cherry to length and width for the four side rails. Make the rail tenon shoulder cuts on your table saw, using a miter gauge and stop block for uniformity (**Fig. 1**). Note that the cuts are $\frac{5}{16}$ in. deep on the outside faces and $\frac{3}{16}$ in. deep on the inside faces. We used a shop-made tenoning jig that slides along the table saw fence to make the tenon cheek cuts (**Fig. 2**).

To make the legs, rip four $1\frac{3}{4}$-in.-square pieces and crosscut each to exact length. Mark the positions of the stopped rabbets and grooves on the legs. Set up your router table to

cut the $\frac{1}{4}$-in. panel groove spaced $\frac{5}{16}$ in. in from the outer faces of the legs and side rails. Then cut the grooves in the rails. To cut the stopped grooves in the legs, first mark the exact position of the bit on the router table fence. Start with the front left and rear right legs. Lower each leg onto the bit at the marked groove end and feed the work to the left to finish each cut (**Fig. 3**). To cut the opposite front right and rear left legs, feed the open top end of each leg into the bit and toward the left, lifting the legs off the bit at the groove ends.

To rout the rabbets, switch to a larger bit and, again, proceed in diagonal pairs. However, instead of pivoting the

Fig. 1 *Use a stop block clamped to an auxiliary miter gauge fence to help accurately position the tenon shoulder cuts.*

Fig. 2 *Make the tenon cheek cuts with a tenoning jig. This shop-made version of a tenoning jig slides along the table saw fence.*

Materials List

Key	No.	Size and description (use)
A	4	$\frac{3}{4}$ x 2 x $16\frac{3}{4}$" cherry (side rail)
B	4	$1\frac{3}{4}$ x $1\frac{3}{4}$ x $36\frac{1}{4}$" cherry (leg)
C	2	$\frac{1}{4}$ x $16\frac{11}{16}$ x $27\frac{11}{16}$" cherry veneer plywood (side)
D1	4	$\frac{3}{4}$ x $\frac{3}{4}$ x $3\frac{1}{2}$" poplar (spacer)
D2	12	$\frac{3}{4}$ x $\frac{3}{4}$ x $6\frac{1}{4}$" poplar (spacer)
E	10	$\frac{3}{4}$ x $1\frac{1}{2}$ x $17\frac{1}{2}$" poplar (guide)
F	5	$\frac{3}{4}$ x 2 x $31\frac{1}{2}$" cherry (front rail)
G1	4	$\frac{3}{4}$ x $1\frac{1}{4}$ x $31\frac{1}{2}$" poplar (rear rail)
G2	1	$\frac{3}{4}$ x $1\frac{1}{2}$ x $31\frac{1}{2}$" poplar (rear rail)
H	10	$\frac{3}{4}$ x $1\frac{1}{2}$ x $16\frac{3}{4}$" poplar (runner)
I	1	$\frac{3}{4}$ x $1\frac{1}{4}$ x $31\frac{1}{2}$" cherry (trim rail)
J	2	$\frac{3}{4}$ x $2\frac{1}{2}$ x 16" poplar (runner)
K	2	$\frac{3}{4}$ x $1\frac{1}{2}$ x $16\frac{3}{4}$" poplar (guide)
L	1	$\frac{3}{4}$ x 2 x 5" cherry (divider)
M	1	$\frac{3}{4}$ x $1\frac{1}{4}$ x 5" poplar (divider)
N	1	$\frac{3}{4}$ x 20 x 36" cherry (top)
O1	2	$\frac{3}{4}$ x $4\frac{7}{8}$ x $15\frac{9}{32}$" cherry (drawer front)
O2	3	$\frac{3}{4}$ x $6\frac{7}{8}$ x $31\frac{13}{32}$" cherry (drawer front)
P1	4	11.5mm x $4\frac{7}{8}$ x $18\frac{7}{8}$" Baltic Birch (drawer side)
P2	6	11.5mm x $6\frac{7}{8}$ x $18\frac{7}{8}$" Baltic Birch (drawer side)
Q1	2	11.5mm x $4\frac{7}{8}$ x $14\frac{7}{8}$" Baltic Birch (drawer back)
Q2	3	11.5mm x $6\frac{7}{8}$ x 31" Baltic Birch (drawer back)
R1*	2	$\frac{1}{4}$ x $14\frac{3}{4}$ x 18" cherry veneer plywood (bottom)
R2*	3	$\frac{1}{4}$ x 18 x $30\frac{7}{8}$" cherry veneer plywood (bottom)
S*	1	$\frac{1}{4}$ x $29\frac{1}{2}$ x $32\frac{1}{2}$" cherry veneer plywood (case back)
T*	1	$\frac{1}{4}$ x $18\frac{1}{2}$ x $31\frac{1}{2}$" cherry veneer plywood (case bottom)
U	10	1" No. 10 panhead screws and washers
V	14	$\frac{3}{4}$" No. 6 panhead screws
W	as reqd.	2" No. 8 fh wood screws
X	as reqd.	$1\frac{1}{4}$" finish nails
Y	10	$\frac{3}{8}$"-dia. x 2" dowels
Z	8	drawer pulls
AA	10	$\frac{1}{2}$" 10-mil nylon tape

Misc.: Glue; sandpaper; medium brown mahogany stain; polyurethane clear satin finish.

* One 4x8 sheet is enough for the case back, bottom, and drawer bottoms.

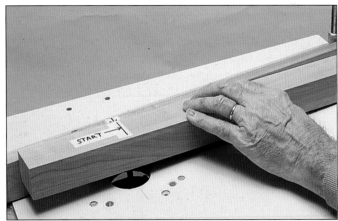

Fig. 3 *To begin a stopped groove at the blind end, lower the leg onto the bit. Then slide the work toward the left to finish the cut.*

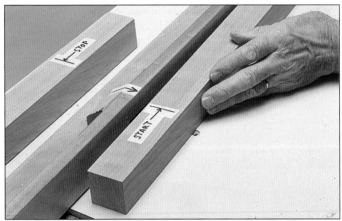

Fig. 4 *Use the same process for the stopped rabbets. An arrow marked on the table fence indicates the exact location of the cut.*

Fig. 5 *Shape the three-quarter-round corner bead by making two half-round passes from adjacent leg surfaces.*

Fig. 6 *After assembling the case ends, glue and nail the drawer guides in place. Use spacers to ensure accurate positioning.*

work down from the top, simply pivot each piece toward or away from the fence at the rabbet ends (**Fig. 4**). Use arrows on the table fence to mark the exact location of the cuts. After the main rabbets have been cut, rout the case-back rabbets in the rear legs.

Use a taper jig on the table saw or the band saw to cut the leg tapers, and smooth the sawn surfaces with a hand plane. Finish the legs by routing the corner bead. Set up an edge-beading bit in your router table so when the half-round cut is made from two adjacent faces of a leg corner, a three-quarter-round bead is produced (**Fig. 5**).

Temporarily clamp the rails and leg assemblies. Hold the parts in alignment with two ¾-in. brads at each joint, using pilot holes to prevent splitting the wood. Then rout the decorative bead around the inside edge of the frame. Finally, cut the plywood panels to size, sand, apply glue to the joints, and assemble the case ends.

Case Assembly

Cut the poplar spacers and drawer guides to size, and attach them to the end assemblies with 1¼-in. finishing nails and glue (**Fig. 6**). Then cut the drawer runners, rails, and center divider to finished size. Use a ¼-in. straight bit in the router table to cut the centered, stopped grooves in the ends of the front and rear members. Then use the table saw's miter gauge and the tenoning jig to shape the tenons in the front-to-rear members. Run the outer edges of the cherry pieces over the edge-beading bit to produce the twin half beads as shown in the drawing (**Fig. 7**). Assemble each frame with glue and clamp. When the glue has set, bore screw holes in the top frame for attaching the case top and add the holes for the small-drawer partition frame. Rout the rabbet for the case back in the bottom frame.

Use partially driven 2-in. finishing nails to temporarily secure each drawer frame to a side drawer guide. Then bore the screw holes for permanently attaching the frames. Dry

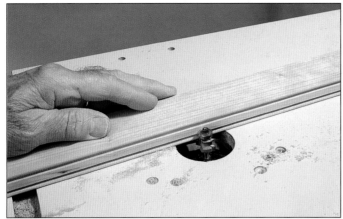

Fig. 7 *Set the height of the beading bit to cut one-half bead. Then rout the upper and lower edge of each front divider piece.*

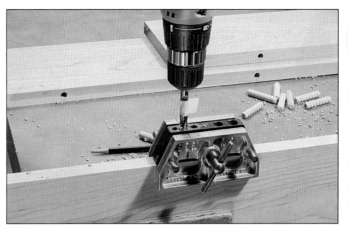

Fig. 8 *Use dowels to join the three boards that make up the top. A doweling jig ensures accurate hole alignment.*

Fig. 9 *To keep the top assembly flat, clamp waxed cauls on each face. Then apply clamps across the top to close the joints.*

Fig. 10 *When the glue is dry, use a cabinet scraper to smooth the top of the dresser. Then cut the top to exact size.*

assemble the case to check for fit. Then disassemble, apply glue, and reassemble the components. Screw the small-drawer partition frame between the two top horizontal frames and add the runners to the frame top and bottom.

Use a doweling jig to bore dowel holes for joining the case-top boards (**Fig. 8**). To ensure a flat assembly, use pairs of waxed cauls clamped across the boards. Then apply glue to the mating surfaces and clamp (**Fig. 9**).

Smooth the top with a cabinet scraper (**Fig. 10**). Then cut it to exact size and rout the top edge with an ogee raised-panel bit. Lay the top upside down and round the edge with a fingernail bit, using a straightedge to guide the router.

The Drawers

We built the drawers with a drawer lock joint (see Drawing Detail 4). After cutting the pieces to exact size, use the tenoning jig to cut the grooves in the ends of the drawer

fronts. Use the miter gauge and repeated cuts to shape the dadoes in the drawer sides, and cut the rabbets in the backs. Rout the grooves for the drawer bottoms.

To assemble the drawers, first apply glue and join a front and rear to a bottom. Then glue the sides to the front, rear, and bottom panels.

Finishing

We finished the cherry wood with a coat of medium brown mahogany stain. We added 10 percent retarder to ease brush application. Follow this with two coats of polyurethane clear satin finish.

Once the finish has dried, complete the dresser assembly. To ensure smooth operation of the drawers, simply apply a strip of self-adhesive nylon tape to each runner. Then secure the dresser top, back, and bottom panels, and install the drawer pulls.

Viewing Habits

Our modified cherry clothespress allows you to unwind by watching TV in bed.

I t's difficult to think of a home appliance that has made a bigger impact on our lives than the television. The myriad images and ideas that come through our sets may entice or irritate, but they are certainly compelling. The box itself is another story. Many people consider the tube unattractive, or, at the very least, not something they want staring back at them 24 hours a day. And while most of us may have come to grips with this Orwellian box in the family room or den, it can still seem out of place in the bedroom. In the hopes of putting a better face on your bedroom TV, we designed this traditional clothespress.

*Key*POINTS

TIME
Prep Time	16 hours
Shop Time	25 hours
Assembly Time	30 hours

EFFORT
Skill Level	intermediate

COST / BENEFITS
Expense: expensive
- Two false drawers with drop-down lids house a VCR or DVD and plenty of movies.
- The cabinet doors practically close flat so they don't obscure your view.

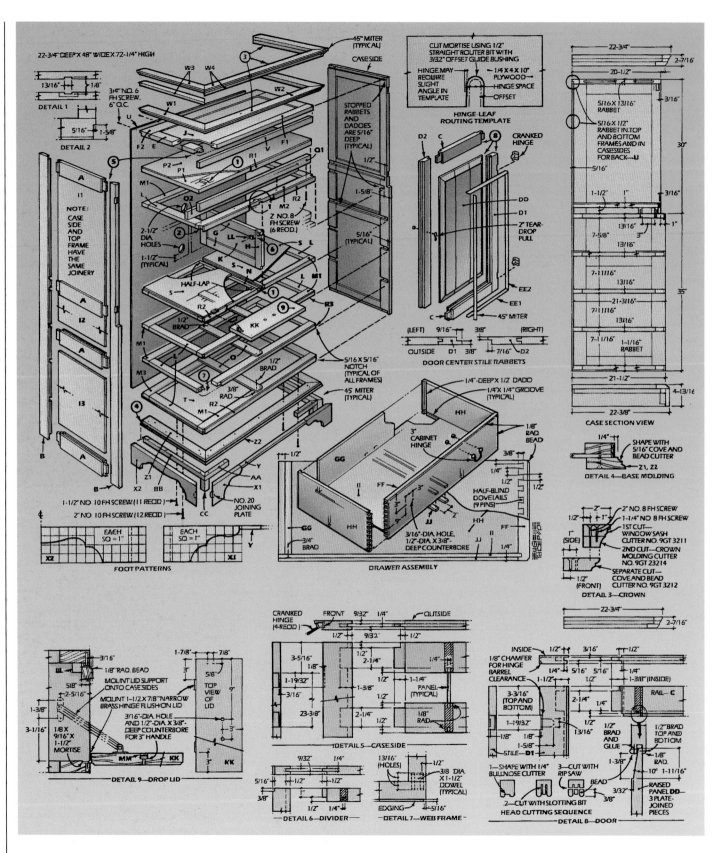

22-3/4" DEEP X 48" WIDE X 72-1/4" HIGH

45° MITER (TYPICAL)

CASE SIDE

CUT MORTISE USING 1/2" STRAIGHT ROUTER BIT WITH 3/32" OFFSET GUIDE BUSHING

HINGE MAY REQUIRE SLIGHT ANGLE IN TEMPLATE

1/4 X 4 X 10" PLYWOOD

HINGE SPACE

OFFSET

HINGE-LEAF ROUTING TEMPLATE

DETAIL 1

13/16" 1/8"

3/4" NO. 6 FH SCREW, 6" O.C.

DETAIL 2

5/16" 1-5/8"

NOTE: CASE SIDE AND TOP FRAME HAVE THE SAME JOINERY

STOPPED RABBETS AND DADOES ARE 5/16" DEEP (TYPICAL)

CRANKED HINGE

DD

D1

2" TEAR-DROP PULL

EE2

EE1

45° MITER

DOOR CENTER STILE RABBETS

OUTSIDE

1/4"-DEEP X 1/2" DADO

1/4 X 1/4" GROOVE (TYPICAL)

DRAWER ASSEMBLY

HALF-BLIND DOVETAILS (9 PINS)

3/16"-DIA. HOLE. 1/2"-DIA X 3/8"-DEEP COUNTERBORE

CASE SECTION VIEW

SHAPE WITH 5/16" COVE AND BEAD CUTTER

DETAIL 4—BASE MOLDING

DETAIL 3—CROWN

FOOT PATTERNS

EACH SQ = 1"

DETAIL 9—DROP LID

DETAIL 5—CASE SIDE

DETAIL 6—DIVIDER

DETAIL 7—WEB FRAME

DETAIL 8—DOOR

Our clothespress can accommodate a full-size TV and VCR or DVD player while still boasting plenty of room for movie storage—thanks to the two false drawers with drop-down lids. Plus, the unit has three spacious drawers for clothes or linens. And we used special cranked hinges that swing 250° instead of the usual 180°, so the doors can open almost flat against the cabinet sides, giving you an unobstructed view of the TV from just about every spot in your bedroom.

The joinery techniques required for this piece run the gamut from mortise-and-tenons, to dowels and plate joints, to traditional dovetails and dadoes. So you'll have a chance to hone a number of different skills before you apply the finish.

Just a word of caution before you begin: This piece was dimensioned to hold the basic 20-in. television. But no matter which brand or model TV you have, be sure to measure it before you start building—and, if necessary, alter our dimensions to suit your particular needs.

Case Construction

Start by cutting the stock to size for the door, side and top rails, and stiles. Note that one door stile is slightly wider than the others to allow for a rear overlap where the two doors meet. Use a dado blade in a table saw to cut the panel grooves in the rails and stiles (**Fig. 1**). Be sure to fabricate the door and case members separately, because the grooves in the case members are centered while those in the door members are off center and of a different dimension. However, since the

Materials List

Key	No.	Size and description (use)
A	8	$^{13}/_{16}$ x $3^{1}/_{4}$ x $17^{1}/_{2}$" cherry (rail)
B	4	$^{13}/_{16}$ x $3^{1}/_{4}$ x 65" cherry (stile)
C	4	$^{13}/_{16}$ x $3^{1}/_{4}$ x $18^{1}/_{2}$" cherry (rail)
D1	3	$^{13}/_{16}$ x $3^{1}/_{4}$ x $29^{3}/_{4}$" cherry (stile)
D2	1	$^{13}/_{16}$ x $3^{5}/_{8}$ x $29^{3}/_{4}$" cherry (stile)
E	2	$^{13}/_{16}$ x $3^{1}/_{4}$ x $17^{1}/_{2}$" cherry (rail)
F1	1	$^{13}/_{16}$ x $2^{1}/_{4}$ x $43^{3}/_{4}$" cherry (stile)
F2	1	$^{13}/_{16}$ x $3^{1}/_{4}$ x $43^{3}/_{4}$" cherry (stile)
G	2	$^{13}/_{16}$ x $1^{1}/_{2}$ x $18^{1}/_{4}$" cherry (rail)
H	2	$^{13}/_{16}$ x 2 x $7^{7}/_{8}$" cherry (stile)
I1	2	$^{1}/_{4}$ x 16 x $24^{1}/_{2}$" cherry plywood (panel)
I2	2	$^{1}/_{4}$ x $9^{1}/_{2}$ x 16" cherry plywood (panel)
I3	2	$^{1}/_{4}$ x 16 x 21" cherry plywood (panel)
J	1	$^{1}/_{4}$ x 16 x $38^{1}/_{4}$" cherry plywood (panel)
K	1	$^{1}/_{4}$ x $5^{7}/_{8}$ x $18^{1}/_{4}$" cherry plywood (panel)
L	10	$^{13}/_{16}$ x 2 x $16^{7}/_{8}$" maple (rail)
M1	8	$^{13}/_{16}$ x 2 x $43^{3}/_{4}$" maple (stile)
M2	1	$^{13}/_{16}$ x 2 x $43^{3}/_{4}$" cherry (stile)
M3	1	$^{13}/_{16}$ x $2^{5}/_{16}$ x $43^{3}/_{4}$" maple (stile)
N	1	$^{13}/_{16}$ x 2 x $20^{7}/_{8}$" maple (crossmember)
O	3	$^{1}/_{4}$ x $1^{1}/_{4}$ x $20^{1}/_{2}$" maple (guide)
P1	1	$^{3}/_{4}$ x $19^{3}/_{4}$ x $43^{3}/_{4}$" fir plywood (shelf)
P2	1	$^{1}/_{4}$ x $19^{3}/_{4}$ x $43^{3}/_{4}$" cherry plywood (veneer)
Q1	1	$^{13}/_{16}$ x $1^{1}/_{2}$ x $43^{1}/_{8}$" cherry (support)
Q2	1	$^{13}/_{16}$ x $1^{1}/_{2}$ x $43^{1}/_{8}$" maple (support)
R1	1	$^{5}/_{16}$ x 1 x $43^{1}/_{8}$" cherry (edge band)
R2	3	$^{5}/_{16}$ x $1^{1}/_{16}$ x $43^{1}/_{8}$" cherry (edge band)
R3	2	$^{5}/_{16}$ x $^{13}/_{16}$ x $43^{1}/_{8}$" cherry (edge band)
S	2	$^{1}/_{4}$ x $20^{7}/_{8}$ x $21^{1}/_{8}$" cherry plywood (platform)
T	1	$^{1}/_{4}$ x $21^{1}/_{4}$ x $43^{1}/_{8}$" plywood (panel)
U	1	$^{1}/_{4}$ x 44 x 64" cherry plywood (back)
V	1	$^{13}/_{16}$ x $1^{1}/_{2}$ x $43^{1}/_{8}$" cherry (rail)
W1	2	$^{13}/_{16}$ x $2^{3}/_{4}$ x $22^{1}/_{8}$" cherry (molding)
W2	1	$^{13}/_{16}$ x $2^{3}/_{4}$ x $46^{1}/_{2}$" cherry (molding)
W3	4	$^{13}/_{16}$ x $2^{3}/_{4}$ x $22^{3}/_{4}$" cherry (molding)
W4	2	$^{13}/_{16}$ x $2^{3}/_{4}$ x 48" cherry (molding)
X1	2	$^{13}/_{16}$ x 4 x $8^{3}/_{4}$" cherry (foot)
X2	2	$^{13}/_{16}$ x 4 x $22^{3}/_{8}$" cherry (foot)
Y	1	$^{5}/_{16}$ x $^{13}/_{16}$ x 29" cherry (filler strip)
Z1	2	$^{13}/_{16}$ x 3 x $22^{3}/_{8}$" cherry (molding)
Z2	1	$^{13}/_{16}$ x 3 x $46^{1}/_{2}$" cherry (molding)
AA	2	$1^{1}/_{8}$ x $1^{1}/_{8}$ x $8^{1}/_{2}$" maple (cleat)
BB	2	$1^{1}/_{8}$ x $1^{1}/_{8}$ x $21^{1}/_{4}$" maple (cleat)
CC	2	$1^{1}/_{2}$ x $1^{1}/_{2}$ x $2^{1}/_{2}$" maple (corner block)
DD	2	$^{5}/_{8}$ x $16^{11}/_{16}$ x $24^{3}/_{16}$" cherry (panel)
EE1	4	$^{1}/_{4}$ x $^{3}/_{8}$ x $16^{5}/_{16}$" cherry (bead)
EE2	4	$^{1}/_{4}$ x $^{3}/_{8}$ x $23^{3}/_{4}$" cherry (bead)
FF	3	$^{13}/_{16}$ x $7^{1}/_{2}$ x 43" cherry (drawer front)
GG	3	$^{1}/_{2}$ x 7 x $42^{1}/_{2}$" poplar (drawer back)
HH	6	$^{1}/_{2}$ x $7^{1}/_{2}$ x $20^{1}/_{2}$" poplar (drawer side)
II	3	$^{1}/_{4}$ x $20^{3}/_{8}$ x $42^{1}/_{2}$" lauan plywood (drawer bottom)
JJ	6	$^{1}/_{4}$ x $^{13}/_{16}$ x $20^{1}/_{4}$" maple (guide)
KK	2	$^{13}/_{16}$ x 7 x $21^{1}/_{16}$" cherry (drop-down front)
LL	2	$^{3}/_{8}$ x $^{5}/_{8}$ x $^{5}/_{8}$" cherry (stop)
MM	4	$^{1}/_{8}$ x $^{1}/_{2}$"-dia. cherry (plug)

Misc.: $1^{1}/_{4}$" No. 8 fh screws; 2" No. 8 fh screws; $1^{1}/_{2}$" No. 10 fh screws; 2" No. 10 fh screws; $^{3}/_{4}$" No. 6 fh screws; $^{1}/_{2}$" brads; $^{3}/_{4}$" brads; No. 20 joining plates; two $5^{1}/_{4}$" lid supports; eight 3" cabinet handles; two 2" teardrop pulls; four $1^{1}/_{2}$ x $^{7}/_{8}$" brass hinges; four cranked hinges; 120- and 220-grit sandpaper; glue; stain; sanding sealer; polyurethane.

Fig. 1 *Cut the stock to size. Then cut panel grooves in the cabinet and door rails and stiles using a dado blade in the table saw.*

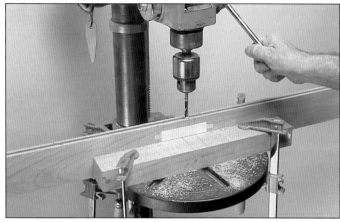

Fig. 2 *Cut joint mortises in the stiles by boring overlapping holes on the drill press. Marked tape on the surface guides spacing.*

Fig. 3 *Clean out all mortises with sharp chisels. Make sure that the mortise walls are pared smooth and square to the edge.*

Fig. 4 *Cut the rail tenons using a dado blade on the table saw. A wood fence and a stop block on the miter gauge ensure identical repeat cuts.*

Fig. 5 *This close-up shows the configuration of the joint. A haunch on the tenon is required to fill the gap in the groove above the mortise.*

TECH *Tips*

Don't Get Burned

Cherry is more prone to burning when you run it through the table saw than just about any other hardwood. When cutting cherry stock, avoid feeding the wood too slowly and never stop in the middle of a cut. Choose your stock carefully since warped wood can cause burning by pushing itself into the blade. If you do encounter some burning, it's a good bet that the problem lies with your setup. Make sure your blades are sharp and that the blade is square to the fence.

top frame members are grooved the same as the side frames, cut these grooves with the same dado setup. You should be aware that our plans show ¼-in.-wide grooves used to seat the plywood panels in the case sides and top frame. Hardwood plywood commonly measures slightly less than ¼ in. thick, so check the thickness of your plywood and size the grooves accordingly.

After the grooves are cut, lay the door rails and stiles facedown on the table saw and cut a ¼-in.-wide setback on the face of the grooved edges. This allows space for the bead molding that will be applied later.

Next, mark the mortise locations on the stiles and use a drill press to bore overlapping holes to remove most of the mortise waste (**Fig. 2**). Then follow up with a sharp chisel to square the corners and smooth the walls (**Fig. 3**).

To cut the tenons, adjust the dado blade to make equal depth cuts on both faces of the side frame rails. Be sure to clamp a stop block on the miter gauge fence to ensure identical repetitive cuts (**Fig. 4**) and to form a haunch on all the tenons to fill the groove holes (**Fig. 5**). Readjust the cutter height, as required, to make the tenon cuts on the ends of the door-frame rails.

Temporarily dry assemble the case side frames and use a ⅛-in.-rad. rounding-over bit to ease the corners that will be visible (**Fig. 6**). Also, hand sand the groove edges with a felt-lined sanding block. Disassemble the frame, and then cut a rabbet in the rear stiles to recess the back panel. Cut the 1-in. setback for the doors in the front stiles.

Next, cut the plywood insert panels to size and sand the faces. Dry assemble the frames again to check the fit of the panels (**Fig. 7**). When satisfied, use hide glue and clamps to assemble the side frame parts. Then make a simple jig to guide your router and cut the stopped dadoes and rabbets in the case sides (**Fig. 8**). A stop block nailed at one end of the jig will control the router's travel. Square the ends of the dadoes with a chisel.

Now, fabricate the maple frames inside the cabinet. Begin by cutting the stock to size, and use a doweling jig to bore the holes for the dowel pins (**Fig. 9**). Note that the VCR-compartment frame receives a half-lapped crossmember that supports a vertical dividing panel. When all the parts are cut, glue and clamp them together. Check each assembly for square, then set them aside to dry. After the glue is set on the VCR shelf, cut a groove in the crossmember—and a dado in the frame parts above—for the compartment divider panel. Assemble the frame and panel that form the top of the case and the TV support slab.

Then dry assemble all the crossframes with one case side lying on the bench. Add the other side and check everything for fit. When satisfied, cut the plywood back panel to size and temporarily tack nail it in place. Then measure the length of the cherry edge banding at each crossframe location. (In theory, they should all be identical, but discrepancies do creep

Fig. 6 *Temporarily dry assemble the side frame, making sure the parts are square. Then round over the inside edges with a router and an ⅛-in.-rad. bit.*

Fig. 7 *Assemble the frame and panels using slow-setting hide glue. Add the second stile only after all other parts are joined.*

Fig. 8 *Cut the shelf dadoes using a router and simple jig made of scrap lumber. A block at the end of the jig stops router travel.*

in, so it's best to measure and cut each to fit its space.) Disassemble the case. Glue and clamp the strips in place on the frames and the TV slab.

Case assembly is best handled in two stages. You'll need eight bar or pipe clamps, two 7-ft. cauls and four more cauls that are about 1 ft. longer than the width of your workbench. Begin by laying one side of the case on your bench. Apply hide glue to all the rabbets and dadoes, then coat the mating edges of the crossframes with hide glue too. Slide all the frames into position and lift the second case side into place. Do not glue the second side to the frames. Install the cauls and clamps, check for square and let the glue dry (**Fig. 10**). When the glue has set, invert the assembly and apply glue to all the joints on the second side, then reinstall the clamps.

Cut the parts for the VCR-compartment divider to size and assemble them. Then slide the assembly into place and secure it with glue and screws. Also, at this time, add the horizontal rails that help to stiffen the TV shelf, and tack nail the back panel in place so you can bore pilot holes for the screws used to attach it permanently. Bore these holes at 6-in. intervals around the perimeter and into each crossframe. Then remove the back, countersink these screw holes, apply glue, and attach the back with the case lying flat down on your workbench.

Case Doors and Drawers

Cut three pieces of stock—slightly oversize—for the door panels, and mark the correct planing direction (with the grain) on each board. Then, using a plate joiner, cut the joining slots—three per edge—in all the mating boards. When this is done, glue and clamp the boards together, keeping all the grain lines pointing in the same direction (**Fig. 11**). Once the glue is dry, use a sharp hand plane to reduce the thickness of the panels to approximately ⅝-in. (**Fig. 12**).

Dry assemble the door-frame members and measure the space between the grooves to establish the size for the door

Fig. 9 *Lay out the dowel locations in the support frame members, then bore dowel holes using a portable drill and a doweling jig.*

Fig. 10 *Glue and clamp the case together. Clamps can bear directly on the case or be attached to cauls and the workbench as shown.*

Fig. 11 *Use plates or dowels to join the stock for the door panels. Place the plates or dowels clear of the area that will be beveled.*

Fig. 12 *Apply glue to the slots, plates, and mating edges, then clamp. When dry, smooth the panel surface with a hand plane.*

panel. Reduce the height dimension by ¹⁄₁₆ in. and the width by about ¼ in. to allow for expansion. Cut the panel to size, then set up a high auxiliary wood fence on your saw's rip fence. Tilt the blade to 10° for making the bevel cuts that create the raised-panel effect (**Fig. 13**). Also use an elevated featherboard to steady the panel. Be sure to make the crossgrain cuts first to prevent tearing out the wood fibers at the panel corners.

The next step is to cut the bead molding that surrounds the door panels. Use a ¼-in. bullnose bit in a table-mounted router. First, make a pass on the edge of both board surfaces. Then use a ¹⁄₁₆-in. slotting bit to extend the width of the bead (**Fig. 14**). Rip the finished ⁵⁄₁₆-in.-wide beads on the table saw and miter their ends to fit the door frames.

Use a 20-gauge brad with a clipped-off head to bore pilot holes in the bead molding. Then install the bead, while the door is still dry assembled, with a slight amount of glue and some ½-in. 20-gauge brads. Do not apply glue to the mitered ends of the bead molding because the frame members must still be taken apart. We didn't bother to countersink the brad heads. A 20-gauge brad is so fine that once the piece is stained and finished, the brad heads are nearly invisible. You should be careful, however, not to nick or dent the molding when hammering the brads flush.

Disassemble, finish sand, and wipe off the dust from all the door parts. Then apply glue to a stile and two rails. Insert the panel and add the second stile (**Fig. 15**), being careful to avoid getting glue on the panel. It must be allowed to float so it can expand. You can, however, drive a small brad near the edge of the upper and lower rails. Locate the brad in the center of the length of the rail. With the panel thus fastened, its expansion will be equalized on both sides of the brad.

Clamp the parts together and then dry install the cranked hinges. To do this, it's necessary to cut mortises on the edge of the rear of each door. Use a simple plywood template and a router with a guide bushing to make these cuts (**Fig. 16**). Note

SKILL*Builder*

Rails 'n' Stiles
Rails and stiles are the backbone of many projects that involve a frame. Regardless of which you're making first (rail or stile) the process begins with a straightedge. Here is a condensed version of rail and stile process principles.

First use a hand plane, power jointer, or stationary jointer to produce a straight edge on a length of lumber. (There are ways to do this with a table saw and even a circular saw, but we'll keep this tutorial brief.)

With a reliable straightedge, rip the rail and stile stock to width, but keep all the pieces slightly wider than they need to be. The straight edge is the one that is run against the table saw fence, and the fence is set far enough from the blade so that there is sufficient stock to plane off.

Assuming you have produced several overwidth strips, feed them a minimum of two at a time through the planer so that you're left with multiple pieces of identical width and parallel edges. (This is a somewhat oversimplified discussion, of course. Sometimes it's better to crosscut the workpieces to finished length and feed them all through the planer, standing on edge, all batched together. Other times you may have to pass a single piece over the jointer to remove a defect that ripping put into it.)

No matter how you process the rails and stiles, the last pass for all the pieces is through the planer. That way all like pieces will be an identical width.

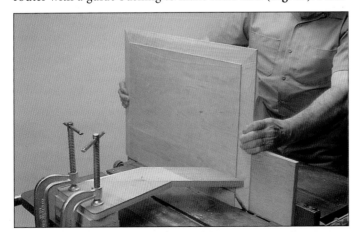

Fig. 13 *Cut the panel bevels on a table saw using a high auxiliary fence and an elevated featherboard as safety precautions.*

Fig. 14 *Cut the bead molding on the router table with two different bits—a bullnose bit first, followed by a slotting bit.*

29

Fig. 15 *Attach the bead to the frame members, then glue and clamp the frame together. Do not glue the panel into the groove—it should float.*

Fig. 16 *Cut the hinge mortises using a router with a guide bushing and two scrap wood jigs—one for the door surface, one for the door edge.*

Fig. 17 *Cut the drawer stock to size then lay out and cut dovetails using a router and a jig. Code mating pieces to avoid mismatches.*

Fig. 18 *Cut the crown with the molding head in the table saw. Use a featherboard and pushstick to keep stock firmly against the fence.*

Safety Sense

FEATHERBOARD, NOT FEATHER HEAD
Building our clothespress requires using your table saw to cut a cove—a change of pace from the ripping and crosscutting for which the saw is most often used.

A disposable workshop safety aid that you shouldn't be without for this type of cutting is a featherboard (also known as a fingerboard), which is simply a board with a row of saw kerfs cut into it. The space between kerfs should be so narrow that the remaining strip of wood is like a feather. When fashioning a board, make the feathers long enough so that they bend easily.

To hold stock securely during a tricky operation, clamp the featherboard so that the workpiece being cut must bend the individual feathers as it passes between the featherboard and the fence. The pressure this exerts holds the workpiece safely in position as it passes over the saw blade, preventing kickback.

that the long leaf on the cranked hinge we used was slightly angled relative to the barrel. This didn't affect its performance, but did require a matching angle in the template cutout. Be sure to check the hinges you buy—before you make the mortises—and follow suit if necessary. And always make test cuts in scrap before cutting the finished mortise on the doors.

To make the drawers, first cut the stock to size, then set up a router dovetail template and cut the half-blind dovetails in the drawer sides and front (**Fig. 17**). Follow these by cutting dadoes in the side members for the backboards and by cutting the grooves for the bottom panel in the sides and front boards. Next, shape the bead around the front with a router, bore the holes for the handle hardware, and sand the inside surface of all parts. Assemble the pieces with glue and clamps, check for square and set aside to dry. Complete the drawers by attaching the guide strips to the bottom panels.

Case Moldings

The crown molding is fabricated from three narrow boards shaped on a table saw fitted with a molding cutter. To build it, glue together the top and middle strips with a ⅜-in. offset. Then attach an auxiliary wood fence to the rip fence on your table saw. This will allow you to adjust the fence properly when making the cove cut. You should also use a raised featherboard to keep the work on a true course (**Fig. 18**).

Cut the first profile with the window-sash cutter, then switch to the cove cutter. Adjust the fence and cut the second shape. The bottom member is shaped with a cove-and-bead cutter, then is glued and screwed to the top assembly. To obtain smooth, non-forced molding cuts, make several incremental passes. Don't try to cut the whole profile in one pass. Miter the corners (**Fig. 19**) and attach the crown to the case top with screws and glue.

Cut the stock for the case feet to size and miter the ends. Then cut the curved profiles on a band or scroll saw. Lay out

the miter faces to receive a single joining plate and cut the slot using a plate joiner. If you don't have a plate joiner, just use a spline set into a saw kerf groove.

Cut the backing cleats for the feet to size and attach them to the case with glue and screws. Then attach the feet, beginning with the front ones. When both front feet are installed, apply glue to the side feet, miter joints, and the plate slots, then insert the joining plates and slide the feet in place (**Fig. 20**). Clamp to the cleats until dry.

Finish the outside of the cabinet and each drawer face. We applied a coat of Behlen's Virginia Cherry Master-Gel Stain, followed with three coats of Minwax Semi-Gloss Polyurethane. We finished the drawers, except for the outside of the fronts, with a single coat of sanding sealer.

SKILL*Builder*

Mortise Know How
Our project calls for producing a mortise that is made by straightening the edges and ends of a row of holes. This is not difficult to do, but you can run into trouble if you use a narrow chisel or rush the process.

In all cases in which you use a chisel to finish a process begun with a machine, use the widest chisel possible. For this project, you may find that it's easier to grip the chisel like a dagger and push it downward by leaning on it with your shoulder. Or you may prefer to tap it into the mortise with a mallet.

Fig. 19 *Join the crown molding parts with glue and screws. Then support the back side of the assembly with scrap block and cut the miters.*

Fig. 20 *Cut the case feet to shape and join them to the mounting cleat. Then glue and screw them to the bottom, using the joining plate to reinforce the corner.*

Field of Dreams

A platform bed that's much more than just a place for your child to sleep.

Beds are for sleeping, right? Well, not if you're a kid. If you're a kid, bed is the place to read, dream, plot, and scheme—or just while away a rainy afternoon. It's gossip central after school is out and the intensive care unit during a bout with the flu. It's the place to return to when the day is done—and, sometimes, it's just the best place to be alone.

Now that you know it's special, your job is to build a bed that's up to snuff. Our design takes care of all the basics, with a little extra just for fun. It's made of plywood and poplar, and we've designed it to be assembled without a cabinet shop full of clamps.

*Key*POINTS

TIME
Prep Time	6 hours
Shop Time	8 hours
Assembly Time	12 hours

EFFORT
Skill Level	intermediate

COST / BENEFITS
Expense: **moderate**
- With ample storage space underneath, **this bed does double duty.**
- Your child will have **easy access** to the items he or she uses the most.

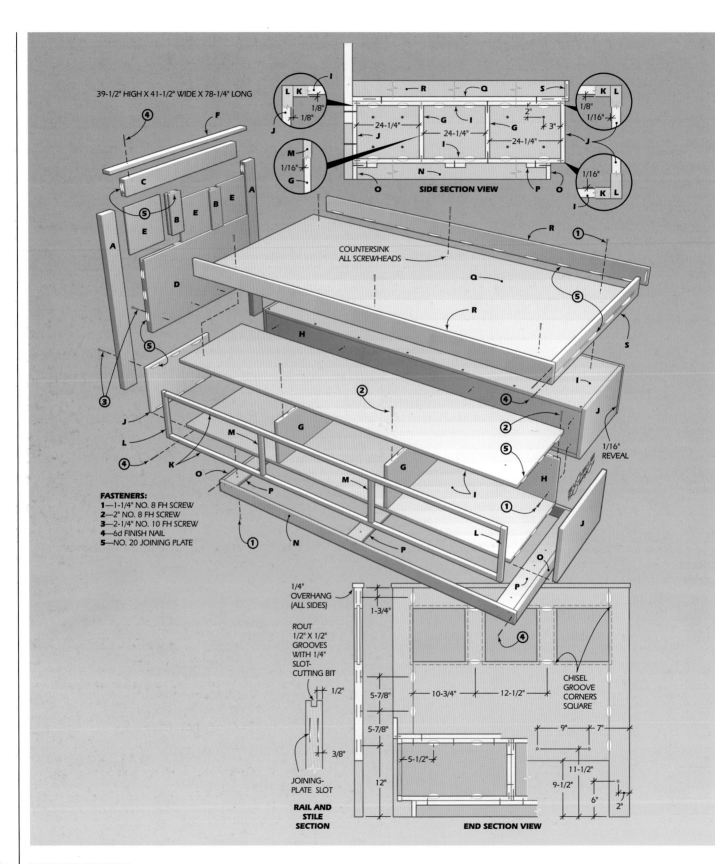

39-1/2" HIGH X 41-1/2" WIDE X 78-1/4" LONG

SIDE SECTION VIEW

1/8"
1/8"
1/8"
1/16"
1/16"

24-1/4"
24-1/4"
24-1/4"
2"
3"

COUNTERSINK
ALL SCREWHEADS

1/16"
REVEAL

FASTENERS:
1—1-1/4" NO. 8 FH SCREW
2—2" NO. 8 FH SCREW
3—2-1/4" NO. 10 FH SCREW
4—6d FINISH NAIL
5—NO. 20 JOINING PLATE

1/4"
OVERHANG
(ALL SIDES)

ROUT
1/2" X 1/2"
GROOVES
WITH 1/4"
SLOT-
CUTTING BIT

1/2"

3/8"

JOINING-
PLATE SLOT

**RAIL AND
STILE
SECTION**

1-3/4"

5-7/8"

5-7/8"

12"

5-1/2"

10-3/4"
12-1/2"

CHISEL
GROOVE
CORNERS
SQUARE

9"
7"

11-1/2"

9-1/2"
6"
2"

END SECTION VIEW

This unique platform bed has ample storage for all the things that occupy kids' time while they're awake. There's enough space for a pile of games, books, clothes—and even the family cat. To give the bed the right look, we've incorporated a strong but simple visual theme that matches the rest of our bedroom suite.

Building the Headboard

First, cut 1½ x 3½-in. poplar to length for the headboard stiles, mullions, and top rail. To make accurate cuts with a circular saw, use a Speed Square to guide the cut (**Fig. 1**). Position the square the appropriate distance from the cutline based on your saw's base plate. Then clamp the square in place.

Prepare the stock for the wide bottom rail by crosscutting the available widths a few inches longer than finished size. Apply glue to the mating edges of each piece and use clamps to pull the joints tight. Add clamps across the thickness of the assembly at each seam to keep the boards aligned (**Fig. 2**).

After about 20 minutes, scrape off any glue that has squeezed out, and let the glue set for at least 1 hour before removing the clamps. Cut the glued-up panel to finished length using a straightedge guide clamped across the work to guide your circular saw.

Mark the locations of joining plate slots for the headboard joints. Note that these joints are formed by a double row of plates. Using a flat table as the registration surface, hold both the joiner and workpiece against the table and cut the slots nearest one face (**Fig. 3**). Then flip each piece over to cut the remaining slots.

Fig. 1 ***Crosscut the 1½-in.-thick poplar headboard pieces to length. A square clamped to the work helps guide the cut.***

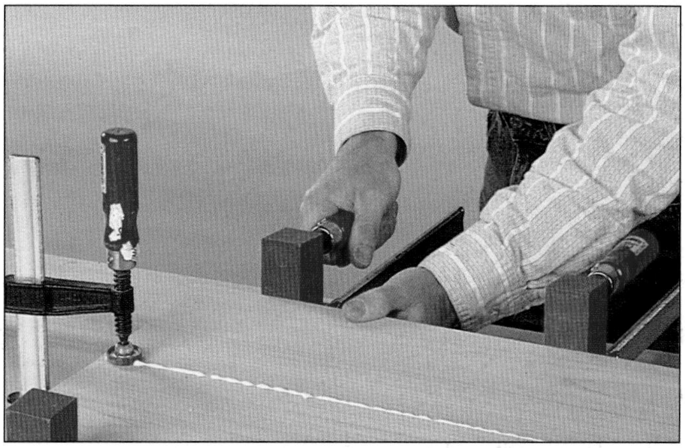

Fig. 2 ***Apply glue to the wide headboard rail pieces and clamp. Use clamps at the ends to help keep the faces aligned.***

Materials List

Key	No.	Size and description (use)
A	2	1½ x 3½ x 38¾" poplar (stile)
B	2	1½ x 3½ x 9" poplar (mullion)
C	1	1½ x 3½ x 34" poplar (rail)
D*	1	1½ x 16¾ x 34" poplar (rail)
E	3	½ x 10 x 10" plywood (panel)
F	1	¾ x 2 x 41½" poplar (cap)
G	4	¾ x 9 x 18¼" plywood (divider)
H	2	¾ x 9 x 74¼" plywood (back)
I	4	¾ x 19 x 74¼" plywood (top/bottom)
J	4	¾ x 10½ x 19" plywood (end)
K	4	¾ x ⅞ x 74 1/16" poplar (facing)
L	4	¾ x ⅞ x 10 9/16" poplar (facing)
M	4	¾ x ⅞ x 8 13/16" poplar (facing)
N	2	¾ x 2¾ x 73¼" plywood (toe kick face)
O	2	¾ x 2¾ x 33" plywood (toe kick end)
P	3	¾ x 3½ x 33" plywood (cleat)
Q	1	¾ x 39½ x 75¾" plywood (platform)
R	2	¾ x 3½ x 76½" poplar (platform edge)
S	1	¾ x 3½ x 39½" poplar (platform end)

Misc.: No. 20 joining plates; 2¼" No. 10 fh wood screws; 2" No. 8 fh wood screws; 1¼" No. 8 fh wood screws; 6d finish nails; glue; sandpaper; latex primer and enamel.

Note: All plywood birch veneer.

* Laminate from narrower stock.

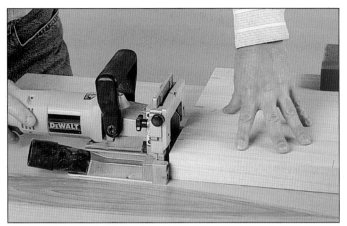

Fig. 3 *To cut the double plate slots, use a flat surface to register the slots on one side. Then flip the work over for the remaining slots.*

Fig. 4 *Dry assemble the headboard with plates and install clamps. Rout the panel grooves with a piloted slotting bit.*

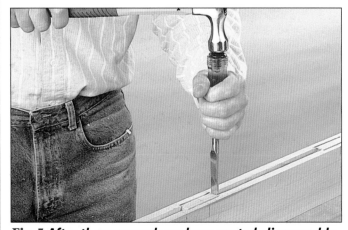

Fig. 5 *After the grooves have been routed, disassemble the headboard and use a sharp chisel to square the rounded ends.*

To cut the headboard panel grooves, first dry assemble the headboard with joining plates and use clamps to hold the joints tight. Next, install a ¼-in. piloted slotting cutter in your router with the pilot bearing mounted on the top of the bit arbor. Then rout a ¼-in.-wide x ½-in.-deep groove around each panel opening and ½ in. from the stock face (**Fig. 4**).

Flip the headboard over, and again run the router around each opening to finish the grooves. Before routing the actual headboard stock, make a test groove in a 1½-in.-thick block to make sure your router is set up correctly.

Disassemble the headboard parts and use a sharp chisel to square the rounded slot ends left by the router (**Fig. 5**). Cut the ½-in.-thick plywood panels to size, lightly sand them, and thoroughly dust them off.

Spread glue in the headboard joint slots and on all joining plates. Insert the plates and join the mullions to the wide rail. Slide the panels in place (**Fig. 6**) and install the top rail. Position the stiles and clamp the assembly. Compare opposite diagonal measurements to check that the assembly is square. If the measurements are different, adjust the clamps until they're the same.

Cut a piece of ¾-in.-thick poplar to size for the headboard cap. Secure the cap to the top of the headboard using glue and nails (**Fig. 7**). Set the nail heads below the surface and fill the holes with wood filler. Sand the entire headboard with 120-, 150-, and 180-grit sandpaper, dusting off the assembly thoroughly between grits. Carefully ease all sharp edges when you sand.

Storage Boxes
The main support for the platform bed is provided by two back-to-back storage box units. Use your circular saw guided by a straightedge to cut the plywood parts for these boxes (**Fig. 8**). Using a fine-tooth blade in your circular saw will minimize tearout.

Fig. 6 *Slide the panels into place, and join the top rail to the mullions. Finish the assembly by joining the stiles to the rail ends.*

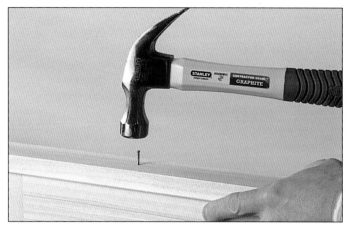

Fig. 7 *Use glue and finish nails to attach the ¾-in.-thick poplar cap to the headboard. Set the nails and fill the nail holes.*

Mark the locations of joining plate slots in the box parts and use your plate joiner to cut the slots. Clamp guides and fences to the panels and worktable to help register the plate joiner when making these cuts (**Fig. 9**). When you cut the slots in the end of a panel, you can use your worktable as the registration surface (**Fig. 10**).

To minimize the need for clamps, some of the plate joints in the bed are used only to align the joint, and screws are used in place of glue. Use dry plates to assemble the partitions, back panels, and top and bottom panels (**Fig. 11**). Then install screws to hold the parts together (**Fig. 12**).

Spread glue in the plate slots and on the joining plates for the end pieces. Position the ends and use 6d finish nails to hold the joints tight (**Fig. 13**). Rip strips of ¾-in. poplar to a width of ⅞ in. for the facing. Cut the pieces to length using a miter box and backsaw.

Apply the facing to the outside edges of the boxes (**Fig. 14**) as shown in the drawing. Pay careful attention to the overhang of each facing strip. Set and fill the nail heads.

Toe Kick and Platform

Cut the parts to size for the toe kick base. Apply glue to the joints and then use clamps to hold the pieces while you nail them together (**Fig. 15**). Secure the cleats with glue and finishing nails.

Cut the platform and poplar edges and end to size. Then cut the joining plate slots for fastening the 3½-in.-high edges and end to the plywood, apply glue to the joints, and assemble the pieces (**Fig. 16**). Use 6d finish nails to hold the joints tight.

Assembly

Start assembling the bed by joining the two storage box units back-to-back. Use clamps to hold the units together while you bore pilot holes and drive screws through the back of one unit into the back of the other.

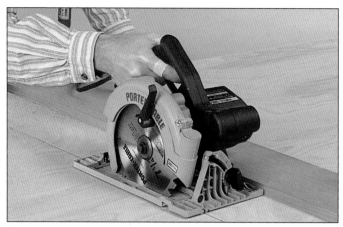

Fig. 8 *To cut the plywood storage box pieces, guide your circular saw with a straightedge clamped to the workpiece.*

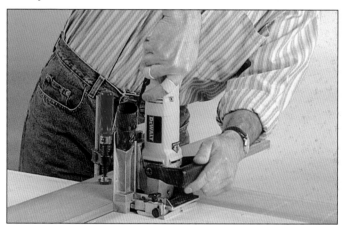

Fig. 9 *Clamp a guide across the top and bottom panels of the storage boxes to help locate the plate joiner when cutting the slots.*

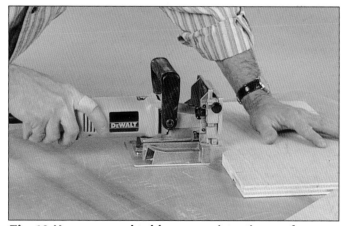

Fig. 10 *Use your worktable as a registration surface when cutting the slots in the ends of the storage box partition panels.*

Fig. 11 *Install the plates and position the partitions followed by the back panels. Finally, place the top panel in position.*

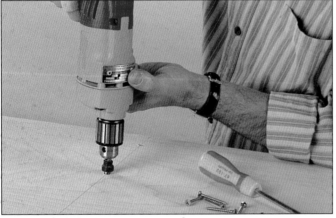

Fig. 12 *With all parts aligned, bore screw holes through the top and secure the panel. Turn the assembly over and fasten the bottom.*

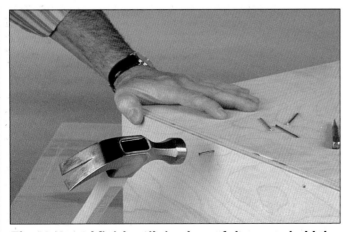

Fig. 13 *Use 6d finish nails in place of clamps to hold the ends tightly in place while the glue on the joining plates sets.*

Turn the box assembly upside down and position the toe kick base so there is a uniform setback on both sides and at the foot of the bed. Fasten the toe kick by screwing through the cleats into the bottom of the box (**Fig. 17**).

Place the panel assembly right side up, position the headboard, and temporarily clamp it in place. Bore and countersink pilot holes and screw the headboard to the end of the base assembly (**Fig. 18**).

Position the platform over the storage boxes, with its open end against the headboard. Bore and countersink pilot holes, then fasten the platform with screws (**Fig. 19**).

Inspect the bed and fill any remaining nail holes with wood filler. Sand all bed parts, finishing with 180-grit sandpaper, and dusting off between grits.

After a final sanding of the bare surfaces, completely dust the bed with a tack cloth. Apply a good quality latex primer to all exposed surfaces. When the primer is dry, lightly sand the bed with 180-grit paper to remove any imperfections. Clean the bed again and follow with two coats of a good latex enamel, following the manufacturer's instructions.

TECH *Tips*

Pressure Reducer
A clamp seems like such a basic tool that most beginning woodworkers hardly give it a moment's thought. That's a mistake. Beginners typically get one thing wrong when they clamp an assembly: More pressure is not better. In fact, just the opposite is true. Always apply just enough pressure to bring the parts into proper position and that's all. One way to tell whether you've got the pressure right is to look at the glue that squeezes from a joint. Assuming you have applied no more than a thin film of glue to each half of the joint, the pressure is correct when the glue that has squeezed out is a series of small round bulges. The glue line should look like it's been pinched off—which it has.

A panel consisting of edge-glued pieces will always arc upward in response to clamping pressure. You can reduce this tendency with proper clamping force, applying clamps above and below the panel. Apply additional clamping force at the ends of the panel with C clamps or similar devices.

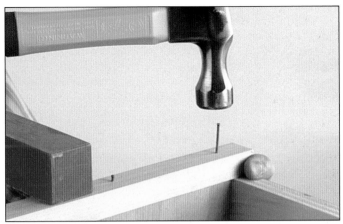

Fig. 14 *Use glue and nails to fasten the facing strips to the storage boxes. Use a clamp to hold the strips while you drive the nails.*

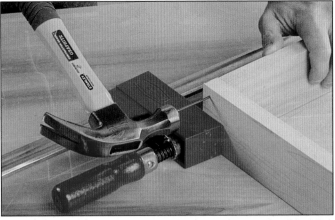

Fig. 15 *Assemble the toe kick base with glue and finish nails. Use clamps to keep the pieces from shifting as you nail.*

Fig. 16 *Join the mattress platform and edges with plates and glue. Drive nails to hold the joints tight while the glue sets.*

Fig. 17 *Turn the storage box assembly upside down and place the toe kick base over it. Secure the base to the box with screws.*

Fig. 18 *Position the headboard and clamp it in place. Bore and countersink pilot holes and screw the headboard to the storage box.*

Fig. 19 *Place the platform assembly on the storage unit and tight against the headboard. Secure the platform with screws.*

Clean Room

Keep everything in your child's room in its right place with this attractive storage shelf.

This storage shelf is designed to be as versatile as possible. In other words, it holds just about anything that is likely to end up scattered all over the floor in your child's room. Its tall spaces are the perfect home for oversize children's books, school notebooks, stacks of games, or stuffed animals. The smaller spaces are proportioned for tapes, CDs, art supplies, and all the odds and ends that inevitably clutter a child's room. The shelf is just the right height for a lamp, radio, and alarm clock, making it ideal for use as a nightstand. And the best part is that you can complete this easy-to-build piece over a long weekend.

*Key*POINTS

TIME
Prep Time	3 hours
Shop Time	6 hours
Assembly Time	8 hours

EFFORT
Skill Level	basic

COST / BENEFITS
Expense: **moderate**

- This versatile shelf functions as **a storage unit and a nightstand.**
- **Tall spaces** hold oversize books, games, and stuffed animals.

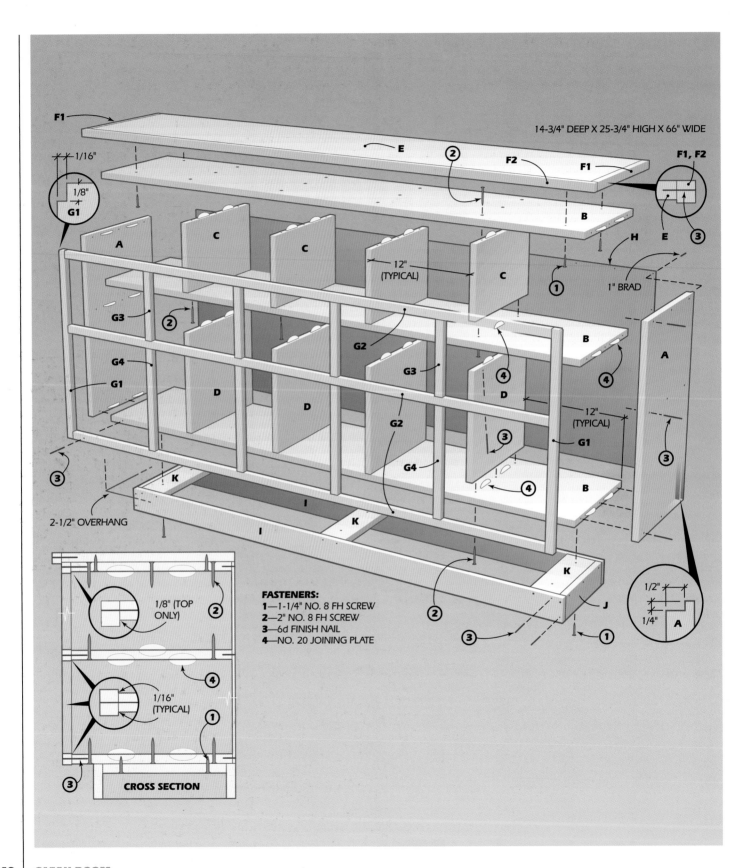

14-3/4" DEEP X 25-3/4" HIGH X 66" WIDE

F1

1/16"

1/8"

G1

F1, F2

E

F2

F1

B

E

3

H

A

C

C

12"
(TYPICAL)

C

1

1" BRAD

B

G3

2

G2

B

G4

G3

4

4

A

G1

D

D

G2

D

3

12"
(TYPICAL)

3

3

G2

G4

4

B

G1

3

K

1/2"

1/4"

A

I

K

2-1/2" OVERHANG

I

K

J

2

3

1

1/8" (TOP
ONLY)

2

FASTENERS:
1—1-1/4" NO. 8 FH SCREW
2—2" NO. 8 FH SCREW
3—6d FINISH NAIL
4—NO. 20 JOINING PLATE

4

1/16"
(TYPICAL)

1

3

CROSS SECTION

The construction of this piece employs the same materials as your child's bed—birch plywood and solid poplar. The assembly techniques rely on a combination of plate joints, screws, and finish nails to draw shelf parts tightly together, so you won't need a bunch of expensive clamps.

Making the Case Parts

Use a circular saw and 40-tooth thin-kerf, crosscut blade to cut the plywood case parts to size. When plywood is cut, there is a tendency for the face veneer to chip where the blade exits the cut. Prevent this chipping by using two techniques. First, clamp a straight board across the panel stock to guide the saw. Next, advance the saw slowly and keep the saw base tight to the guide strip (**Fig. 1**).

Set up the router with a straight bit and an accessory edge guide. Adjust the router to cut the rabbet at the back edge of the case sides. Test the setup on a piece of scrap stock. Then clamp a case side to the workbench and cut the rabbet (**Fig. 2**). If you use a router bit with a ½-in.-dia. shank, you can make the cut in one pass. If you are using a bit with a ¼-in.-dia. shank, you should take two passes to cut the rabbet.

Mark the locations of plate joint slots in the cabinet sides, shelves, and partitions. Note that the middle shelf has staggered slots on the top and bottom surfaces. It's important to stagger the slots to prevent too much wood from being removed in one location. Clamp a guide block to the case sides and shelves to help locate the plate joiner when cutting the slots in the center of a panel (**Fig. 3**). When you cut the slots in the sides for the case top and bottom, you can use the fence on the plate joiner to register the cuts (**Fig. 4**).

Use the workbench top as the registration surface when you cut the slots in the ends of the shelves and partitions. Firmly hold both the plate joiner and the workpiece to the benchtop when making the cuts. Keep your fingers well away from the cutting area to avoid accidents. Countersink pilot holes through the top, bottom, and middle shelves.

Fig. 1 *Clamp a straightedge across the workpiece and crosscut it with a circular saw. Support the piece that will be cut off.*

Fig. 2 *Use a straight bit in the router and the edge guide attachment to cut a rabbet along the back edge of the side panels.*

Materials List

Key	No.	Size and description (use)
A	2	³/₄ x 13¼ x 22¼" plywood (side)
B	3	³/₄ x 13 x 63" plywood (shelf, top, bottom)
C	4	³/₄ x 8 x 13" plywood (partition)
D	4	³/₄ x 12 x 13" plywood (partition)
E	1	³/₄ x 14 x 64½" plywood (top)
F1	2	³/₄ x ⁷/₈ x 14" poplar (edging)
F2	1	³/₄ x ⁷/₈ x 66" poplar (edging)
G1	2	³/₄ x ⁷/₈ x 22⁵/₁₆" poplar (facing)
G2	3	³/₄ x ⁷/₈ x 62⁷/₈" poplar (facing)
G3	4	³/₄ x ⁷/₈ x 7¹³/₁₆" poplar (facing)
G4	4	³/₄ x ⁷/₈ x 11⁷/₈" poplar (facing)
H	1	¼ x 22¹/₄ x 64" plywood (back)
I	2	³/₄ x 2³/₄ x 59½" plywood (toe kick)
J	2	³/₄ x 2¼ x 10" poplar (toe kick)
K	3	³/₄ x 3½ x 10" plywood (cleat)

Misc.: No. 20 joining plates; 2" No. 8 fh wood screws; 1¼" No. 8 fh wood screws; ¾" No. 6 fh wood screws; 6d finish nails; glue; sandpaper; latex primer and enamel.

Fig. 3 *Clamp a fence across a case side and use it to guide the plate joiner when cutting the plate slots for the shelves.*

Fig. 4 *Clamp the case sides upright in a vise and cut the slots along their upper edge using the plate joiner's fence for alignment.*

Fig. 5 *The short partitions are attached to the panel above with screws, so there is no need to use glue with the joining plates.*

Case Assembly

Begin the case assembly process by joining the case top to the short partitions (**Fig. 5**). Install the joining plates in their slots and position the short partitions over them. You do not need to use glue on these plates because they merely locate the joint. Turn the assembly over, and bore pilot holes in the partitions (**Fig. 6**). Then screw the partitions to the top panel.

Spread glue in the joining plate slots for the joints between the short partitions and the middle shelf. Place the middle shelf over the short partitions, bore pilot holes into the partition ends, and fasten the shelf and partitions with screws.

Next, install joining plates in the slots for the joints between the bottom and the tall partitions. Assemble the partitions and bottom and fasten them with screws. Spread glue in the slots and on the plates for the joints between the tall partitions and the middle shelf. Install the plates, clamp the assembly together, and drive 6d finish nails through the middle shelf into the short partitions (**Fig. 7**).

Spread glue in the slots and on the joining plates for the joints between the middle shelf, top and bottom, and the case sides. Assemble the parts and drive 6d finish nails to fasten the joints.

Rip and crosscut the edge strips for the top. Apply glue to them, clamp them to the top, and nail the parts together. Apply poplar facing to the front of the sides, top, bottom, middle shelf, and partitions. Start with the case sides, then apply the facing to the horizontal parts and finally to the partitions. Note that the strips overhang the plywood panels by $1/16$ in. on each edge except for the case top, which has a $1/8$-in. overhang. Use a chisel to cut the notch at the top outside corners of the facing strips (**Fig. 8**).

Place the top panel upside down on the work surface and invert the case assembly over it. Bore pilot holes and screw the top to the assembly. Complete the case by nailing on the back.

Rip and crosscut the pieces of poplar and plywood for the toe kick assembly. Clamp the assembly together and join the parts with glue and 6d finish nails. Clamp the toe kick assembly to the bottom. Then bore and countersink pilot holes through the cleats into the bottom. Screw the cleats to the bottom.

Finishing

Set the heads of all finish nails below the surface. Fill the holes with a wood filler (**Fig. 9**). Mound the filler slightly over each hole since it shrinks when it dries. Sand the cabinet, inside and out, with 120-, 150-, and 180-grit sandpaper (**Fig. 10**). Carefully ease all sharp edges with a sanding block (**Fig. 11**). Remove all sanding dust by vacuuming and using a tack cloth before applying the primer.

Use a small-diameter paint roller to apply a coat of latex primer to all cabinet surfaces. When the primer is dry, sand it lightly with 220-grit paper. Complete the project by applying two coats of latex semigloss paint for an attractive finish.

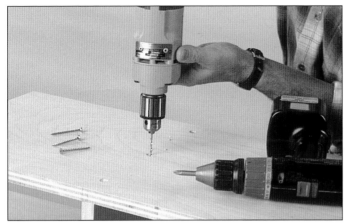

Fig. 6 *Bore and countersink pilot holes into the top of the short partitions. Then drive screws to fasten the partitions and panel.*

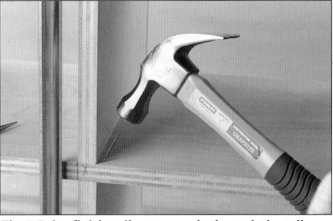

Fig. 7 *Drive finish nails at an angle through the tall partitions and the middle shelf and into the short partitions.*

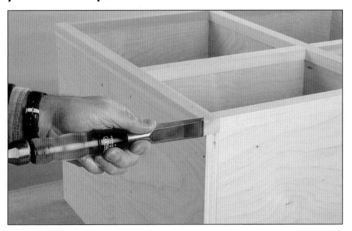

Fig. 8 *Use a chisel to cut a small clearance notch in the top outside corner of each vertical facing strip. Cut in toward the case.*

Fig. 9 *Use a putty knife to press drying filler into the nail holes. Slightly mound the filler and let it harden before sanding.*

Fig. 10 *Sand the surfaces carefully using a random-orbit block sander. This tool is small enough to fit into the compartments.*

Fig. 11 *Put a small, crisp bevel on the facing and edge strips with a sanding block that you move perpendicular to the strip's edge.*

Stay Tuned

Put the information age at your child's fingertips with our computer desk.

Kids are not known for their neat work habits—neither are many adults, for that matter. But at least with kids, there's always hope that they can learn something better. The right desk can mark the first step on the path to neatness and organization. Our design provides sufficient work surface and storage space. The desktop is large enough to accommodate a computer monitor and keyboard, and it still has room for software, papers, and books. The pedestal provides a drawer for smaller loose items, and two deep shelves can hold a small printer and other supplies. And the storage shelf has lots of space for CDs, tapes, and collectibles.

*Key*POINTS

TIME
Prep Time . . . . **6 hours**
Shop Time . . . . **14 hours**
Assembly Time . . . . **14 hours**

EFFORT
Skill Level . . . . **intermediate**

COST / BENEFITS
Expense: **moderate**
• Our design has room for a computer, printer, books—**with extra workspace to spare.**
• The desk **disassembles easily** to make moving from workshop to bedroom a snap.

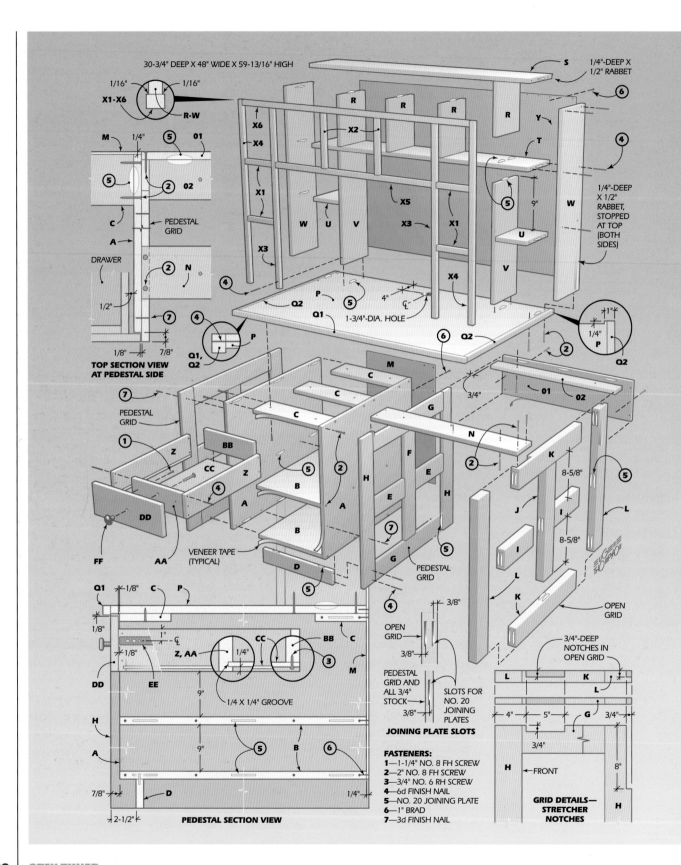

30-3/4" DEEP X 48" WIDE X 59-13/16" HIGH

1/4"-DEEP X 1/2" RABBET

1/16" 1/16"
X1-X6
R-W

1/4"-DEEP X 1/2" RABBET, STOPPED AT TOP (BOTH SIDES)

TOP SECTION VIEW AT PEDESTAL SIDE

M 1/4" 5 01
5 2 02
C
PEDESTAL GRID
A
DRAWER
2 N
1/2"
7
1/8" 7/8"

S
X6
X4
X2
X1
X3
W U V
X5
X3 X1
R R R R Y
T
W
9"
U
V
X4
P
Q2 Q1 5 4"
1-3/4"-DIA. HOLE
Q2
6
2
P
1"
1/4"
Q2

Q1, Q2

7
PEDESTAL GRID
1
Z
CC
A
DD
FF AA
VENEER TAPE (TYPICAL)
M
C C
C
B
B
D
5
5
4
BB
5
2
A
H
5
7
G
F
E
E
H
G
PEDESTAL GRID
3/4"
01 02
N
2
K
8-5/8"
J
I
8-5/8"
L
I
L
K
5
L
OPEN GRID

4
OPEN GRID
3/8"
3/8"
PEDESTAL GRID AND ALL 3/4" STOCK
3/8"
SLOTS FOR NO. 20 JOINING PLATES
JOINING PLATE SLOTS

PEDESTAL SECTION VIEW

Q1 1/8" C P
1/8"
DD
EE
1/8"
1"
CC BB
Z, AA
1/4"
3
C
M
9"
1/4 X 1/4" GROOVE
H
A
9"
5 B 6
7/8"
D
2-1/2"
1/4"

3/4"-DEEP NOTCHES IN OPEN GRID
L K
L
4" 5" G 3/4"
3/4"
H FRONT
8"
H
GRID DETAILS— STRETCHER NOTCHES

FASTENERS:
1—1-1/4" NO. 8 FH SCREW
2—2" NO. 8 FH SCREW
3—3/4" NO. 6 RH SCREW
4—6d FINISH NAIL
5—NO. 20 JOINING PLATE
6—1" BRAD
7—3d FINISH NAIL

The desk is built from birch plywood with poplar edge-banding, and the parts are held together with joining plates, nails, screws, and glue. Any beginner can build it. Its construction is so rugged, it's just about impossible to damage it, and it disassembles to make it easier to move—a handy feature when transporting it from your shop to the bedroom.

Making the Pedestal Parts

First, rip and crosscut the plywood pieces to size. Guide the circular saw using a straightedge clamped to the panel (**Fig. 1**). Note that a 40-tooth thin-kerf, crosscut blade was used for these cuts. Next, use a clothes iron to apply birch veneer edge tape to the plywood pieces (**Fig. 2**). Let the veneer cool to room temperature before trimming it to length and width using a sharp chisel (**Fig. 3**). If the veneer tears out as it is trimmed, cut from the opposite direction.

Next, mark the locations of the joining plate slots in the pedestal parts. The joining plates hold the parts in position, and screws are used to pull the parts together. The screw heads are hidden under the applied grids.

Cut the joining plate slots in the pedestal parts using the plate joiner. For the slots at the top and bottom of the pedestal sides, clamp a tall fence to the workbench. Then clamp a pedestal side to the fence, and cut the slots with the plate joiner held against the workbench (**Fig. 4**). To cut the slots in the center of a panel, clamp a straightedge across the panel to guide the plate joiner (**Fig. 5**). To cut the slots in the shelf ends and cleats, hold the workpiece to the bench and use the top as the registration surface (**Fig. 6**).

Fig. 1 *To cut the plywood desk parts to size, use a circular saw guided by a straightedge clamped to the panel's face.*

Materials List

Key	No.	Size and description (use)
A	2	$3/4$ x 25 x $28^7/8$" plywood (side)
B	2	$3/4$ x 15 x $28^7/8$" plywood (shelf)
C	3	$3/4$ x 5 x 15" plywood (cleat)
D	1	$3/4$ x $2^3/4$ x $16^1/2$" poplar (toe kick)
E	4	$3/4$ x $3^1/2$ x $9^3/4$" poplar (short rail)
F	2	$3/4$ x $3^1/2$ x $20^3/4$" poplar (mullion)
G	4	$3/4$ x $3^1/2$ x 23" poplar (rail)
H	4	$3/4$ x $3^1/2$ x $27^3/4$" poplar (stile)
I	2	$1^1/2$ x $3^1/2$ x $9^3/4$" poplar (short rail)
J	1	$1^1/2$ x $3^1/2$ x $20^3/4$" poplar (mullion)
K	2	$1^1/2$ x $3^1/2$ x 23" poplar (rail)
L	2	$1^1/2$ x $3^1/2$ x $27^3/4$" poplar (stile)
M	1	$1/4$ x $16^1/2$ x 25" plywood (back)
N	1	$3/4$ x 5 x $28^1/2$"plywood (cleat)
O1	1	$3/4$ x 8 x $28^1/2$" plywood (back cleat)
O2	1	$3/4$ x 3 x 27" plywood (cleat)
P	1	$3/4$ x 30 x $46^1/2$" plywood (desktop)
Q1	1	$3/4$ x $7/8$ x 48" poplar (edging)
Q2	2	$3/4$ x $7/8$ x 30" poplar (edging)
R	4	$3/4$ x 8 x 9" plywood (partition)
S	1	$3/4$ x $8^1/4$ x 45" plywood (top)
T	1	$3/4$ x 8 x 45" plywood (shelf)
U	2	$3/4$ x 6 x 8" plywood (shelf)
V	2	$3/4$ x 8 x $20^3/4$" plywood (side)
W	2	$3/4$ x $8^1/4$ x $31^1/4$" plywood (side)
X1	4	$3/4$ x $7/8$ x $5^7/8$" poplar (facing)
X2	2	$3/4$ x $7/8$ x $8^7/8$" poplar (facing)
X3	2	$3/4$ x $7/8$ x $30^7/16$" poplar (facing)
X4	2	$3/4$ x $7/8$ x $31^5/16$" poplar (facing)
X5	1	$3/4$ x $7/8$ x $31^3/8$" poplar (facing)
X6	1	$3/4$ x $7/8$ x $44^7/8$" poplar (facing)
Y	1	$1/4$ x $31^3/4$ x 46" plywood (back)
Z	2	$3/4$ x 4 x 18" poplar (drawer side)
AA	1	$3/4$ x 4 x $12^1/2$" poplar (drawer front)
BB	1	$3/4$ x $3^1/2$ x $12^1/2$" poplar (drawer back)
CC	1	$1/4$ x 13 x $17^1/2$" plywood (drawer)
DD	1	$3/4$ x $5^1/4$ x $14^3/4$" poplar (drawer face)
EE	1	18" drawer tracks
FF	1	$1^1/4$"-dia. knob

Misc.: No. 20 joining plates; 2" No. 8 fh wood screws; $1^1/4$" No. 8 fh wood screws; $3/4$" No. 6 rh wood screws; 6d and 3d finish nails; 1" wire brads; birch veneer; grommet; glue; sandpaper; latex primer and enamel.

Notes: All plywood birch veneer; dimensions include veneer tape where applicable.

Bore and countersink pilot holes through the pedestal sides for joining the sides, shelves, and cleats. Install joining plates in the side panels, and check the pieces' fit before the assembly sequence (**Fig. 7**).

Desk Construction

Now assemble the pedestal sides, shelves, and cleats without using glue in the plate joints. Bore pilot holes into the ends of the shelves and cleats. Then drive the screws to fasten the sides to these parts (**Fig. 8**).

Rip and crosscut the poplar toe kick to size, and cut the joining plate slots in its top edge. Spread glue in the slots and on the plates. Clamp it in place until the glue sets.

Rip and crosscut all the grid parts and mark the parts for joining plates. Use two plates at each joint on the open grid. When cutting slots in the endgrain of the poplar pieces, clamp the workpiece to the bench.

To assemble either grid, first spread glue on the joining plates and in the plate slots. Glue and clamp together the crosspieces in the center of the grid (**Fig. 9**). When the glue is dry, glue and clamp the horizontal pieces to the top and bottom of the cross, and then glue and clamp the two vertical pieces to the assembly.

Cut the cleat notch on the top of the pedestal grid and the open grid. Then cut the ¾-in.-deep rabbet on the open grid stile using a router and straight bit. After it is cut, square its ends with a chisel (**Fig. 10**).

Place the pedestal on its side, and position one of the pedestal grids on it. Clamp the grid to the pedestal, and nail it in place without using glue. Nail the grid to the toe kick using 6d finish nails (**Fig. 11**).

Cut out the pedestal back and nail it in place. Next, apply birch veneer edge tape to the exposed edges of the front and back cleats that join the pedestal and open grid. Cut joining

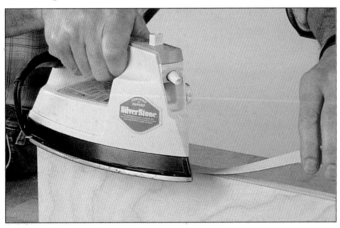

Fig. 2 *Use a household iron to apply heat to the birch veneer tape. The banding has heat-sensitive adhesive on its back.*

Fig. 3 *Use a sharp chisel to trim the birch veneer tape to width. Cut from the opposite direction if the tape tears out.*

Fig. 4 *To cut joining plate slots on the panel's face, clamp the panel upright and slide the plate joiner on the work surface.*

Fig. 5 *To cut plate slots in the panel's center, clamp a fence across the panel to guide the vertically positioned plate joiner.*

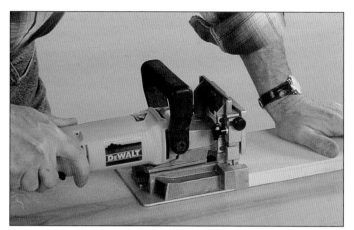

Fig. 6 *To cut plate slots in the end of plywood parts, hold the workpiece down and slide the plate joiner on the bench.*

Fig. 7 *Bore and countersink the pilot holes in the pedestal sides, then test fit the parts before the final assembly.*

plate slots in the vertical back cleat and in the edge of the rear cleat. Install joining plates with glue and clamp these cleats together. This cleat assembly is installed when the pedestal and open grid are joined.

Rip and crosscut the poplar edges for the desktop. Glue and clamp them to the top, and fasten them with 6d finish nails so they are flush with the top, but overhang the bottom by ⅛ in.

Building the Storage Shelf

Use a router and straight bit to cut the notch in the back of the desktop (**Fig. 12**). Square the ends of the cut with a chisel. Next, bore the grommet hole in the top.

Apply birch veneer tape to the top edges of the storage shelf sides. Then use the router with an edge guide to cut the stopped rabbet on the sides. Use a chisel to cut the end of the rabbet square (**Fig. 13**).

Cut the joining plate slots for the storage shelf. Begin the storage shelf assembly by spreading glue in the slots and on the plates for the joints between the partitions and the top. Join these parts, and drive 6d finish nails to fasten the joints (**Fig. 14**). Clamp these joints until the glue sets.

Glue and clamp the short shelves to the inner sides. Then glue and clamp those sides to the bottom of the middle shelf (**Fig. 15**). Glue and clamp the top and shelf assembly, then drive finish nails through the shelf into the top of the inner side (**Fig. 16**).

Glue and nail the poplar facing in place. Next, cut the joining plate slots in the desktop to locate the storage shelf. Install the plates with glue, then place the storage shelf on the desktop. Screw the desktop to the storage shelf (**Fig. 17**).

Make the poplar drawer pieces, clamp the parts together, and use glue and 6d finish nails to fasten them (**Fig. 18**). Install the drawer bottom.

Install the drawer tracks on the pedestal sides and the drawer sides. Then test fit the drawer in the pedestal. Cut the

Fig. 8 *Clamp the pedestal parts together, bore pilot holes into the shelves and cleats, and drive the screws to secure the sides.*

Fig. 9 *Begin the assembly of the open grid by gluing and clamping together the center horizontal and vertical pieces.*

Fig. 10 *Cut the stopped rabbet in the open grid using a router and straight bit. Then cut the end of the rabbet square using a chisel.*

Fig. 11 *Clamp the grid to the desk pedestal. Nail the grid to the pedestal sides with 3d nails and to the toe kick with 6d nails.*

Fig. 12 *Use a router to cut the notch in the top of the desk. The first cut forms a rabbet, and the second cut completes the notch.*

drawer face to size and screw it to the drawer box. Then install the drawer pull.

Use screws—but not glue—to fasten the cleats between the open grid and the pedestal.

Place the desktop shelf assembly over the base. Then bore and countersink pilot holes through the cleats and into the bottom of the desktop. Screw the desktop and storage shelf to the base (**Fig. 19**).

To finish the desk, set all finish nails and fill the holes. Sand all the surfaces using 180-grit sandpaper and ease the edges. Apply a coat of latex primer. Lightly sand the primer, then apply two coats of latex semigloss paint.

TECH *Tips*

Tale of the Tape
Birch veneer tape is a handy material for disguising edge joints, but it can be very difficult to pare to the width of the panel.

Since birch is known for tearout, it demands razor-sharp tools. Unless you can sharpen your chisel or block plane so that it is sharp enough to shave with, use another edge-banding material.

In the event of tearout, cut from the opposite direction. If that doesn't work when using a chisel, switch to a low-angle block plane. If the tape is still tearing out, the problem may be that the tape is not properly adhered and is flexing away from the panel's edge.

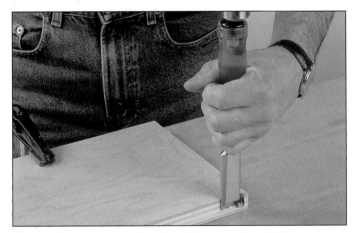

Fig. 13 *Cut a stopped rabbet in each side of the storage shelf using a router with an edge guide. Then square the rabbet using a chisel.*

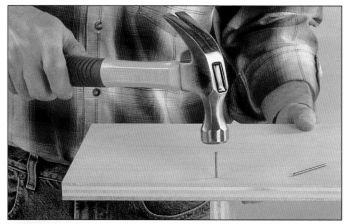

Fig. 14 *Begin the shelf assembly by joining the top and partitions with joining plates and glue. Also nail the pieces together.*

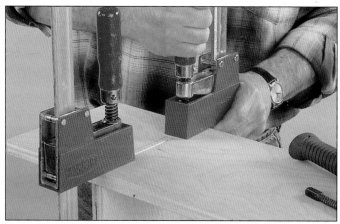

Fig. 15 *Join the short shelves and inner sides. Then use glue, plates, and clamps to join these parts to the middle shelf.*

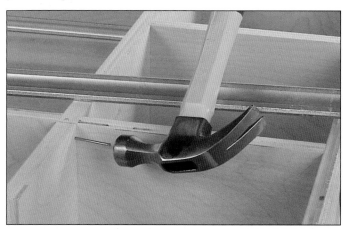

Fig. 16 *While holding the parts in position with clamps, drive a nail through the shelf and into the top of the inner side.*

Fig. 17 *Place the storage shelf on the desktop. Fasten the shelf to the desktop by driving screws through the desktop and into the shelf sides.*

Fig. 18 *Spread glue on the endgrain joints of the drawer box parts, and clamp them together. Also fasten them with finish nails.*

Fig. 19 *Drive screws through the cleats into the bottom of the desk top to fasten the top and bottom subassemblies.*

Top Drawer

Our roomy four-drawer dresser will help keep your child's clothes off the floor.

While it may seem that some kids are content to wear the same T-shirt and pair of jeans almost every day, most have an appetite for clothes that can strain even the biggest budgets. And where do you put it all? Well, before you decide to build an addition on the house, take a look at our less expensive solution.

Designed to match the rest of our bedroom suite, this dresser features four generous drawers that slide effortlessly on ball-bearing-equipped tracks, and sturdy plywood construction with solid poplar detailing. And we've made the job easier by employing simple and fast glue-and-nail joints to streamline drawer construction.

Key POINTS

TIME
Prep Time .... 4 hours
Shop Time .... 10 hours
Assembly Time .... 10 hours

EFFORT
Skill Level .... intermediate

COST / BENEFITS
Expense: moderate
• Four large drawers provide a spacious home for an entire wardrobe.
• This sturdy dresser is easy to build—and built to last.

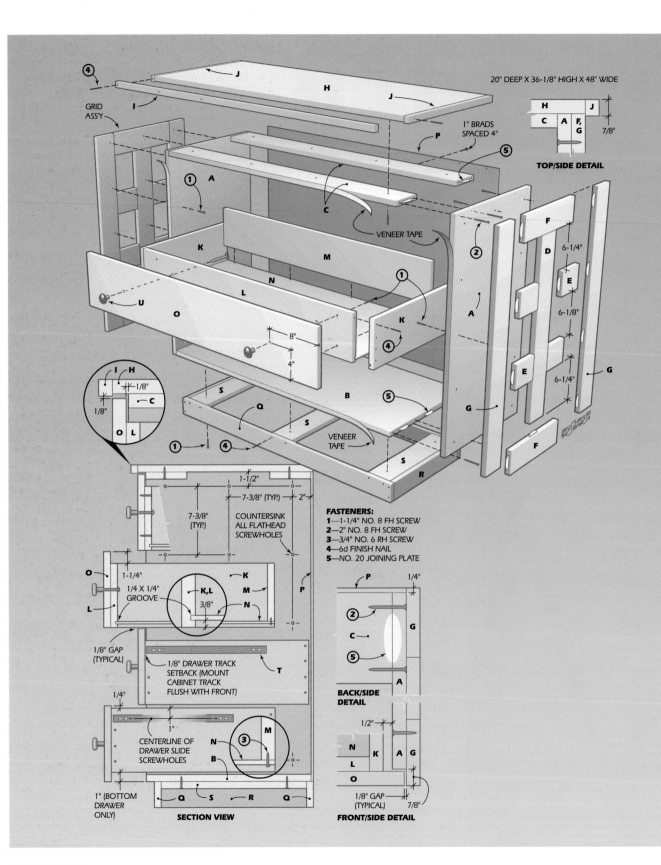

20" DEEP X 36-1/8" HIGH X 48" WIDE

TOP/SIDE DETAIL

GRID ASS'Y

1" BRADS SPACED 4"

VENEER TAPE

VENEER TAPE

6-1/4"

6-1/8"

6-1/4"

8"

4"

1/8"

1/8"

FASTENERS:
1—1-1/4" NO. 8 FH SCREW
2—2" NO. 8 FH SCREW
3—3/4" NO. 6 RH SCREW
4—6d FINISH NAIL
5—NO. 20 JOINING PLATE

1-1/2"

7-3/8" (TYP.)   2"

7-3/8" (TYP.)

COUNTERSINK ALL FLATHEAD SCREWHOLES

1-1/4"

1/4 X 1/4" GROOVE

3/8"

1/8" GAP (TYPICAL)

1/8" DRAWER TRACK SETBACK (MOUNT CABINET TRACK FLUSH WITH FRONT)

1/4"

1"

CENTERLINE OF DRAWER SLIDE SCREWHOLES

1" (BOTTOM DRAWER ONLY)

SECTION VIEW

1/4"

BACK/SIDE DETAIL

1/2"

1/8" GAP (TYPICAL)

7/8"

FRONT/SIDE DETAIL

We've accessorized our dresser with a wall-mounted storage unit. This piece is based on the shelf assembly featured with our desk (see "Stay Tuned," page 46). To build the wall-mounted unit, follow the instructions given for the desk unit, but eliminate the leg sections and cut the end panels to 10½ in. long.

Case Construction

Equip your circular saw with a fine-tooth blade to cut the plywood case parts to size. For accuracy, use a straightedge positioned at the appropriate distance from your cutline. With the guide square to the edge of the panel, hold the saw base against the guide while moving the saw slowly forward.

Fig. 1 *Heat the hot-melt adhesive on the back of the veneer tape with an iron. Slowly advance the iron with firm pressure.*

Fig. 2 *Use a sharp chisel to trim the overhanging edges of the veneer tape. If the tape begins to tear, reverse the cutting direction.*

Use an iron to apply veneer tape to the front edges of the plywood case sides, bottom, and front cleat (**Fig. 1**). Set the iron to its highest setting and advance it slowly while you press down firmly. Position the ¹³⁄₁₆-in.-wide tape so there's a slight overhang on each side of the panel. Trim the excess tape flush to the panel faces with a razor-sharp chisel. If the tape tends to tear, reverse the direction of the chisel (**Fig. 2**).

Mark the locations of joining plate slots on the plywood case parts. First cut the slots in the ends of the cleats and bottom. For good joint registration, hold both the piece and plate joiner tight to your worktable. To cut the slots in the case sides, first clamp a tall fence to the worktable. Use this fence as a support to hold the sides in a vertical position while cutting the slots (**Fig. 3**).

Bore screw clearance holes through the case sides and countersink the holes so that the screw heads will be slightly recessed. Install joining plates in the case joints. Since these joints depend on screws for their strength, don't apply glue to the plates. Then assemble the case parts. Use clamps to hold the parts together while you bore pilot holes into the panel edges and drive the screws (**Fig. 4**). Set this assembly aside

Materials List

Key	No.	Size and description (use)
A	2	³⁄₄ x 18⅛ x 32⅝" plywood (side)
B	1	³⁄₄ x 18⅛ x 43½" plywood (bottom)
C	2	³⁄₄ x 4½ x 43½" plywood (cleat)
D	2	³⁄₄ x 3½ x 25⅝" poplar (mullion)
E	8	³⁄₄ x 3½ x 4⅜" poplar (short rail)
F	4	³⁄₄ x 3½ x 12¼" poplar (rail)
G	4	³⁄₄ x 3½ x 32⅝" poplar (stile)
H	1	³⁄₄ x 19¼ x 46½" plywood (top)
I	1	³⁄₄ x ⅞ x 48" poplar (edge)
J	2	³⁄₄ x ⅞ x 19¼" poplar (edge)
K	8	³⁄₄ x 6¾ x 18" poplar (drawer side)
L	4	³⁄₄ x 6¾ x 41" poplar (drawer front)
M	4	³⁄₄ x 6⅛ x 41" poplar (drawer back)
N	4	¼ x 17½ x 41½" plywood (drawer bottom)
O	4	³⁄₄ x 8 x 44¾" poplar (drawer face)
P	1	¼ x 32⅝ x 45" plywood (back)
Q	2	³⁄₄ x 2¾ x 43" poplar (toe kick face)
R	2	³⁄₄ x 2¾ x 16" poplar (toe kick side)
S	3	³⁄₄ x 4 x 16" plywood (cleat)
T	4	18" drawer tracks
U	8	1¼"-dia. knobs

Misc.: No. 20 joining plates; 2" No. 8 fh wood screws; 1¼" No. 8 fh wood screws; ¾" No. 6 rh wood screws; 6d finish nails; 1" brads; birch veneer tape; glue; sandpaper; latex primer and enamel.

Notes: All plywood birch veneer; dimensions include veneer tape where applicable.

while you construct the poplar grids. Using a square to guide your circular saw, cut the poplar grid pieces to length. Then lay out the joining plate slot locations and cut the slots. When cutting into endgrain, especially on short pieces, clamp the part to the worktable (**Fig. 5**).

Apply glue to the slots and plates for the joints between the mullion and the short, center rails. Join the rails to the mullion (**Fig. 6**), and then use clamps to pull the joints tight until the glue sets. Next, join the top and bottom rails to the mullion ends. Again, clamp the joints (**Fig. 7**). Finally, join the two stiles to the rail ends.

Making the Grids

Use a clamp at each rail to ensure that the joints are tight. Compare opposite diagonal measurements of the grid assembly to be sure that it is square. If the measurements differ, adjust the clamps until they are the same.

Assembly and Top

Position a grid assembly against each plywood case side, adjusting for the proper overhang at the front and back edges. Use clamps to temporarily hold the parts together and bore and countersink pilot holes through the case sides. Pay attention to the hole locations as shown in the plans so you do not place screws where they might interfere with the drawer track installation. Fasten the grids with 1¼-in. No. 8 fh screws (**Fig. 8**).

Use your circular saw and rip guide to cut edge strips for the dresser top, and then crosscut the strips to length. Apply glue to one end of the top panel and position a strip so it's flush with the top surface and overhanging ⅛ in. on the bottom. Clamp the strip while you drive 6d finish nails. The clamp will keep the strip from moving, ensuring that it stays flush with the top of the panel. Apply the strip at the opposite end of the panel, and add the front edge. Set the nail heads.

Fig. 3 *Use a plate joiner to make the slots for the case. Clamp the case sides vertically and register the slots against your work surface.*

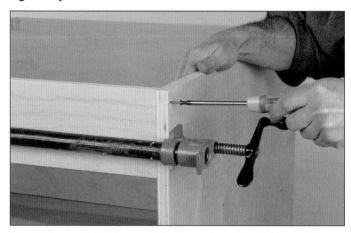

Fig. 4 *Assemble the case by screwing the sides to the cleats and bottom. Use clamps to hold the pieces while you drive the screws.*

Fig. 5 *Cut plate slots in the grid assembly components. Clamp pieces to your work surface for safe and accurate cuts.*

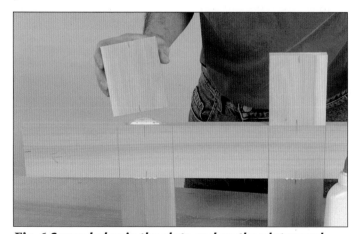

Fig. 6 *Spread glue in the slots and on the plates and assemble the short rails to the mullion. Clamp the subassembly until the glue sets.*

Clamp the top in place while you bore and countersink pilot holes through the cleats (**Fig. 9**). Fasten the top to the case with 1¼-in. No. 8 fh screws.

The Drawers

Rip and crosscut the drawer parts to finished dimension. Use a ¼-in. straight bit and an edge-guide accessory to rout the grooves in the drawer sides and fronts for the bottom panels (**Fig. 10**).

Sand the interior drawer surfaces with 120-, 150-, and 180-grit sandpaper before assembly. Then dust off the pieces and assemble the drawers. Apply glue to the mating surfaces, and use clamps to hold the parts together while you drive 6d finish nails (**Fig. 11**).

Cut the ¼-in. plywood drawer bottom panels to size and sand them, finishing with 180-grit sandpaper. After dusting off the bottom panels, slide each one into the grooves of an assembled drawer.

Then drill pilot holes and drive screws through the panels into the drawer backs to secure the panels (**Fig. 12**). Glue or screws are not used in the panel grooves.

Mount the drawer rails to the drawer sides (**Fig. 13**). Drive screws through the vertical slots at the ends of each rail to allow for adjustment after installation. The rails must be mounted ⅛ in. back from the front edge of the box.

Lay the case on its side on your worktable to mount the remaining track halves (**Fig. 14**). Drive screws through the horizontal slots at each end of the slides to allow for track adjustment. This time, position the track halves so that the front ends are flush with the front edge of the dresser case.

Final Steps

Cut the back panel to size. Compare opposite diagonal measurements of the case to be sure that it is square. Then nail the back in place with 1-in. brads (**Fig. 15**).

To install the drawers, engage the drawer rail under the small hooks at the back edge of the tracks, then lower the drawer over the plastic clips until you hear them click into place (**Fig. 16**).

Cut poplar stock to size for the drawer faces. Starting with the bottom drawer, clamp the face to the box, bore screw holes from inside, and drive screws to fasten the face to the box (**Fig. 17**). After all four faces are installed, check their alignment and adjust the slides to achieve a uniform ⅛-in. space around each. Drive screws into all the remaining track-mounting holes.

Bore holes for the drawer knobs and mount the knobs with 1⅛-in.-long mounting screws. Remove the drawers for painting.

Use glue and 6d finish nails to assemble the toe kick base. Lay the cabinet on its back and clamp the base to the case bottom while you bore pilot holes and screw the toe kick in place (**Fig. 18**).

Fig. 7 *Apply glue to the end rail joints and clamp to the mullion. After the glue has set, attach the grid stiles with glue and plates.*

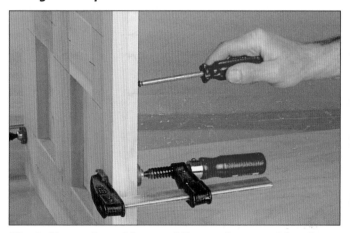

Fig. 8 *Clamp the grid assemblies to the case sides. Bore and countersink screw pilot holes and drive screws to fasten the grids.*

Fig. 9 *After gluing the edges to the plywood top, clamp the top in place, and bore screw holes. Then screw the case to the top.*

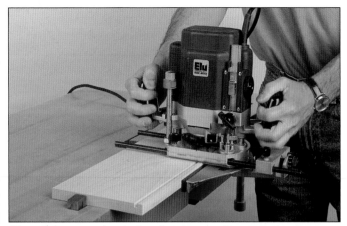

Fig. 10 *Rout grooves for the drawer bottoms in the drawer front and side panels. Use a ¼-in. straight bit and router edge guide.*

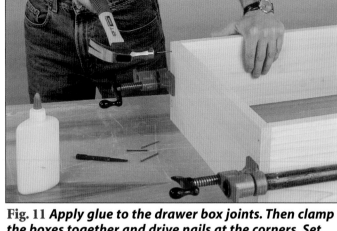

Fig. 11 *Apply glue to the drawer box joints. Then clamp the boxes together and drive nails at the corners. Set the nail heads.*

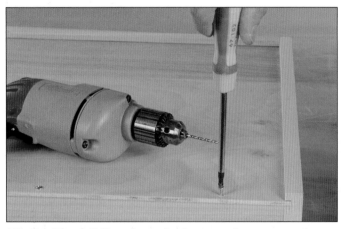

Fig. 12 *After sliding the ¼-in. bottom drawer panels in place, secure them to the drawer backs with ¾-in. No. 6 rh screws.*

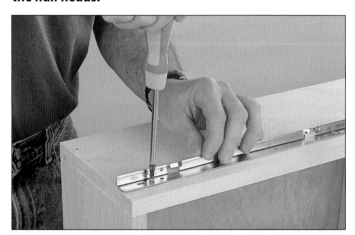

Fig. 13 *Fasten the drawer halves of each track to the drawer sides with screws driven through the vertical slotted holes.*

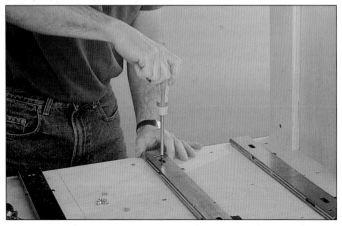

Fig. 14 *Install the case tracks by screwing through the horizontal slotted holes. Place the tracks flush with the front edges of the case.*

Fig. 15 *After measuring the case to ensure that it's square, install the ¼-in. back panel with 1-in. brads driven about 4 in. apart.*

Set all nail heads and fill the holes with wood filler. Sand the case and drawer parts, finishing with 180-grit paper, and clean away the dust. Apply a good latex primer to all cabinet surfaces and drawer faces. If you wish to finish the drawer boxes, use two coats of shellac.

When the primer is dry, use 180-grit paper to lightly sand all surfaces. Then dust it off before painting. Apply two coats of a quality latex semigloss enamel, following the directions supplied by the manufacturer. When the paint is dry, reinstall the drawers.

TECH *Tips*

Slide Home

Commercial side-mount drawer slides (those that you don't make yourself out of wood) are designed for kitchen cabinet shops and mill workshops. The people who install them are usually so familiar with them that they don't need the instructions, which are often pretty sketchy. Simply put, you're on your own. But there are several things you can do to make the job a bit easier and increase your odds of getting the installation right the first time.

First, you may find it easier to install the slides before the top or bottom of the furniture is installed. Of course, whether that is practical depends on the construction of the particular piece of furniture.

Another way to help yourself is to use positioning jigs, which you can make from scrap wood. To ensure that the slide is correctly positioned on the drawer side and on the case piece, draw lines on the jig that correspond with the proper alignment of the slide components.

You may find it easiest to drive just enough screws so that hardware is held in place. That way you don't have to go through too much trouble if you need to remove the hardware and reposition it for a correct fit. Drive the rest of the screws after the drawer is operating correctly.

Finally, what do you do if the case or the drawer is slightly out of square or the wrong size, and you just can't get the hardware to work properly? A down and dirty trick is to use brass shim stock to position the parts properly. This material is available in a wide range of thicknesses and is sold through model-building catalogs, on the Web, and through machine-shop supply houses.

Fig. 16 *Install each drawer by engaging the drawer member with the hook at the back of the track. Then lower the front of the drawer.*

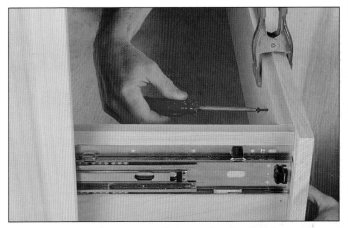

Fig. 17 *Clamp the drawer face to the drawer box. Then bore and countersink screw pilot holes. Attach each face and check alignment.*

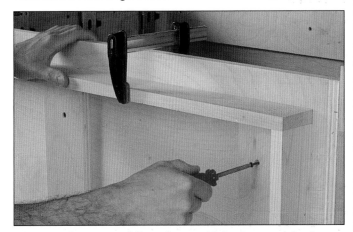

Fig. 18 *After assembling the toe kick pieces with glue and nails, clamp the base to the dresser, bore screw holes, and drive screws.*

Child's Play

This easy-to-build toy chest is a parent's dream: it's both kid-proof *and* kid-friendly.

One of the great joys in life is watching a child at play, especially when it's with some of his or her favorite toys. But one of the most persistent parent-child confrontations centers around what to do with all these toys when playtime is over. Here's a solution—or at least part of one.

Our durable toy chest holds a bunch of easily accessible toys and turns into a convenient bench when the top is closed. And we've added a nifty safety feature to help put your mind at ease: The lid is controlled by a spring-tensioned support that prevents accidental slamming on little fingers.

*Key*POINTS

TIME
Prep Time . . . . **2 hours**
Shop Time . . . . **8 hours**
Assembly Time . . . . **6 hours**

EFFORT
Skill level . . . . **basic**

COST / BENEFITS
Expense: **low**
• This kid-friendly chest puts kids' favorite **treasures easily within their reach.**
• **Durable construction** means that your children's children may also enjoy it.

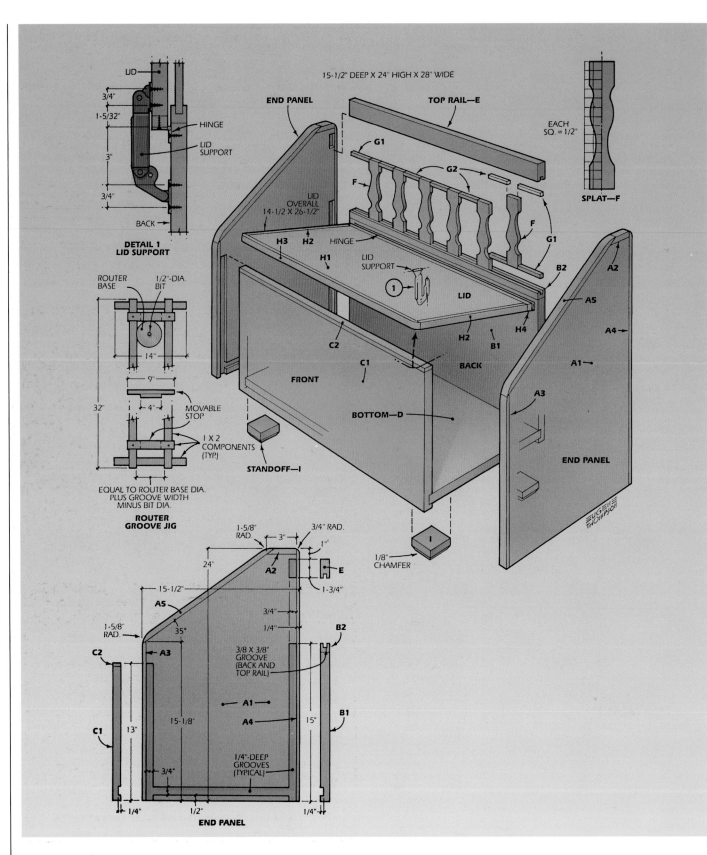

DETAIL 1
LID SUPPORT

LID
3/4"
1-5/32"
3"
3/4"
HINGE
LID SUPPORT
BACK

ROUTER BASE
1/2"-DIA. BIT
14"
9"
4"
32"
MOVABLE STOP
1 X 2 COMPONENTS (TYP.)
EQUAL TO ROUTER BASE DIA.
PLUS GROOVE WIDTH
MINUS BIT DIA.
ROUTER GROOVE JIG

END PANEL
15-1/2" DEEP X 24" HIGH X 28" WIDE
TOP RAIL—E
G1
G2
F
F
G1
B2
A2
A5
A4
A1
A3
END PANEL
EACH SQ. = 1/2"
SPLAT—F

LID OVERALL 14-1/2 X 26-1/2"
H3 H2 HINGE
H1
LID SUPPORT
1
LID
H2
H4
B1
C2
C1
FRONT
BACK
BOTTOM—D
STANDOFF—I
I
1/8" CHAMFER

1-5/8" RAD.
3"
3/4" RAD.
1"
24"
A2
E
15-1/2"
1-3/4"
A5
3/4"
1/4"
B2
1-5/8" RAD.
35°
C2
A3
3/8 X 3/8" GROOVE (BACK AND TOP RAIL)
A1
A4
B1
15"
C1
13"
15-1/8"
3/4"
1/4"-DEEP GROOVES (TYPICAL)
1/4"
1/2"
1/4"
END PANEL

Making the Panels

Begin construction using a smooth cutting blade. A simple way to handle the large crosscuts is to tack a strip of wood to each panel's back. The strip is sized to slide easily in the miter gauge slot (**Fig. 1**). To make the strip slide smoothly, rub some wax on its edges.

Next, rip and crosscut maple edge banding and glue it to the panels (**Fig. 2**). We used 3-way clamps, but you can try bar clamps or even masking tape. Note that the top edge bands of the end panels are slightly long, so they'll be sawn at an angle when the ends are cut to shape. Also, use three 19-gauge brads partially driven into each edge band to keep it from sliding. Band all the panels in this fashion—except the lid, which gets its edge bands after the chest is assembled.

After the glue dries, scrape off glue beads and plane edge bands flush to the panel surfaces.

Next, set the table saw miter gauge to 35° and make the angled cuts on the end panels (**Fig. 3**). Glue and clamp the edge bands onto the sawn surface.

We cut the panel dadoes and grooves with a router and a ½-in.-dia. straight bit. A rectangular frame is used to guide the router to make these cuts (**Fig. 4**). Be sure that the side rails are parallel and are spaced to fit the diameter of your router base, plus the difference between the diameter of the router bit and the width of the required dado or groove. You must precisely measure the thickness of the plywood before setting

Fig. 1 *Tack nail a strip to the back of each panel. The strip should ride in the miter gauge groove as the panel is being cut.*

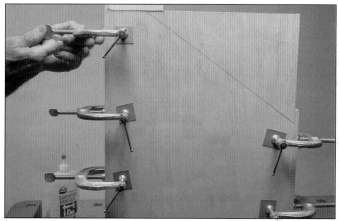

Fig. 2 *Glue and clamp each of the edge bands to the panels. Note that the top edge band of the end panel is just slightly long.*

Materials List

Key	No.	Size and description (use)
A1	2	³/₄ x 15 x 23¹/₂" maple plywood (end)
A2	2	¹/₂ x ³/₄ x 3" maple (band)
A3	2	¹/₄ x ³/₄ x 15¹/₈" maple (band)
A4	2	¹/₄ x ³/₄ x 24" maple (band)
A5	2	¹/₂ x ³/₄ x 16¹/₈" maple (band)
B1	1	³/₄ x 14¹/₈ x 27" maple plywood (back)
B2	1	³/₄ x ⁷/₈ x 27" maple (splat band)
C1	1	³/₄ x 12³/₄ x 27" maple plywood (front)
C2	1	¹/₄ x ³/₄ x 27" maple (band)
D	1	³/₄ x 14 x 27" maple plywood (bottom)
E	1	³/₄ x 1¹/₄ x 27" maple (rail)
F	6	³/₈ x 1³/₈ x 7" maple (splat)
G1	4	³/₈ x ³/₈ x 2¹³/₁₆" maple (filler block)
G2	10	³/₈ x ³/₈ x 2⁵/₈" maple (filler block)
H1	1	³/₄ x 13³/₈ x 25¹³/₁₆" (lid)
H2	2	¹/₄ x ³/₄ x 13³/₈" maple (band)
H3	1	¹/₂ x ³/₄ x 26⁵/₁₆" maple (band)
H4	1	¹/₂ x ³/₄ x 26⁵/₁₆" maple (band)
I	4	³/₄ x 2¹/₄ x 2¹/₄" maple (standoff)

Misc.: 1¹/₂ x 26¹/₄" brass-plated hinge; center-mounted hinge support; glue; polyurethane.

Fig. 3 *Using the miter gauge, cut the sloping edge on the end panels. Afterward, apply edge banding to the sawn surface.*

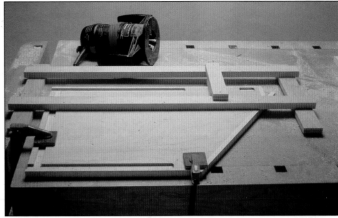

Fig. 4 *Cut grooves and dadoes in the end panels with a router and a straight bit. Then tack nail a block across the rails to stop the cut.*

the distance between the rails. (Hardwood plywood is always slightly thinner than its stated dimension.) Tack nail a movable stop across the rails to control the length of the cut, and cut each groove or dado in two passes. Then, using a chisel, cut the ends of the grooves square.

Making the Splat Rail and Assembly

Cut the splats to shape, then smooth their edges. The pieces will be too small to clamp to a bench. Instead, use a $\frac{1}{16}$-in.-rad. corner-rounding bit in the router table for the job (**Fig. 5**).

With the dado head in the table saw, cut the groove in the top rail and the edge band on the back panel. Then cut the filler blocks to length, leaving the four end blocks $\frac{1}{2}$ in. longer than the others. Remember to round off the rail edges before assembling the workpieces.

Use glue sparingly as you fit the splats and filler blocks in the top rail (**Fig. 6**). When they're all in place, briefly insert

Fig. 5 *Since the splats are so small, it's best to round over their edges on a router table. A ball-bearing bit usually works best.*

MATERIAL *Matters*

Working With Plywood
Plywood is often the material of choice in furniture construction. It's stable in response to humidity and temperature, and when you put an edge band on it, it can often pass for a panel that has been glued up out of narrower strips. Here are some tips for getting the most out of your plywood.

Like any lumber, plywood is expensive, and just one little mistake can ruin an entire sheet. So unless you are absolutely sure about your cutting sequence, begin by marking the

sheet with a light-colored chalk to establish how many parts you will get from the sheet. This will also help you plan your cutting sequence.

When working in a small shop, you're probably better off reducing the panel size with a circular saw before moving on to final cutting on the table saw. Cutting the parts to rough size may seem like a waste of time at first, but anybody who has ever wrestled a full sheet of $\frac{3}{4}$-in. plywood over the top of a small table saw (or even a full-size saw) will agree that it's easy to get the cut wrong. Rough cutting the sheet into smaller pieces will also put less physical strain on you.

TECH *Tips*

Glue Guru

Glue is a messy necessity in woodworking. It often squeezes out of joints and generally finds its way onto surfaces where it doesn't belong. Here are some easy steps you can take to avoid the hassle and eliminate the mess.

When gluing up panels or gluing together joints, use a razor-sharp chisel to pare away the glue that squeezes out of a joint. Do this when the glue is rubbery—don't wait until it has fully cured. Removing hardened glue can be tough on you and your tools, and it can also damage the wood. Hardened glue is actually stronger than the wood itself and scraping and paring hardened glue may actually tear loose wood fibers.

When paring away this rubbery gunk from a panel, skim the chisel along the surface with the chisel's bevel facing down. When paring the glue that has squeezed out of a mortise-and-tenon joint (for example), you may find just the opposite is true. Hold the chisel flat against the surface. A well-polished, razor-sharp chisel will skim the glue right off the surface. Keep a moistened rag handy to clean the chisel as you go.

Fig. 6 *Insert the splats and spacer blocks in the top rail. After the glue has dried, repeat the procedure on the back panel.*

Fig. 7 *Begin the assembly by inserting the back into an end panel. Next, add the bottom and front, then the other end.*

the subassembly into the groove in the back panel—but don't use glue to secure it. After the glue in the top rail has set, repeat the procedure, applying glue and spacing each block to secure the splats in the back panel. During both subassembly stages, temporarily test fit the back to the side panels to ensure later realignment.

When the back assembly is dry, complete the project in the following sequence: Insert the back panel into the groove (**Fig. 7**). Join the bottom and front to this subassembly, then add the second end and lay the chest on its back. Next, glue and clamp the entire assembly together (**Fig. 8**) and check it for square.

Cut the lid panel to size, glue and clamp the side bands to it, and then add the front and back bands. Install the hinge and lid support, attach the standoffs and relieve any sharp corners with fine sandpaper. Finally, apply several coats of polyurethane to finish off the project.

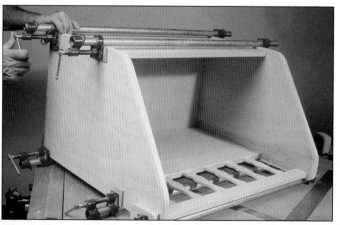

Fig. 8 *Clamp the chest using five bar or pipe clamps. Be sure to check the assembly for square before allowing the glue to set.*

Warming Trend

Add beauty and warmth to your bedroom with this traditional cherry blanket chest.

There was a time when a blanket chest could be found in just about every home. In the days before built-in closets, these chests were used to store clothing, linen, and blankets. Today, even though closets are found in every home, blanket chests are becoming popular again, not only because of their practicality, but also because of their beauty.

Our cherry blanket chest features a traditional design that will fit comfortably in all but the most contemporary of settings. It's lined with aromatic cedar, and its roomy storage drawer is sturdily constructed with handcut dovetail corners.

*Key*POINTS

TIME
Prep Time . . . . **4 hours**
Shop Time . . . . **10 hours**
Assembly Time . . . . **12 hours**

EFFORT
Skill Level . . . . **intermediate**

COST / BENEFITS
Expense: **moderate**
• A beautiful accent piece that **adds warmth to any room.**
• Cedar-lined drawers **extend the life of your linens.**

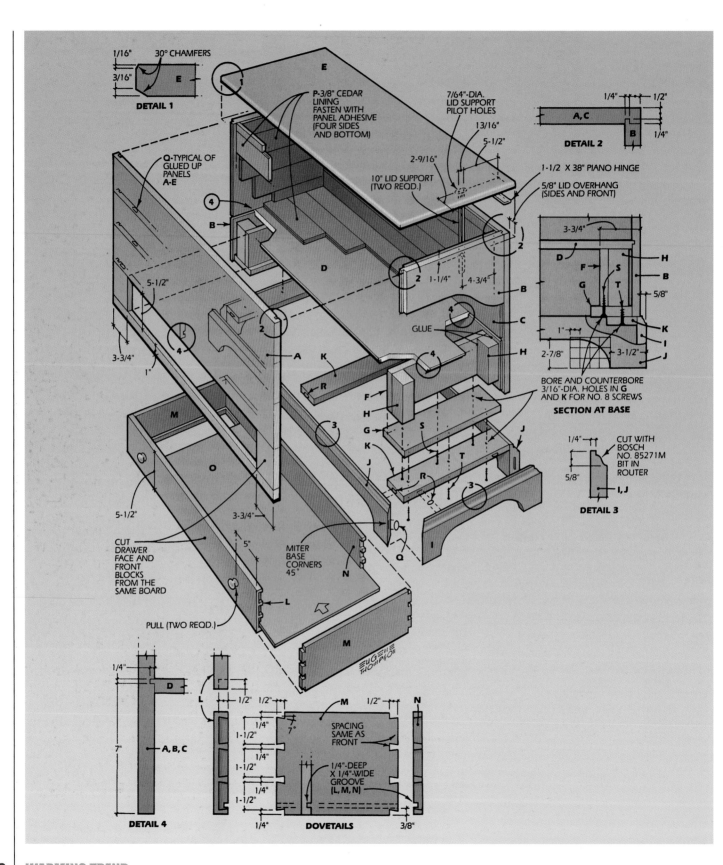

DETAIL 1

1/16"
3/16"
30° CHAMFERS
E
E

DETAIL 2

1/4"
1/2"
A, C
B
1/4"

P-3/8" CEDAR LINING FASTEN WITH PANEL ADHESIVE (FOUR SIDES AND BOTTOM)

7/64"-DIA. LID SUPPORT PILOT HOLES

13/16"

5-1/2"

2-9/16"

10" LID SUPPORT (TWO REQD.)

Q-TYPICAL OF GLUED UP PANELS A-E

4

B

D

E

2

2

2
1-1/4"
4-3/4"

B

C

GLUE

4

H

1-1/2 X 38" PIANO HINGE

5/8" LID OVERHANG (SIDES AND FRONT)

3-3/4"

D

F
S

G
T

H

B

5/8"

1"

K

I

2-7/8"

3-1/2"

J

BORE AND COUNTERBORE 3/16"-DIA. HOLES IN G AND K FOR NO. 8 SCREWS

SECTION AT BASE

5-1/2"

3-3/4"

1"

A

K

R

F

H

G

S

K

J

J

4

3

1/4"

5/8"

CUT WITH BOSCH NO. 85271M BIT IN ROUTER

I, J

DETAIL 3

M

O

5-1/2"

3-3/4"

5"

MITER BASE CORNERS 45°

N

T

R

J

3

O

Q

I

CUT DRAWER FACE AND FRONT BLOCKS FROM THE SAME BOARD

PULL (TWO REQD.)

L

M

DETAIL 4

1/4"

D

7"

A, B, C

L

1/2"

1/2"

1-1/2"

1/4"

1-1/2"

1/4"

1-1/2"

1/4"

1/4"

M

7°

SPACING SAME AS FRONT

1/2"

N

1/4"-DEEP X 1/4"-WIDE GROOVE (L, M, N)

DOVETAILS

3/8"

As a shop project, the blanket chest is appropriate for a woodworker of intermediate skill. To build the chest, you need basic shop tools: a table saw, router, band saw or jigsaw, and hand tools. And as far as finishing is concerned, we kept things as simple as possible. We used a basic oil finish to give the chest a warm glow and a silky feel.

Building the Chest

Rip and crosscut each board to rough size and edge joint each. Then select the boards for each panel and mark the joining plate slot positions at 6- to 8-in. intervals (**Fig. 1**). Place the boards on a flat surface and cut the plate slots (**Fig. 2**). When laying out the boards for the chest front, rip and joint one board to 5½ in. wide. Cut the drawer face and the panel pieces that are at both ends of the drawer face from this piece. Cutting these pieces from one board produces a continuous grain pattern across the panel and the drawer.

Apply glue to the joining plate slots, plates, and board edges, then clamp the assembly (**Figs. 3 and 4**). After 20 to 30 minutes, scrape off the glue that has squeezed out. Allow the glued assembly to cure. Use a cabinet scraper to smooth the panel surfaces.

Rip and crosscut the panels to finished size, and cut the rabbets and dadoes. We used a router, straight bit, and edge guide to make these cuts (**Fig. 5**). There are two things to be aware of: First, test the router setup on some scrap before making the cuts. Second, note that the grooves on the front

Fig. 1 *Lay out the boards for each panel. Then mark the location of the joining plates 6 to 8 in. between the plate centers.*

Fig. 2 *Cut joining plate slots at each layout mark. Make sure that the tool and the workpiece are positioned on a flat surface.*

Materials List

Key	No.	Size and description (use)
A	1	¾ x 24 x 38¾" cherry (front)
B	2	¾ x 14½ x 24" cherry (side)
C	1	¾ x 24 x 38¾" cherry (back)
D	1	¾ x 14½ x 37¾" poplar (shelf)
E	1	¾ x 16⅛ x 40" cherry (lid)
F	2	¾ x 5½ x 14" poplar (side guide)
G	2	1 x 4 x 14" poplar (runner)
H	4	1½ x 2 x 5½" poplar (blocking)
I	2	¾ x 5 x 16¾" cherry (base)
J	2	¾ x 5 x 40" cherry (base)
K	3	¾ x 3 x 15¼" poplar (cleats)

Key	No.	Size and description (use)
L	1	¾ x 5½ x 31¼" cherry (drawer front)
M	2	½ x 5½ x 14½" cherry (drawer sides)
N	1	½ x 5½ x 31¼" cherry (drawer back)
O	1	¼ x 14 x 30¾" maple plywood (drawer bottom)
P	as reqd.	⅜" tongue-and-groove aromatic cedar lining
Q	as reqd.	No. 20 joining plates
R	as reqd.	No. 0 joining plates
S	6	2" No. 8 fh wood screws
T	6	1½" No. 8 fh wood screws

Misc.: 1½ x 38" piano hinge; 10" lid support; drawer pulls; carpenter's glue; panel adhesive; sandpaper; Danish oil; steel wool.

Fig. 3 *Apply glue to the joining plate slots, the plates, and the board edges. Be sure to apply glue sparingly on all surfaces.*

Fig. 4 *Use bar clamps to pull the joints together. Wait 20 to 30 minutes, then scrape off the glue that has oozed out.*

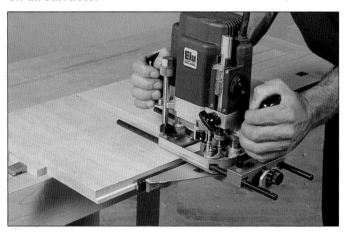

Fig. 5 *Use a router and a straight bit to cut the rabbets and dadoes in the panels. Make test cuts before proceeding.*

and back panels that seat the poplar shelf are stopped short of the panel ends. If the grooves extend to the panel ends, they'll be visible after the box is assembled.

Do a test assembly first and sand or plane any joints that fit too tightly. Proceed with the assembly in stages. Join the shelf and sides to the front panel (**Fig. 6**), apply as many clamps as needed to pull the joints tight, then let the glue set. Remove the clamps and install the back panel. Again, use plenty of clamps to pull the joints tight.

Next, rip and crosscut the blocking, drawer compartment side guides, and bottom runners from poplar. Invert the chest and glue the blocking in the drawer compartment (**Fig. 7**). Then install the side guides by gluing them to the blocking and the underside of the shelf. Glue and screw the bottom runners to the side guides.

To apply the pieces of cedar closet lining, begin with the poplar shelf. Cut the cedar boards to length, apply a bead of

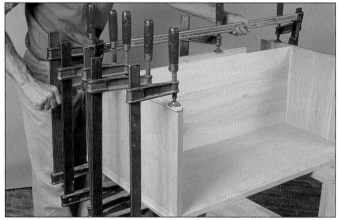

Fig. 6 *Glue and clamp one side to the chest front, then follow with a second side and the shelf. Let the glue set before you move on.*

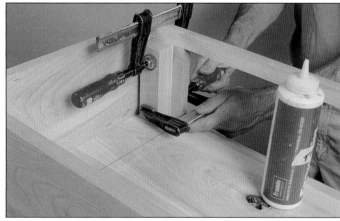

Fig. 7 *After inverting the chest, use glue to install the blocking in the drawer compartment. These blocks guide the drawer.*

panel adhesive on each and slide it into position. Proceed up each side, and rip the last board ⅟₁₆ in. wider than required. Use spring clamps to maintain a tight joint between the cedar and the cherry on this last piece. After the adhesive has cured, plane the cedar flush to the cherry.

Adding the Lid

Bore the pilot holes through the lining and into the chest for the lid support. Install the support after the chest is finished. Cut the panel for the chest lid to finished size, and use a 30° chamfer bit in the router to cut the profile around the lid.

Next, use a hacksaw to cut the piano hinge to length. Bore ⅟₁₆-in.-dia. pilot holes for the mounting screws, then bore the pilot holes for the lid support. You will eventually attach the hinge to the lid and the lid to the chest, but don't actually install the hinge and lid until the chest is attached to the base. The chest must be inverted to mount the base, and this will be easier if the hinge and lid have not been installed.

Making the Base

Rip stock for the chest base to finished width, and crosscut it slightly overlength. Use an ogee bit in the router table to cut the molded edge at the top of each piece (**Fig. 8**). We recommend using the router table for this operation, as opposed to routing freehand. Cutting the molded edge with the router table ensures that the edge will be uniform along its length and will match perfectly at the mitered ends.

Cut the joining plate slots for No. 20 plates in the mitered ends of the base parts (**Fig. 9**). Lay out and cut slots for No. 0 joining plates to form the joints between the base sides and the cleats. The smaller plates are used here to avoid cutting through the molded edge at the top of the base.

The next step is to cut the base parts to shape on the band saw. Carefully remove the saw marks on the curved areas using rasps and sandpaper (**Figs. 10 and 11**).

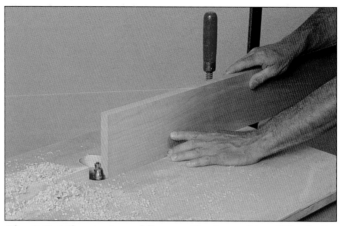

Fig. 8 *Cut the ogee molding on the top edge of the base pieces. Use a router table for each of these cuts to ensure uniform results.*

Fig. 9 *Tip the plate joiner's fence so the tool can cut a slot in the mitered ends of a base piece. The work surface must be clean.*

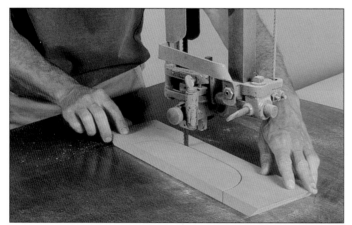

Fig. 10 *Trace the profile on each base piece, and then cut it out with a band saw. Cut just to the waste side of the layout line.*

Fig. 11 *Clamp the base piece in the bench vise. Remove saw marks and smooth the curved areas with a rasp and sandpaper.*

Dry clamp the entire base assembly before using glue. Check that the assembly is square and make any necessary adjustments. Apply glue to the mating edges of the front and back base pieces, the base cleats, the joining plate slots, and the plates themselves. Clamp the front and back base pieces to the base cleats (**Fig. 12**). After the glue has set, clamp the end base pieces to the base cleats. It may be difficult to align the miter joints, so apply pressure with clamps from two directions if necessary.

Sand both the chest and base with 120-grit sandpaper, then invert the chest and position the base over it. Adjust the base to provide an even ⅛-in.-wide reveal on all sides, and make a series of counterbored pilot holes through the cleats and into the blocking next to the drawer compartment. Screw the base to the chest (**Fig. 13**).

Drawer Construction and Finish

Rip and crosscut the drawer parts to size. Next, use a marking gauge to scribe a baseline on both ends of the drawer side, the back, and the drawer front (**Fig. 14**).

Lay out the dovetail spacing on the drawer sides using a dovetail template or sliding bevel gauge (**Fig. 15**). Mark the waste areas to prevent cutting in the wrong area.

Clamp both drawer sides together and make the cuts with a dovetail saw. You should stop the cuts at the baseline.

Next, clamp each side to the workbench, over a piece of scrap, and use a sharp chisel to remove the waste between the dovetails (**Fig. 16**). Alternate vertical and horizontal cuts and chop only halfway through the board, then turn over the drawer side and complete the cuts. Approach the scribed baseline in stages and finish by placing the chisel in the scribe mark to make the final cut.

Put the drawer back vertically in the bench vise and place a drawer side over it. Trace the outline of the dovetails using a sharp knife. Also use the knife to mark the pin cuts on the

Fig. 12 *To complete the base assembly, clamp the base ends to the front and back pieces. Apply pressure from two directions.*

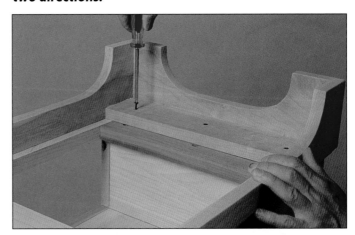

Fig. 13 *Align the base over the chest so that there's an even ⅛-in.-wide reveal on all sides. Screw the base to the chest.*

Fig. 14 *Set the marking gauge a hair thicker than the stock thickness. Scribe a baseline on the drawer side, back, and front.*

Fig. 15 *Use a dovetail template or a sliding bevel gauge to lay out the dovetail spacing on the drawer sides. Mark the waste areas to avoid cutting in the wrong spot.*

drawer face (**Fig. 17**). Use a square to extend the scribed lines down the drawer face and the back of the face. Clamp the drawer back in the bench vise, and saw down to the baseline along each angled mark. Then use a chisel to get rid of the waste between the pins.

Clamp the drawer face in the vise and hold the saw at a sharp angle to start the cuts for the pins (**Fig. 18**). Cut only as far as the layout lines, then use a sharp chisel to remove the waste. Test fit each drawer joint (**Fig. 19**). It should be snug, but able to slide together with gentle mallet taps. Pare with a chisel to loosen tight spots.

Use the table saw and dado blade to cut the groove for the drawer bottom in the sides, front, and back. Sand the inside of the drawers with 120- and 220-grit sandpaper, but do not sand the joint surfaces. Dust off the surfaces thoroughly.

Use a small glue brush to apply glue to the drawer joints, then join the face and back to a side, slide in the bottom, and

install the other side. If the joints fit properly, clamping should not be necessary. Check the assembly for square and adjust as necessary.

After the glue has dried, test the drawer in its opening, then patiently sand or plane to eliminate any tight spots. Install the drawer pulls.

Finish sand the chest with 220-grit sandpaper, and remove the dust with a tack cloth. We used three coats of Watco Danish Oil to finish the outside of the chest. Apply the oil with a rag or brush, let it soak in for 30 minutes, then wipe it off. After letting it dry overnight, repeat the process. Apply a third coat the same way, and when it has dried, buff it with 4/0 steel wool and polish the chest with a soft cloth.

Finish the underside of the lid, the drawer compartment, and the drawer with a quality paste wax. The cedar should be left unfinished. Finally, install the lid, the lid support, and the drawer pulls.

Fig. 16 *Remove waste in the dovetails with a chisel. Cut halfway through from one side, then flip over the drawer side, and finish chiseling from the other side.*

Fig. 17 *Lay the completed sides over the front of the drawer, then trace the outline of the dovetails and mark the pin cuts using a sharp knife.*

Fig. 18 *Clamp the drawer front upright in a vise and saw along the layout lines. Finish cutting the joints with a chisel.*

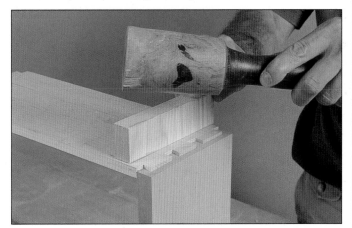

Fig. 19 *Test fit the drawer. The parts should require only light taps of a mallet to be driven together. Use a chisel to loosen tight spots.*

Dressed Up

Fine wood and fine lines make this tall, mahogany dresser an instant classic.

For this dresser, we have combined solid mahogany with figured pomele sapele veneer and wenge. The six drawers are mounted on top of the line, full-extension slides that provide complete access to drawer space while remaining almost invisible to the user. In the tradition of the finest furniture, we have included a completely finished back, so this piece looks great from any angle. The dresser's legs, rails, back-panel assembly, and drawer fronts are all cut from solid mahogany. You may need to order this often hard-to-find hardwood from a mail-order company or online, but you won't mind the extra effort once you see the finished product.

*Key*POINTS

TIME
Prep Time . . . . 10 hours
Shop Time . . . . 20 hours
Assembly Time . . . . 20 hours

EFFORT
Skill Level . . . . intermediate

COST / BENEFITS
Expense: **expensive**
• Solid mahogany construction means this dresser is **built to last.**
• **Spacious drawers** offer plenty of room for clothing and linens.

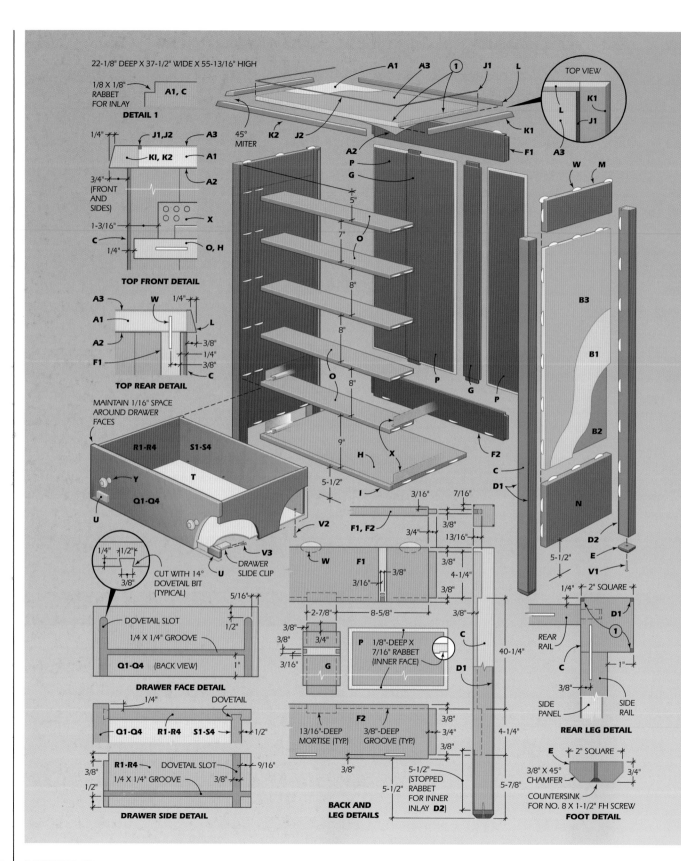

22-1/8" DEEP X 37-1/2" WIDE X 55-13/16" HIGH

1/8 X 1/8" RABBET FOR INLAY **A1, C**
DETAIL 1

1/4" **J1,J2** **A3**
KI, K2 **A1**
A2
3/4" (FRONT AND SIDES)
1-3/16" **X**
C
1/4" **O, H**
TOP FRONT DETAIL

A3 **W** 1/4"
A1 **L**
A2
3/8"
1/4"
F1 3/8"
C
TOP REAR DETAIL

MAINTAIN 1/16" SPACE AROUND DRAWER FACES

R1-R4 **S1-S4**
Y
T
Q1-Q4
U

1/4" 1/2"
3/8"
CUT WITH 14° DOVETAIL BIT (TYPICAL)
V3
U
DRAWER SLIDE CLIP

5/16"
DOVETAIL SLOT 1/2"
1/4 X 1/4" GROOVE
Q1-Q4 (BACK VIEW) 1"
DRAWER FACE DETAIL

1/4" DOVETAIL
Q1-Q4 **R1-R4** **S1-S4** 1/2"

R1-R4 DOVETAIL SLOT 9/16"
3/8"
1/4 X 1/4" GROOVE 3/8"
1/2"
DRAWER SIDE DETAIL

A1 A3 **1** **J1** **L**
45° MITER
K2 **J2**
A2
P
G
5"
7" **O**
8"
8" **O**
8"
H **X**
9"
5-1/2"
I

TOP VIEW
L **K1**
J1

K1
F1 **A3**

W **M**

B3

B1

B2

F2
C
D1

N

D2
E
V1

3/16" 7/16"
F1, F2 3/8"
3/4" 13/16"
V2

W **F1**
3/16"
3/8"
2-7/8" 8-5/8"
3/8"
3/8" 3/4"
G
3/16"

P 1/8"-DEEP X 7/16" RABBET (INNER FACE)
1
C
D1
40-1/4"

F2
3/8"
13/16"-DEEP MORTISE (TYP.) 3/8"-DEEP GROOVE (TYP.) 3/4"
3/8"
3/8"
5-1/2" (STOPPED RABBET FOR INNER INLAY **D2**)
5-1/2"
BACK AND LEG DETAILS

3/8"
4-1/4"
3/8"
4-1/4"
5-7/8"

1/4" 2" SQUARE
D1
1
REAR RAIL
C
3/8"
SIDE PANEL SIDE RAIL
REAR LEG DETAIL

E 2" SQUARE
3/8" X 45° CHAMFER 3/4"
COUNTERSINK FOR NO. 8 X 1-1/2" FH SCREW
FOOT DETAIL

5-1/2"

It's an old rule in veneer work that a panel should be balanced in its construction. This means that veneer of similar grain and density should be applied to both faces of the panel to keep it from warping. We used pomele sapele on the outer face and mahogany on the inside face. These woods are close enough in density and expansion properties to ensure a balanced panel.

Veneering the Panels

We used a book-matched grain pattern on our panels. To do this, two adjacent veneer sheets are cut to the same size and grain layout. Then one of the sheets is turned over to form a mirror image of the first sheet.

First, stack two sheets of veneer so that their grain is aligned. Mark a line across the top sheet and use a veneer saw guided by a straightedge to cut the veneer to size (**Fig. 1**). Cut gently at the sheet's edge to avoid tearing it. It's also important to note that the adjacent sheet edges must meet perfectly. If necessary, join two sheets together and plane their edges so they are smooth and straight.

Next, use perforated paper veneer tape to join two adjacent sheets together. Moisten the veneer tape with a damp sponge and place it across the veneer's seam at 4- to 6-in. intervals (**Fig. 2**). Then run a continuous piece of veneer tape along the seam's length.

Fig. 1 *Place veneers on a surface into which you can cut. Slice through the stack with a veneer saw guided by a straightedge.*

Materials List

Key	No.	Size and description (use)
A1	1	$3/4$ x $20^5/8$ x $35^1/4$" MDF (top core)
A2	as reqd.	mahogany (bottom veneer)
A3	as reqd.	pomele sapele (top veneer)
B1	2	$3/4$ x 17 x $34^3/4$" MDF (side core)
B2	as reqd.	mahogany (inner veneer)
B3	as reqd.	pomele sapele (outer veneer)
C	4	2 x 2 x $54^1/4$" mahogany (leg)
D1	12	$1/8$ x $1/8$ x $54^1/4$" wenge (inlay)
D2	4	$1/8$ x $1/8$ x $5^1/2$" wenge (inlay)
E	4	$3/4$ x 2 x 2" wenge (feet)
F1	1	$3/4$ x 5 x $33^1/2$" mahogany (top rail)
F2	1	$3/4$ x 5 x $33^1/2$" mahogany (bottom rail)
G	2	$3/4$ x $3^5/8$ x 41" mahogany (mullion)
H	1	$3/4$ x 19 x 32" birch plywood (bottom)
I	1	$3/4$ x $3/4$ x 32" mahogany (edge band)
J1	2	$1/8$ x $1/8$ x $20^1/2$" wenge (inlay)
J2	1	$1/8$ x $1/8$ x $35^1/4$" wenge (inlay)
K1	2	$13/16$ x $1^1/8$ x $22^1/8$" mahogany (edge)
K2	1	$13/16$ x $1^1/8$ x $37^1/2$" mahogany (edge)
L	1	$13/16$ x $3/8$ x $35^1/4$" mahogany (edge)
M	2	1 x 5 x 17" mahogany (rail)
N	2	1 x $9^3/4$ x 17" mahogany (rail)
O	5	$3/4$ x 6 x 32" mahogany (rail)
P	3	$1/2$ x 9 x $40^1/4$" mahogany plywood (panel)
Q1	1	$3/4$ x $4^7/8$ x $31^7/8$" mahogany (drawer front)
Q2	1	$3/4$ x $6^7/8$ x $31^7/8$" mahogany (drawer front)
Q3	3	$3/4$ x $7^7/8$ x $31^7/8$" mahogany (drawer front)
Q4	1	$3/4$ x $8^7/8$ x $31^7/8$" mahogany (drawer front)
R1	2	$1/2$ x $4^1/8$ x $18^5/8$" maple (drawer side)
R2	2	$1/2$ x $6^1/8$ x $18^5/8$" maple (drawer side)
R3	6	$1/2$ x $7^1/8$ x $18^5/8$" maple (drawer side)
R4	2	$1/2$ x $8^1/8$ x $18^5/8$" maple (drawer side)
S1	1	$1/2$ x $3^3/8$ x $30^7/8$" maple (drawer back)
S2	1	$1/2$ x $5^3/8$ x $30^7/8$" maple (drawer back)
S3	3	$1/2$ x $6^3/8$ x $30^7/8$" maple (drawer back)
S4	1	$1/2$ x $7^3/8$ x $30^7/8$" maple (drawer back)
T	6	$1/4$ x $18^1/8$ x $30^7/8$" birch plywood (drawer bottom)
U	12	$1/2$ x 1 x $2^1/2$" mahogany (block)
V1	4	$1^1/2$" No. 8 fh wood screws
V2	24	$1^1/2$" No. 8 rh wood screws
V3	24	$5/8$" No. 6 fh wood screws
W	as reqd.	No. 20 plates
X	6 pr	drawer slides
Y	12	drawer pulls

Misc.: Veneer tape; glue; 120-, 220-, and 320-grit sandpaper; 4/0 steel wool; clear shellac; Waterlox Original Sealer/Finish.

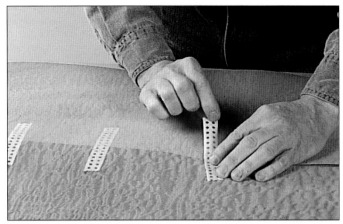

Fig. 2 *Make the edges of two book-matched veneers perfectly straight and smooth, then join the sheets with veneer tape.*

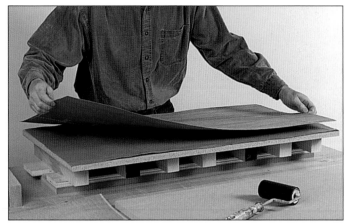

Fig. 3 *Place the bottom veneer facedown against a sheet of kraft paper on top of a platen, cauls, and blocking.*

Fig. 4 *Cut the veneered panel to finished length and width, then remove the veneer tape using a sharp cabinet scraper.*

Fig. 5 *Clamp a leg securely to the bench. Using a router and straight bit, cut a stopped rabbet on the inside of the leg.*

To glue and clamp veneer to a panel, you need to evenly distribute the pressure from the head of the clamp to the entire surface of the veneer. Make cauls from scrap 2x4 lumber and plane a ⅛-in. crown into one edge of each. Cut two pieces of ¾-in. plywood to the same dimensions as the panel you are gluing up. These are called platens. The cauls take the force from the clamp and spread it out, the platens further spread the clamping force from the cauls. The result is evenly applied pressure that bonds every square inch of the veneer to the core.

To begin the glue-up process, place scrap wood blocking on the workbench to provide clearance for the head of the clamps. On top of the blocking, place the cauls, crown side up. Place a platen on the cauls and a sheet of kraft paper on top of the platen. Finally, place the veneer on the paper, with the veneer tape facing the paper (**Fig. 3**).

Next, use a foam roller to coat one surface of the core panel with glue. Place the glue-covered face of the core against the

sheet of veneer. Then apply glue to the other face of the core. Position the sapele veneer, tape side up, over the core. Place a sheet of kraft paper over the veneer and a platen over the paper followed by the cauls, crown side down.

Position clamps at the center of the panel assembly and apply pressure. Place clamps outward from the center and keep applying pressure until the veneer is properly bonded to the panel. Let the glue cure for 2 hours, then remove the panel and let it air-dry. Scrape off the veneer tape and any glue that bled through the veneer face (**Fig. 4**). Use the table saw to cut the panel to finished dimension.

Legs, Rails, Stiles, and Panels

Rip and crosscut the mahogany for the legs. Next, use a router, fence, and straight bit to cut the rabbet and stopped rabbet for the leg inlay (**Fig. 5**). Joint one edge of the inlay straight and smooth, then rip the inlay slightly overwidth using a band saw

(**Fig. 6**). Glue and tape the inlay to the leg. When the glue has dried, trim the inlay flush using a block plane. Cut the feet to size and fasten them to the legs. Cut the chamfer on the feet using a sharp plane or on the table saw.

Use a plunge router, fence, and spiral up-cutting bit to cut the rail mortises in the legs (**Fig. 7**). Then cut the ends of the mortise square with a chisel (**Fig. 8**). Use the same setup to cut the panel grooves in the legs.

Rip and crosscut the material for the back panel assembly. To cut the tenons on the rails, mullions, and panels, install a dado blade in the table saw and an auxiliary fence. Butt the workpiece to the fence and run it over the blade (**Fig. 9**).

Case Assembly

Use a plate joiner to cut the necessary slots in those pieces that are joined with plates and glue. Begin the assembly process by gluing and clamping together the side panels and the rails. Next, glue and clamp the legs to the panel/rail assembly (**Fig. 10**). After the glue is dry, cut the plate slots for the bottom assembly and the drawer rails (**Fig. 11**). Use a straightedge to guide the plate joiner.

For the back assembly, glue and clamp the mullions to the bottom rail, then slide the center panel into its groove (**Fig. 12**). Glue and clamp the top rail to this assembly.

Rip and crosscut the edge banding for the bottom panel and glue it to the panel's front edge (**Fig. 13**). Trim the banding flush to the panel face. When the bottom is finished, glue and clamp it to the back subassembly and check that the two are square to each other. Next, slide in another back panel, and join the back/bottom assembly to a case side.

With that subassembly completed, use a straight piece of scrap lumber to maintain a square assembly and proper drawer rail spacing, then use plates, glue, and clamps to join the drawer rails to the case side (**Fig. 14**). Complete the case by

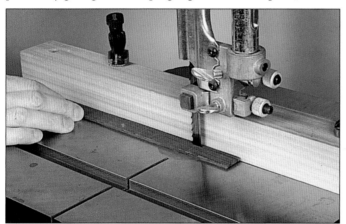

Fig. 6 *Rip the leg inlay into slightly overwidth strips. Guide the cut with a straightedge clamped to the band saw table.*

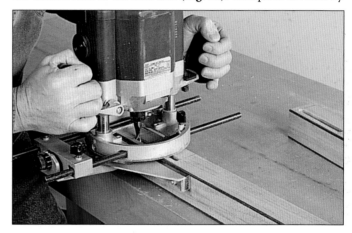

Fig. 7 *Cut mortises in the legs after the inlay is trimmed flush. Use a plunge router and spiral up-cutting bit to cut the mortises.*

Fig. 8 *Cut the bulk of each mortise with a router and mortising bit. Cut the ends of each mortise square with a sharp chisel.*

Fig. 9 *Cut the tenons on the rails and stiles using a dado blade in the table saw. Butt the workpiece against a fence.*

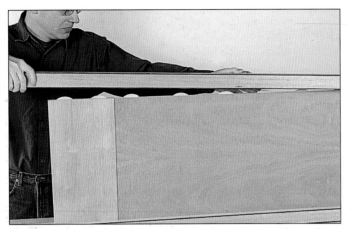

Fig. 10 *Glue and clamp together the side panels and rails. Then test fit this assembly with the legs before gluing and clamping.*

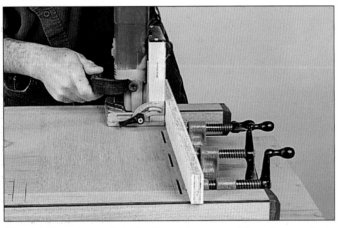

Fig. 11 *Cut plate slots in the side assembly using a plate joiner. Hold the joiner along a straight piece of scrap to ensure accuracy.*

Fig. 12 *Glue and clamp together the two center stiles and one rail. Slide in the center panel before attaching the other rail.*

sliding in the remaining panel, then gluing and clamping the second side in position.

Rip and crosscut the edge banding and inlay for the top. After cutting the rabbet in the top, glue the edge banding and inlay in place as was done on the legs. Trim these parts flush to the panel. Next, cut the bevel on the banding using a razor-sharp block plane (**Fig. 15**). Cut the joining plate slots in the top, then use glue, clamps, and joining plates to join the top to the case.

Drawer Assembly and Finishing

Rip and crosscut the materials for the drawers, then use a dovetail bit in a router to cut the dado slot for the front and back. Use a straightedge clamped across a workpiece to guide the router when cutting the dovetail slots (**Fig. 16**). Use a straight bit and fence on a plunge router to cut the groove in the front and sides for the drawer bottom (**Fig. 17**). Cut the dovetails on the drawer sides with the same router bit, but install the router in a router table and move the workpiece over the bit. If you use a traditional router table that holds the router vertically, you will also have to fashion a support to hold the drawer pieces upright as they move past the bit. Another option is to mount the router in an upright panel, then slide the workpiece horizontally under the bit.

No matter which method you use, cut the dovetails on some long pieces of scrap and fine-tune the setup before cutting an actual workpiece. Dry fit the parts for each drawer after all the parts are cut. Then glue and clamp the drawer parts together.

The drawer slides used on this project require that stopped holes be bored in the drawer back. Use a piece of masking tape wrapped securely around the bit to act as a depth gauge, and then bore the holes (**Fig. 18**). Also, install blocks under each drawer and against each drawer's front. Install the drawer slides per the manufacturer's instructions. Mount the drawers, test fit them, and adjust as required. Remove the drawers and drawer hardware before moving on to finishing.

Finish the inside of the case and the drawers with clear shellac. Do not use the Waterlox finish on the inside because the strong odor it imparts to the wood does not dissipate in a closed space and can be transferred to clothing stored in the case. Apply three coats to each surface. Let each coat dry and sand it with 320-grit sandpaper before applying the next. Smooth the last coat with 4/0 steel wool.

Finish the outside of the case and each drawer face with finish. We used Waterlox Original Sealer/Finish. Apply a liberal coat and wipe off the excess after about 30 minutes. Leave the surface damp with finish, and let it dry overnight. Scuff the surface with 320-grit sandpaper, and apply a second coat using the same method. Apply the third coat in the same manner, then burnish it with 4/0 steel wool when it is dry. Install the knobs on the drawers and reinstall the drawer hardware to complete the project.

Fig. 13 *Glue and clamp the edge banding to the case bottom. When the glue is dry, plane the banding flush to the panel.*

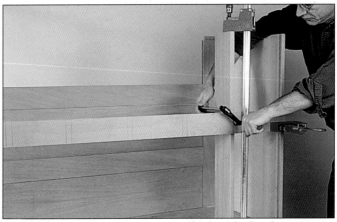

Fig. 14 *Use a piece of scrap marked with the drawer divider positions to ensure that the dividers are square to the case side.*

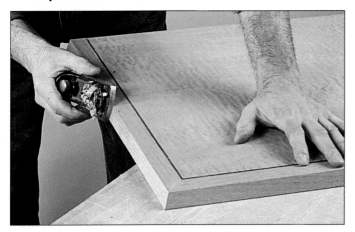

Fig. 15 *After the edge banding is glued and clamped to the top, plane it flush to the panel, then cut the bevels with a block plane.*

Fig. 16 *Cut the dovetail slots in the drawer front and sides with a router and dovetail bit. Guide the router with a straightedge.*

Fig. 17 *Install a straight bit in the router. Then, using the tool's fence, cut the drawer bottom groove in the front and sides.*

Fig. 18 *Use a piece of masking tape on a drill bit to mark a hole's depth, then bore the stopped holes in the back of each drawer.*

Gentleman's Wardrobe

This spacious wardrobe features solid poplar construction and a white pickled finish.

Even those of us lucky enough to have really big bedroom closets often find that we *still* don't have enough space for all of our clothes and accessories. Our wardrobe, also known as a clothespress or an armoire, presents an elegant solution to this problem by combining the benefits of a dresser and a closet in one piece of furniture. The wardrobe's drawers and shelves keep you organized by helping you find whatever it is you're searching for at a glance. our wardrobe's construction is straightforward, emphasizing clean lines. Design details like paneled doors and a wide crown molding give it a distinctive flair.

*Key*POINTS

TIME
Prep Time . . . . **10 hours**
Shop Time . . . . **20 hours**
Assembly Time . . . . **20 hours**

EFFORT
Skill Level . . . . **intermediate**

COST / BENEFITS
Expense: **moderate**
• A hanging pole, drawers, and shelves provide more than enough **storage for all of your clothes and accessories.**

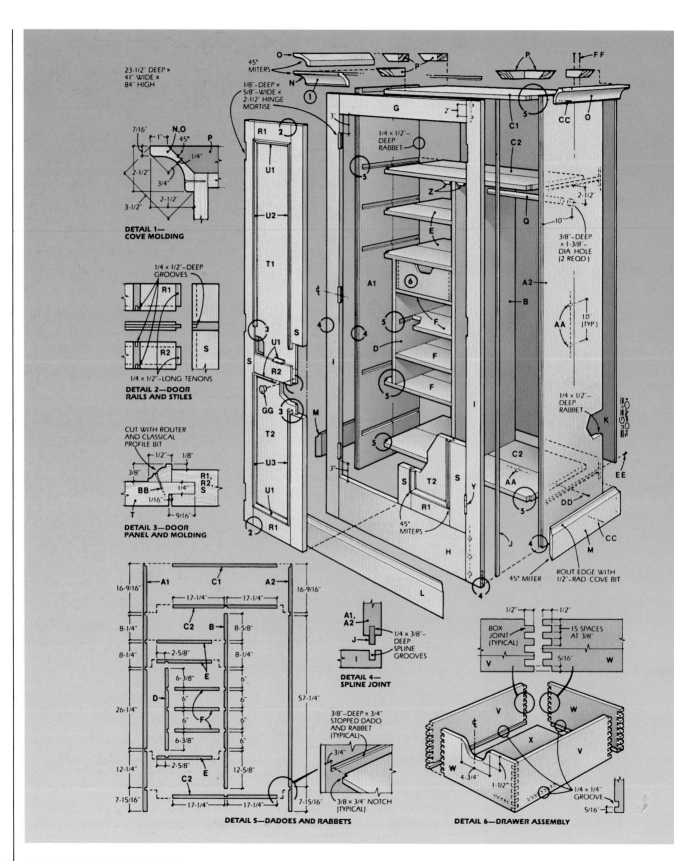

23-1/2" DEEP ×
41" WIDE ×
84" HIGH

45° MITERS

1/8"-DEEP ×
5/8"-WIDE ×
2-1/2" HINGE
MORTISE

DETAIL 1—COVE MOLDING

7/16" 1" 45°
N,O P
2-1/2" 1/4"
3/4"
2-1/2"
3-1/2"

DETAIL 2—DOOR RAILS AND STILES

1/4 × 1/2"-DEEP GROOVES
R1
R2
S
1/4 × 1/2"-LONG TENONS

DETAIL 3—DOOR PANEL AND MOLDING

CUT WITH ROUTER AND CLASSICAL PROFILE BIT
1/2" 1/8"
3/8"
BB 1/4"
T 1/16"
9/16"
R1, R2, S

1/4 × 1/2"-DEEP RABBET
3/8"-DEEP × 1-3/8"-DIA HOLE (2 REQD)
2-1/2"
10"
1/4 × 1/2"-DEEP RABBET
10" (TYP)

ROUT EDGE WITH 1/2"-RAD COVE BIT
45° MITER

45° MITERS
3"
3"

DETAIL 5—DADOES AND RABBETS

16-9/16"
A1 C1 A2
16-9/16"
17-1/4" 17-1/4"
C2 B
8-1/4" 8-5/8"
8-1/4" 2-5/8" 8-1/4"
E
6-3/8"
26-1/4" D 6"
6" 6"
F
6"
6-3/8"
57-1/4"
12-1/4" 2-5/8" 12-5/8"
E
C2
7-15/16" 17-1/4" 17-1/4" 7-15/16"

DETAIL 4—SPLINE JOINT

A1, A2
J
I
1/4 × 3/8"-DEEP SPLINE GROOVES

3/8"-DEEP × 3/4" STOPPED DADO AND RABBET (TYPICAL)
3/4"
3/8 × 3/4" NOTCH (TYPICAL)

DETAIL 6—DRAWER ASSEMBLY

1/2" 1/2"
BOX JOINT (TYPICAL)
15 SPACES AT 3/8"
V W
5/16"
X
W
4-3/4"
1-1/2"
1/4 × 1/4" GROOVE
5/16"

This project is well within the capability of a woodworker with a reasonably well-equipped shop. You'll need a table saw and the usual portable power tools: circular saw, drill, and router. As with all large case pieces, the cutting and fitting here will challenge your skills. But we believe that you'll find your efforts well rewarded in the finished piece.

Preparing the Stock

Begin construction by ripping and crosscutting the stock to rough size for all of the parts. Joint the mating edges of the stock to be used for the case panels. Then, using a doweling jig and portable drill, bore holes 8 to 10 in. apart along the edges for $\frac{1}{4}$-in.-dia. dowels.

Glue and clamp up the panels slightly oversize to allow for final trimming. When the glue has dried, sand the panels smooth with a belt sander. Rip the panels to finished width on a table saw. Then cut them to length, using a straightedge and a circular saw (**Fig. 1**).

Lay out the position of the dadoes and rabbets on the case sides, partitions, and shelves. Note that the dadoes for the case assembly are stopped $\frac{3}{4}$ in. short of the case front. Use a straightedge clamped across the workpiece to guide the router (**Fig. 2**). Use a sharp chisel to square the end of each dado.

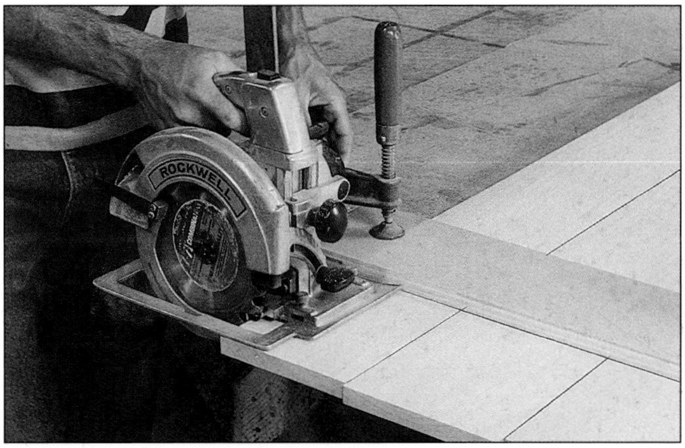

Fig. 1 ***Clamp a straight-edged board square to the panel's edge. Guide the saw along it when crosscutting panels to size.***

Next, use the router with an edge-guide attachment to cut the $\frac{1}{4}$ x $\frac{1}{2}$-in. rabbet along the back inside edge of the case sides (**Fig. 3**). Cut the notches in the front edges of shelves and partitions.

Mark the position of the closet pole on the right case side and the center partition. Use a $1\frac{3}{8}$-in.-dia. multispur or Forstner bit to bore a $\frac{3}{8}$-in.-deep mortise to carry the pole (**Fig. 4**). Use a roughing gouge to turn down a $1\frac{5}{8}$ in. sq. x 20 in. long poplar blank on the lathe. Use a parting tool (**Fig. 5**) to mark the end cuts.

Materials List

Key	No.	Size and description (use)
A1	1	$\frac{3}{4}$ x $20\frac{1}{4}$ x $82\frac{1}{2}$" poplar (left side)
A2	1	$\frac{3}{4}$ x $20\frac{1}{4}$ x $82\frac{1}{2}$" poplar (right side)
B	1	$\frac{3}{4}$ x 20 x 58" poplar (partition)
C1	1	$\frac{3}{4}$ x 20 x $35\frac{1}{4}$" poplar (top)
C2	2	$\frac{3}{4}$ x 20 x $35\frac{1}{4}$" poplar (bottom, top shelf)
D	1	$\frac{3}{4}$ x 20 x 27" poplar (partition)
E	3	$\frac{3}{4}$ x $17\frac{5}{8}$ x 20" poplar (shelf)
F	3	$\frac{3}{4}$ x $14\frac{5}{8}$ x 20 " poplar (shelf)
G	1	$\frac{3}{4}$ x 4 x 30" poplar (case top rail)
H	1	$\frac{3}{4}$ x 8 x 30" poplar (case bottom rail)
I	2	$\frac{3}{4}$ x 3 x $82\frac{1}{2}$" poplar (case stile)
J	2	$\frac{1}{4}$ x $\frac{3}{4}$ x $82\frac{1}{2}$" poplar plywood (spline)
K	1	$\frac{1}{4}$ x $35\frac{1}{2}$ x $75\frac{1}{8}$" poplar plywood (back)
L	1	$\frac{3}{4}$ x 5 x $37\frac{1}{2}$" poplar (front baseboard)
M	2	$\frac{3}{4}$ x 5 x $21\frac{3}{4}$" poplar (side baseboard)
N	1	1 x $3\frac{1}{2}$ x 41" poplar (front cove molding)
O	2	1 x $3\frac{1}{2}$ x $23\frac{1}{2}$" poplar (side cove molding)
P	6	$1\frac{1}{2}$ x 3 x 5" poplar (glue block)
Q	1	$1\frac{3}{8}$"-dia. x $17\frac{5}{8}$" poplar (closet pole)
R1	4	$\frac{3}{4}$ x 3 x $9\frac{15}{16}$" poplar (door rail)
R2	2	$\frac{3}{4}$ x 3 x $9\frac{15}{16}$" poplar (center door rail)
S	4	$\frac{3}{4}$ x 3 x $70\frac{3}{8}$" poplar (door stile)
T1	2	$\frac{1}{2}$ x $9\frac{15}{16}$ x 38" poplar plywood (upper door panel)
T2	2	$\frac{1}{2}$ x $9\frac{15}{16}$ x $25\frac{3}{8}$" poplar plywood (lower door panel)
U1	8	$\frac{3}{8}$ x $\frac{1}{2}$ x $8\frac{15}{16}$" poplar (door molding)
U2	4	$\frac{3}{8}$ x $\frac{1}{2}$ x 37" poplar (door molding)
U3	4	$\frac{3}{8}$ x $\frac{1}{2}$ x $24\frac{3}{8}$" poplar (door molding)
V	8	$\frac{1}{2}$ x $5\frac{15}{16}$ x $19\frac{3}{4}$" poplar (drawer side)
W	8	$\frac{1}{2}$ x $5\frac{15}{16}$ x $13\frac{3}{4}$" poplar (drawer end)
X	4	$\frac{1}{4}$ x $13\frac{1}{4}$ x $19\frac{1}{4}$" poplar plywood (drawer bottom)
Y	6	$1\frac{3}{4}$ x $2\frac{1}{2}$" cabinet hinges
Z	2	magnetic catches
AA	as reqd.	$\frac{1}{4}$"-dia. x 2" spiral-groove hardwood dowels
BB	as reqd.	$\frac{3}{4}$" brads
CC	as reqd.	3d finish nails
DD	as reqd.	4d finish nails
EE	as reqd.	$\frac{5}{8}$" No. 5 rh screws
FF	12	2" No. 8 fh screws
GG	2	$1\frac{1}{4}$"-dia. brass knobs

Misc.: White wood filler; 120- and 220-grit sandpaper; vinyl primer sealer; 220-grit no-fill sandpaper; glue; satin polyurethane varnish.

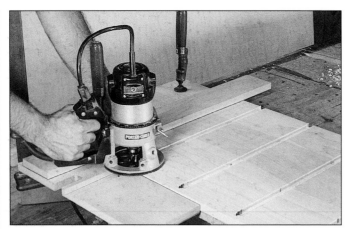

Fig. 2 *Use a shop-made T square to guide the router while cutting the dadoes. Note that the dadoes stop ¾ in. short of the front edge.*

Fig. 3 *Cut the rabbet on rear edge of each case side to receive the back panel. Use a router with an edge guide or rabbeting bit.*

Fig. 4 *Use a Forstner or multispur bit chucked in a portable power drill to bore the shallow mortises that hold 1⅜-in.-dia. closet rod.*

With a ¼-in. slotting cutter and 1-in.-dia. ball-bearing pilot in the router, cut a groove in the front edge of the case sides to receive the splines that join the face frame to the case (**Fig. 6**). Finally, sand all interior case parts.

Assembling the Case

For ease of assembly, interior case pieces are assembled with glue and 4d finish nails. Join the small shelves to the short left-hand partition and center partition. Spread glue in the dadoes and on the shelf ends and drive in the finishing nails. Set the nail heads and fill the holes with white wood filler. Check the assembly for square and let the glue dry (**Fig. 7**).

Glue and nail the case bottom and top shelf to the center partition. Then glue and clamp the left and right case sides to the top, the top shelf, and bottom, remembering to install the closet pole. Check for square and let the glue dry.

Start on the face frame by ripping and crosscutting stock to size. Mark the position for the dowel pins that will join the frame together, then use a doweling jig to bore ¼-in.-dia. x 1¹⁄₁₆-in.-deep holes for 2-in.-long, spiral-grooved dowels (**Fig. 8**). Insert the dowels, glue, and clamp the frame together. Check for square and let it dry. After the glue has dried, use a router and an edge-guide attachment to cut the ¼ x ⅜-in.-deep grooves in the face frame using a ¼-in.-dia. straight bit (**Fig. 9**).

Cut the splines to size and spread glue in the spline grooves in both the frame and case sides. Spread glue on the front edge of the case top and the front edge of the case bottom, slide the splines into the case grooves, and position the face frame on the case. Clamp it in place until the glue dries.

Cutting and Fitting the Trim

With a ½-in.-rad. cove bit in a router table or router, cut the profile on the top front edge of the base trim pieces. Cut the miter on their ends, then apply glue to the miters, and nail the baseboard in place with 3d finishing nails.

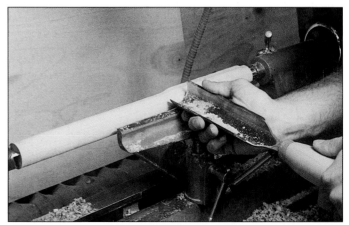

Fig. 5 *Use a roughing gouge to turn down a poplar blank for the closet pole. Mark the end cuts using a parting tool.*

You may be able to get crown molding at your local lumber supplier. If not, it's relatively simple to make. Begin by ripping 1-in.-thick stock to 5 in. wide. Lower the table saw blade below the table and clamp a straightedge board across the table at a 55° angle. The edge of the board should be 2½ in. from the blade measured from the centerline of the arbor.

Raise the blade to a height of ¹⁄₁₆ in. above the table. Using pushsticks, advance the workpiece over the blade. Repeat the process, raising the blade ¹⁄₁₆ in. at a time, until the blade is ¾ in. above the table (**Fig. 10**). Rip the board to the specified width, set the saw blade at a 45° angle, and make the angled cuts on the molding's front and back. Scrape the saw marks out of the cove and finish sand it with 120-grit followed by 220-grit sandpaper (**Fig. 11**).

Making the Doors

Rip and crosscut the stock for the door rails, stiles, and panels. Use the table saw with dado blades to cut the tenons on the rails. Readjust the height of the dado blades and cut the ¼ x ½-in.-deep groove in the stiles and rails.

Use a router with a ¾-in. straight bit and edge guide to cut the ¼-in.-deep x ⁹⁄₁₆-in.-wide rabbet around the back edge of the door panels (**Fig. 12**).

Glue and clamp the door stiles, rails, and panels. Check diagonal measurements for square and let the glue dry. If you decide to make the panels from solid wood, do not glue them in place.

To make the panel molding, plane some stock to ½ in. thick. Using a router table and a bit with a profile similar to the one shown, cut the molding on the edge of the stock (**Fig. 13**). Rip molding off the stock and repeat the process to make enough molding for both doors. Using the miter box, cut the molding to length and nail it to the door panels.

Lay out the location of the door hinges on the face frame stiles and chisel out the mortises. Install the hinges. Position one door at a time in its opening and transfer the location of the hinges to the door stiles. Chisel out matching mortises and screw the hinges to the door. Test fit each door and trim it where necessary using a block plane.

Fitting the Crown

Miter the crown molding to length using a miter box, spread glue on the miters, and nail the pieces to the case with the 3d finishing nails. Then cut the reinforcing blocks—which help support the crown molding—to size. Spread glue between the blocks and the back of the molding and screw the blocks to the top of the case.

Making the Drawers

Rip and crosscut stock for the drawers, the corners of which meet in a finger joint. To cut this joint, first clamp all like parts together in a stack. Then make repeated cuts to the proper depth, using dado blades on a table saw (**Fig. 14**).

Fig. 6 *Use a ¼-in.-slotting cutter with a 1-in.-dia. ball-bearing pilot to cut the spline slots in the front edges on the two case sides.*

Fig. 7 *Glue and nail together the inside case pieces, then check the assembly for square. Set all nail heads and fill the holes.*

Fig. 8 *Mark the locations for the dowel joints in the stiles and rails of the face frame. Use a dowel jig when boring the holes.*

Cutting Corners
Cutting mitered joints is a fundamental woodworking skill that requires several things:

1. You need good light to mark and cut a miter. If your shop lighting is dim, then you'll have trouble both marking and cutting on the mark.

2. The mark is crucial. A No. 2 pencil is fine for finish carpentry, and many woodworkers also use them to mark miter cuts in furniture construction. But it's often better to mark the cut using a penknife or marking knife. A mark cut into the wood won't smudge, and you can actually rest the saw teeth in it. If the knife mark is hard to see, lightly mark on top of it with a pencil.

3. Whether you are using a power or handsaw miter box, it will probably need to be "zero adjusted." Consult the owner's manual for help. Adjustment screws position the saw relative to the worktable. After the miter box is properly adjusted, loosen and relocate the pointer so it rests on zero.

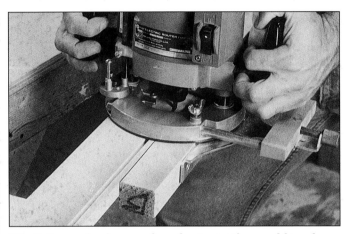

Fig. 9 *Securely clamp a face frame to the workbench and then cut spline grooves with a ¼-in.-dia. straight bit and router.*

Fig. 10 *Cut the cove in the crown molding by making repeated passes on the table saw. Raise the blade ¹⁄₁₆ in. per pass.*

Fig. 11 *Secure the crown molding to the bench. Remove saw marks from the cove with a gooseneck scraper, then smooth with 220-grit sandpaper.*

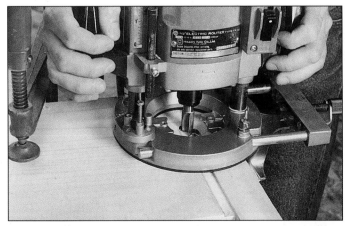

Fig. 12 *Clamp the door panels in place and then cut the rabbet along the back edges with a router and a ⁹⁄₁₆-in.-dia. straight bit.*

Measure and mark the spacing of the fingers on the miter gauge, then clamp a stop block to the first mark. Butt the stack of drawer parts against the stop and make the first cut. Then move the stop block to the next mark, and cut again. Repeat this process until the entire joint is cut. Use the same dado blade to cut the groove in the drawer parts to carry the drawer bottom.

Use a jigsaw to shape the handhold cutouts in the front of each drawer. Next, finish sand the inside faces of all drawer parts with 120-grit, followed by 220-grit sandpaper. Glue and clamp the drawer sides and ends together, but do not glue in the drawer bottoms. Check each assembly for square, then when the glue is dry, check each drawer for proper fit in the case. Sand or plane each as necessary.

Finishing the Case

Finish sand the wardrobe exterior of the case with 120-grit, then 220-grit sandpaper. Dust it thoroughly and wipe it down with a tack cloth.

Our "pickled" finish is actually a paint used as a stain. We used a vinyl primer sealer thinned 30 to 40 percent with water. Brush the paint onto the piece, working in sections of no more than 8 sq. ft. at a time. Let the paint stand on each section for 5 to 10 minutes, then use a clean rag to wipe it off in the direction of the wood grain, and proceed to the next section (**Fig. 15**). After the pickling process is complete, let the wardrobe dry overnight.

After the finish has dried, sand the wardrobe lightly with 220-grit no-fill sandpaper, which is available at auto body or auto parts stores. Dust it off and then wipe it with a tack cloth. Apply two coats of satin polyurethane varnish, sanding lightly between coats. When the finish has dried, install the case back, the doors, their knobs, and magnetic catches on the partition to keep the doors closed.

TECH *Tips*

In a Pickle
An antique pickled finish is easy to create, but still merits a word of caution. Before you apply any finish you've never worked with before, apply it to a test surface first. Take a piece of scrap material that is large enough to give you a good look at the finish, and sand it in the same manner as the real piece of furniture. In other words, make the test piece as close to identical to the furniture as you can. It's extra work, but it's better than realizing you don't like a finish only after you've applied it to your furniture!

Fig. 13 *Cut the profile of panel molding on ½-in.-thick stock, using a router table. Then rip it to finished size on the table saw.*

Fig. 14 *Cut the finger joints on the drawer pieces using dado blades in a table saw. Clamp the parts together and cut simultaneously.*

Fig. 15 *The pickled finish is no more than latex paint used as a stain. Brush it on, let it sit, then wipe it off and let it dry.*

A Place for Everything

Three modular wall units will help you dig out from under the mess in your bedroom closet.

It seems that storage space is always at a premium. No matter how many times we vow to keep the attic, basement, or garage under control, the ever-growing volume of possessions seems to undermine our best intentions. Nowhere is this situation more frustrating than in a bedroom closet. That old jacket that defined something special years ago, those beaten-up work boots that served for so long, and the countless other objects that we don't use much but still can't part with all seem to come to rest there. We've come up with an easy solution: a three-piece wall unit for everything from socks to sweaters and just about any knickknack that needs a home.

Key POINTS

TIME
Prep Time	8 hours
Shop Time	20 hours
Assembly Time	20 hours

EFFORT
Skill Level	intermediate

COST / BENEFITS
Expense: **moderate**

- These attractive wall units are an economical way to **get rid of closet clutter.**
- The units are based on the same model, so they **can be adapted to suit your needs.**

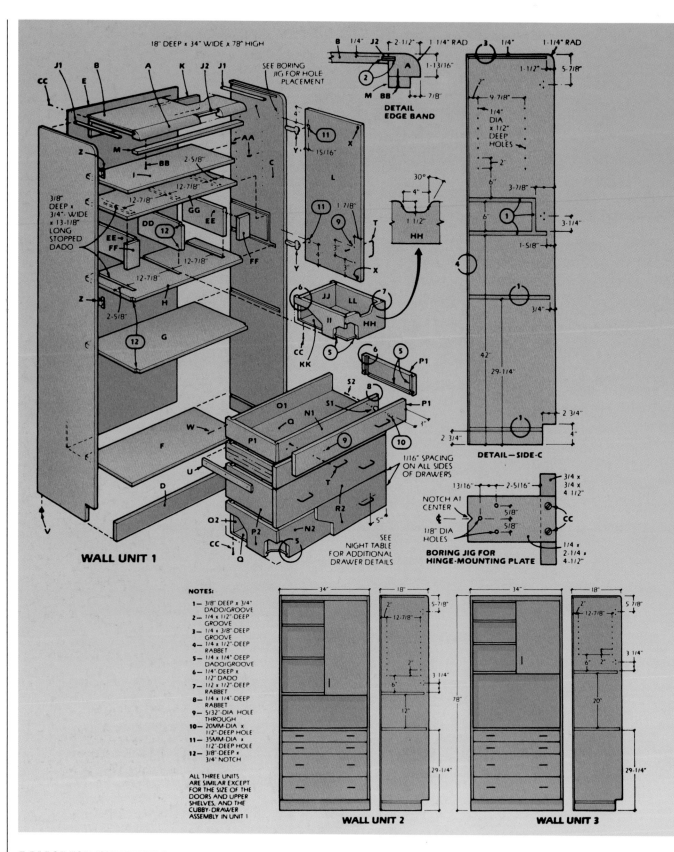

18" DEEP x 34" WIDE x 78" HIGH

DETAIL EDGE BAND

DETAIL—SIDE-C

WALL UNIT 1

BORING JIG FOR
HINGE-MOUNTING PLATE

3/8" DEEP x 3/4"- WIDE x 13-1/8" LONG STOPPED DADO

SEE BORING JIG FOR HOLE PLACEMENT

1/16" SPACING ON ALL SIDES OF DRAWERS

SEE NIGHT TABLE FOR ADDITIONAL DRAWER DETAILS

NOTES:
1— 3/8" DEEP x 3/4" DADO/GROOVE
2— 1/4 x 1/2"-DEEP GROOVE
3— 1/4 x 3/8"-DEEP GROOVE
4— 1/4 x 1/2"-DEEP RABBET
5— 1/4 x 1/4"-DEEP DADO/GROOVE
6— 1/4"-DEEP x 1/2" DADO
7— 1/2 x 1/2"-DEEP RABBET
8— 1/4 x 1/4"-DEEP RABBET
9— 5/32"-DIA HOLE THROUGH
10— 20MM-DIA x 1/2"-DEEP HOLE
11— 35MM-DIA x 1/2"-DEEP HOLE
12— 3/8"-DEEP x 3/4" NOTCH

ALL THREE UNITS ARE SIMILAR EXCEPT FOR THE SIZE OF THE DOORS AND UPPER SHELVES, AND THE CUBBY-DRAWER ASSEMBLY IN UNIT 1

WALL UNIT 2

WALL UNIT 3

Designed to be versatile and easy to build, these three pieces are all based on the same module. Each case has the same overall dimensions and requires the same construction techniques. The differences lie in the sizes of the display areas and the presence (or absence) of cubby drawers in the upper section of each unit. By rearranging the details presented in each case, you can customize the cabinets to suit your needs. We explain how to build unit No. 1 in the directions and materials list. The others are constructed the same way except for the cubby drawers and their support framework.

Construction Details

Cut the case top and edge banding slightly oversize, then rout the spline groove on the front edge of the top using a ¼-in. slotting cutter. Cut a matching groove in the edge banding, also using the slotting cutter. Then cut stock for the splines from ¼-in.-thick plywood or hardboard. Be sure that the spline sock is thick enough to yield a snug fit.

Apply glue to the spline groove, spline, and mating edges, and clamp the edge banding to the case top. When the glue has set, use the 1¼-in.-rad. rounding-over bit to rout the profile on the edge banding. Use the table saw to rip and crosscut each top to finished dimension.

With a 1¼-in.-rad. bit in the router, shape the edge of a scrap block of poplar. Using this scrap as a pattern, trace the radius onto the corner of a piece of MDF that is at least 24 in. square. Using a jigsaw, carefully cut the fiberboard to shape keeping the blade on the waste side of the line. Then refine the profile by sanding it smooth and check against the poplar block for accuracy. The MDF will serve as a template to shape each of the case sides.

Materials List

Key	No.	Size and description (use)
A	1	1¹³⁄₁₆ x 2½ x 32½" poplar (edge band)
B*	1	¾ x 15½ x 32½" MDF (top)
C*	2	¾ x 18 x 78" MDF (side)
D*	1	¾ x 4 x 41" MDF (toeboard)
E	1	¼ x 33½ x 77¾" hardboard (back)
F*	1	¾ x 15 x 33¼" MDF (bottom)
G*	1	¾ x 17¾ x 33¼" MDF (divider shelf)
H*	1	¾ x 16⅞ x 33¼" MDF (fixed shelf)
I*	2	¾ x 13⅞ x 32⅜" MDF (adjustable shelf for Unit 1 only; for Units 2 and 3 the shelves measure ¾ x 16⅞ x 32⅜" MDF)
J1	2	¼ x ⅞ x 15" hardboard (spline)
J2	1	¼ x 1 x 32½" hardboard (spline)
K	1	¾ x 4 x 32½" poplar (cleat)
L*	2	¾ x 16⁵⁄₃₂ x 34⅛" MDF (doors for Units 1 and 3; for Unit 2 the doors measure ¾ x 16⁵⁄₃₂ x 26⅞" MDF)
M*	1	¾ x 1⅝ x 32½" MDF (doorstop)
N1	2	½ x 4 x 31" Baltic Birch plywood (drawer front)
N2	2	½ x 7½ x 31" Baltic Birch plywood (drawer front)
O1	2	½ x 3½ x 31" Baltic Birch plywood (drawer back)
O2	2	½ x 7 x 31" Baltic Birch plywood (drawer back)
P1	4	½ x 4 x 16" Baltic Birch plywood (drawer side)
P2	4	½ x 7½ x 16" Baltic Birch plywood (drawer side)
Q	4	¼ x 15¼ x 31" birch plywood (drawer bottom)
R1*	2	¾ x 4½ x 32⅜" MDF (drawer face)
R2*	2	¾ x 8 x 32⅜" MDF (drawer face)
S1	8	drawer front adjusters
S2	8	8-32 x ¾" rh machine screws
T	8	3" gray nylon wire pulls
U	4 pr.	16" full-extension drawer slides
V	4	⅝"-dia. steel furniture glides
W	as reqd.	¾" brads
X	4	self-sticking plastic door cushions
Y	2	95° self-closing hinges
Z	2	176° self-closing hinges with inset plate (left door on Unit 1 and both doors on Units 2 and 3)
AA	8	adjustable shelf pins
BB	3	1¼" No. 8 fh screws
CC	as reqd.	⅝" No. 5 rh screws
DD*	1	¾ x 6¾ x 13⅞" MDF (center partition Unit 1 only)
EE*	2	¾ x 6¾ x 13⅛" MDF (side partition Unit 1 only)
FF*	2	¾ x 3⅜" x 6" MDF (partition cap Unit 1 only)
GG*	1	¾ x 13⅞ x 33¼" MDF (upper fixed shelf Unit 1 only)
HH*	2	¾ x 5¹⁵⁄₁₆ x 12¹³⁄₁₆" MDF (cubby drawer front Unit 1 only)
II	4	½ x 5¹⁵⁄₁₆ x 13⅝" Baltic Birch plywood (cubby drawer side Unit 1 only)
JJ	2	½ x 5⁷⁄₁₆ x 12⁵⁄₁₆" Baltic Birch plywood (cubby drawer back Unit 1 only)
KK	2	¼ x 12⁵⁄₁₆ x 13⅛" birch plywood (cubby drawer bottom Unit 1 only)

Misc.: Glue; 120-, 220-, and 320-grit sandpaper; polyurethane; mineral spirits; wax; interior enamel undercoat primer; gloss enamel paint.
Note: These storage units are all based on the same module, so they can be arranged and customized to suit individual needs.
* MDF stands for medium-density fiberboard.

Next, cut the case sides to size, and using the template, rout the corner profile on each side. Use a ½-in. straight bit with a pilot bearing. Then lay out the notch for the toe space in each side and use a jigsaw or band saw to make the cutout.

Using the router with ½-in. or ¾-in. straight bit and an edge guide, cut the rabbet for the case back on each case side.

Be sure to stop the rabbet ¼ in. shy of the top edge and use a sharp chisel to square the end of the cut. Use the same router setup to cut the rabbet on the back edge of case top.

Now cut and attach the wall cleat to the back edge of the case top using glue and clamps. When this assembly is dry, cut stock for the upper case doorstop and screw it to the underside of the edge banding.

Using the drawing as a guide, lay out the dadoes on each case side (**Figs. 1 and 2**). Note that all the dadoes, except those for the case bottom, are stopped short of the case front. Cut these dadoes using a router with a ¾-in. straight bit and a straightedge guide. When all the dadoes are cut, use a sharp chisel to square the ends of the stopped dadoes. Finish routing the side by cutting the spline grooves for the side-to-top joint. Use a ¼-in. straight bit and a straightedge guide. Note that these grooves are stopped 1½ in. short of the case front. Cut the shelves and cubby drawer assembly parts to size (**Fig. 3**). Then using a table saw, band saw, or jigsaw, cut the required notches in the front corners of the shelves and partition. Finally, lay out and rout the dadoes in the shelves for the cubby drawer assembly.

Assembly

Glue and clamp the cubby drawer assembly together and set it aside to dry (**Fig. 4**). Then cut all the splines to proper length. To assemble the case, begin by laying one side on the bench with the inside surface facing up. Apply the glue to all dadoes and spline grooves, shelf ends, and splines. Insert the shelves and top assembly into the side. Then apply glue to dadoes in

Fig. 1 *Cut the side panels to size, then lay out and rout shelf dadoes in the sides using a ¾-in. straight bit and a straightedge guide.*

Fig. 2 *On case No. 1, lay out and rout additional dadoes to house the cubby drawer assembly. Guide the router with a straightedge.*

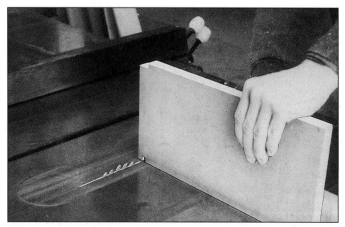

Fig. 3 *Cut fixed shelves, bottoms, and partitions (where required) to size. Then cut notches in the front corners to the size shown on the drawing.*

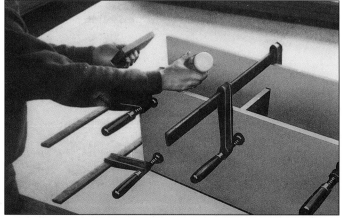

Fig. 4 *Preassemble cubby drawer unit for case No. 1 using glue and clamps. Check for square and readjust the clamps if necessary.*

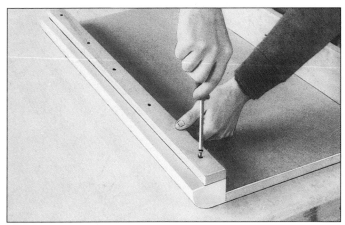

Fig. 5 *Glue and clamp the wall cleat and edge banding to the top panel. Rout a profile on the edge banding and attach the doorstop to bottom edge.*

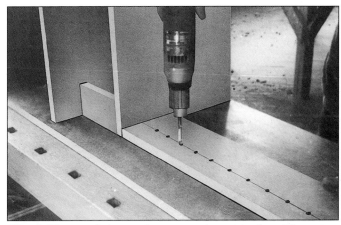

Fig. 6 *Glue and clamp the case parts together. Then bore adjustable-shelf pinholes in the sides. Use a prebored pattern jig for accuracy.*

the opposite side and place it over the existing assembly. Clamp the entire case together, using cauls under the clamp jaws to evenly distribute the pressure. Check the case for square by comparing opposite diagonal measurements and readjust the clamps if necessary.

Cut the toeboards for the toe spaces to size, then glue and clamp in place (**Fig. 5**). Next, cut the case back to size from 1/4-in.-thick hardboard. Set the back aside. It will be installed after the finishing process is complete.

Then lay out the position of the adjustable-shelf holes inside each case (**Fig. 6**). By making a template from a piece of scrap plywood or MDF, you can simplify this process. Bore a series of 1/4-in.-dia. holes 2 in. on center, along the length of the template. Clamp the template in the proper position, then bore the pinholes right through the template into the side. Cut the adjustable shelves to size and set aside for finishing.

Building the Doors

Cut stock to size for the cabinet doors, then use a 35-mm bit to bore the hinge holes in the doors (**Fig. 7**). (These bits are available from mail-order hardware and tool suppliers.) It's a good idea to clamp a fence to the drill press table, so you can easily locate the holes a uniform distance from the door edges. When the holes are bored, mount the hinges using the specified screws (**Fig. 8**). We used self-closing hinges on the doors to eliminate the need for door catches. We also specified 95° hinges on the right door of unit No. 1 to prevent the door from swinging into the wardrobe ("Closet Control," page 100). If you aren't building the wardrobe, or placing it adjacent to the wall units, use wider-swinging 176° hinges throughout.

Using the drawing as a guide, make a template for boring the mounting plate holes and the case sides. Align the template as shown on the drawing, then bore the holes and mount the plates (**Fig. 9**). We used Blum hinges for this project. If you choose other hinges, the hinge locations may be different.

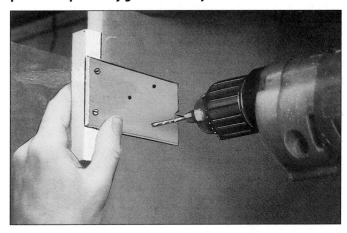

Fig. 7 *Construct a jig—as shown on the drawing—for boring the door-hinge pilot holes. Properly position the jig on the case sides and bore holes.*

Fig. 8 *Temporarily attach the hinge-mounting plates to the case sides. They will be removed later to make the finishing process easier.*

Hang the door on the cases by sliding the hinges onto the plates and tightening the mounting screws. Adjust the doors, then lay out and bore clearance holes for the door pulls.

Drawer Assembly and Finishing

Cut the parts for the cubby drawers to size (**Fig. 10**). Then use the template shown in the drawing to trace the finger-pull cutouts on the drawer fronts. Make the cutouts with a jigsaw, then sand the edge smooth.

Use the dado blades on the table saw to make the required dado and rabbet cuts in drawer parts (**Figs. 11 and 12**), then cut drawer bottoms to size. Assemble the drawers with glue and brads and check for square. Slide the drawer bottoms in place and fasten with screws to the bottom edge of the drawer back. Sand the drawers thoroughly. Keep in mind that these two drawers will be finished entirely with the enamel paint.

Next, cut the parts for the bottom case drawers from ½-in.-thick Baltic Birch plywood. Use dado blades in a table saw to cut the groove for the drawer bottom in the drawer sides and fronts. Then readjust the saw to cut the dadoes for drawer fronts and backs in the sides, and to cut the rabbets on the ends of the drawer fronts. Cut the drawer bottoms to size from a sheet of ¼-in.-thick birch plywood.

Assemble the drawers using glue and brads (**Fig. 13**). Fasten the bottoms to drawer backs using screws. Mount the drawer slides following the manufacturer's instructions (**Fig. 14**).

Next, cut the drawer faces to size. Clamp each drawer face to its respective drawer box. Then bore pilot holes through the drawer front into the face to mark the position of the drawer front adjusters (**Fig. 15**). Remove the face and number it for easy reassembly later. Bore the holes for the drawer front adjuster in the back of the drawer face then tap the adjusters into place (**Fig. 16**). Lay out and bore the holes for the drawer pulls, being sure to countersink these holes on the back side of the drawer face so the screw heads won't project above the surface. Attach the pulls, then reattach the drawer faces and install the drawers in the case. Adjust the slides, if necessary, for smooth operation, then adjust the drawer faces to yield uniform spacing around each.

Remove all doors, drawers, and hardware, then separate the drawer faces from drawers. If the cases are to be used in a side-by-side configuration, temporarily clamp the cases together and bore 5/16-in. holes for the connecting screws. While the exact location of these holes is not important, it's best if they are placed within the upper and lower cabinet enclosures so they won't be visible when the doors and drawers are closed.

Finish the lower drawers with a clear polyurethane varnish. Thin the first coat 25 percent with mineral spirits, then let it dry overnight. Sand lightly with 220-grit paper before applying a second coat full strength. (If desired, apply a third coat.) For directions on how to apply the enamel finish to the rest of the unit, see "Closet Control," page 106.

When the finish has dried, reattach the drawer faces and install the case back. Remount all hardware, hang the doors, and slide the drawers in place. Make any final adjustments for proper door and drawer alignment and the cases are complete.

Fig. 9 *Carefully locate the hinge positions on the door backs, then bore hinge-mounting holes. Push the hinge into the hole and attach with screws.*

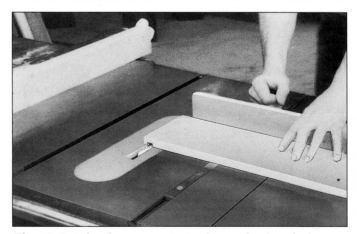

Fig. 10 *Cut the drawer parts to size and using dado blades in the table saw, cut dadoes in the side to receive the drawer fronts and backs.*

Fig. 11 *Cut rabbets in the ends of the drawer fronts using a ¹/₄-in. wide dado blade in the table saw. Be sure to keep the board tight to the fence.*

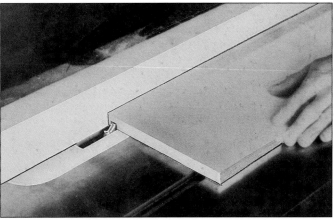

Fig. 12 *Readjust the table saw fence and cut ¹/₄-in. grooves in the drawer sides, fronts, and backs to receive the drawer bottom panel.*

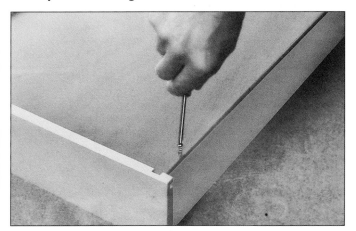

Fig. 13 *Cut the bottom panels to size, then assemble the drawer parts with glue and brads. Slide the bottoms into place and attach them with screws.*

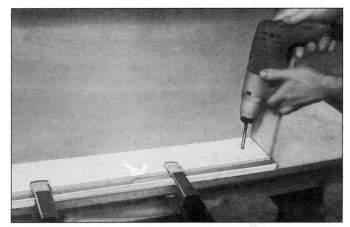

Fig. 14 *Cut the drawer faces to size and clamp them to the drawer fronts. Bore pilot holes through the front into the face to locate the drawer adjusters.*

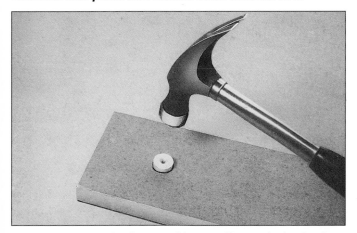

Fig. 15 *Remove the face and bore adjuster holes in the back sides. Tap the adjusters into place, then attach the face to the front using adjuster screws.*

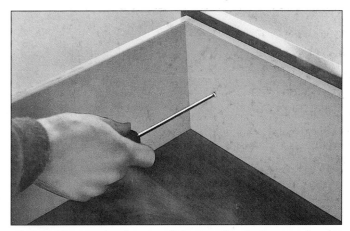

Fig. 16 *Mount the drawer slides on the drawer and case, install the drawer, and check for fit. Loosen the screws to adjust the drawer face and retighten.*

Closet Control

This impressive stand-alone wardrobe decreases your worries by increasing your closet space.

Though we designed this wardrobe as a companion piece to the wall units described in "A Place for Everything" (page 92), it can also stand on its own in almost any contemporary environment. By increasing the cabinet depth, we created enough space for hanging clothes, which should relieve some pressure on your crowded bedroom closets. We also incorporated a combination of open shelves and cubby drawers for keeping smaller items organized. If you would prefer more room for hanging clothes, or fewer drawers and more open shelves, you can easily modify the dimensions to suit your individual needs.

*Key*POINTS

TIME
Prep Time .... 6 hours
Shop Time .... 20 hours
Assembly Time .... 20 hours

EFFORT
Skill Level .... intermediate

COST / BENEFITS
Expense: moderate
• The design can be **easily customized** to add more open shelves or drawers.
• This wardrobe **can stand alone or act as a companion** to the wall units.

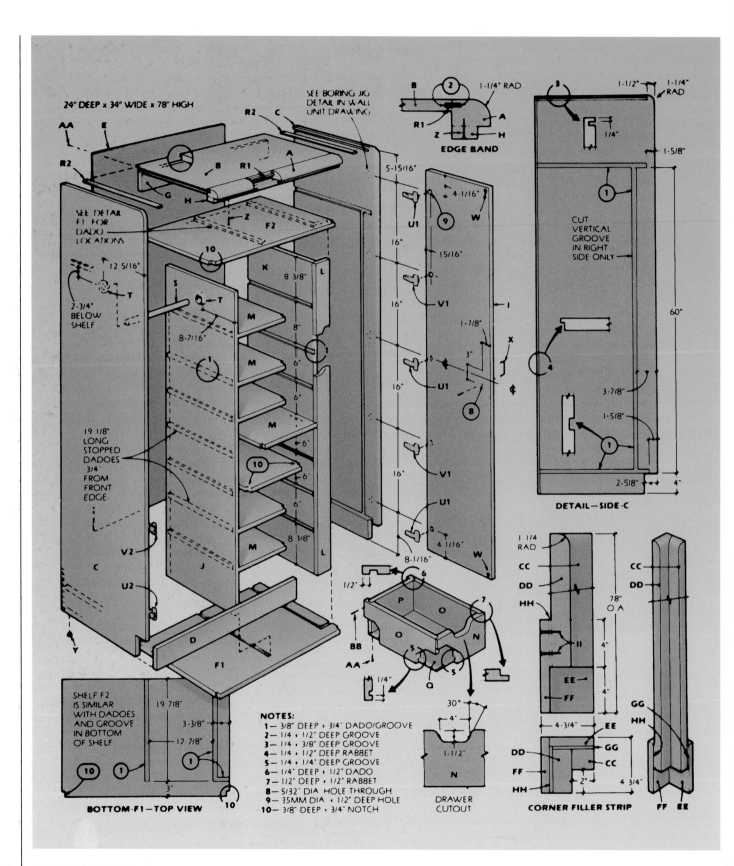

24" DEEP x 34" WIDE x 78" HIGH

SEE BORING JIG
DETAIL IN WALL
UNIT DRAWING

EDGE BAND

1-1/4" RAD

1-1/2"
1-1/4" RAD

CUT
VERTICAL
GROOVE
IN RIGHT
SIDE ONLY

DETAIL—SIDE-C

1/4"

1-5/8"

60"

3-7/8"

1-5/8"

2-5/8"   4"

SEE DETAIL
F1 FOR
DADO
LOCATIONS

12 5/16"

2-3/4"
BELOW
SHELF

8-7/16"

19 1/8"
LONG
STOPPED
DADOES
3/4"
FROM
FRONT
EDGE

8 3/8"

8"

6"

6"

6"

6"

6"

8 3/8"

5-15/16"

4-1/16"

16"

15/16"

16"

1-7/8"

3"

16"

16"

4 1/16"

8-1/16"

1/2"

1/4"

BB

AA

DRAWER
CUTOUT

30°

4"

1-1/2"

N

1 1/4
RAD

CC

DD

HH

78"
O A

4"

4"

EE

FF

4-3/4"

DD

FF

HH

CORNER FILLER STRIP

2"

EE

GG

CC

CC

DD

GG

HH

FF EE

4 3/4"

SHELF F2
IS SIMILAR
WITH DADOES
AND GROOVE
IN BOTTOM
OF SHELF

19 7/8"

3-3/8"

17 7/8"

3"

BOTTOM-F1—TOP VIEW

NOTES:
1 — 3/8" DEEP • 3/4" DADO/GROOVE
2 — 1/4 • 1/2" DEEP GROOVE
3 — 1/4 • 3/8" DEEP GROOVE
4 — 1/4 • 1/2" DEEP RABBET
5 — 1/4 • 1/4" DEEP GROOVE
6 — 1/4" DEEP • 1/2" DADO
7 — 1/2" DEEP • 1/2" RABBET
8 — 5/32" DIA HOLE THROUGH
9 — 35MM DIA • 1/2" DEEP HOLE
10 — 3/8" DEEP • 3/4" NOTCH

Construction Details

Begin by cutting the panel for the case top slightly oversize in both length and width, and cut the 8/4 poplar edge banding to length. Use a $\frac{1}{4}$-in. slotting cutter and router to cut the spline grooves in the mating edges of the top panel and the edge banding. Cut stock for the spline from $\frac{1}{4}$-in.-thick hardboard or plywood. Then apply glue to the spline, groove, and mating edges, and clamp all parts together. After the glue has dried use a $1\frac{1}{4}$-in. rounding-over bit to rout the top corner of the edge banding.

Next, rip and crosscut the case top and sides to finished dimension. Then use the template made for the wall units ("A Place for Everything," page 92) to guide the router in shaping the upper corners of the case sides. Clamp the sides over the template with the edges flush and use a $\frac{1}{2}$-in. straight bit to trace the template. Lay out the toe-space notch and use a jigsaw or band saw to make the cutouts.

Dadoes and Rabbets

Use the router with a $\frac{1}{4}$-in. straight bit and edge guide to cut the grooves in the case sides for joining them to the top. Note that these grooves are stopped $1\frac{1}{2}$ in. short of the front edge of the sides. Then, using a $\frac{1}{4}$-in. slotting cutter, cut the matching spline grooves in the edges of the case top.

Using a $\frac{1}{2}$- or $\frac{3}{4}$-in. straight bit and edge guide, rout the rabbets in the case top and sides to receive the case back. Note that the rabbet in the case sides is stopped $\frac{1}{4}$ in. shy of the top edge. Use a chisel to square the ends of these stopped cuts. Lay out the dadoes for the case bottom and top shelf in the sides, and use a $\frac{3}{4}$-in. straight bit to rout the dadoes **(Fig. 1)**. Be sure to use a straightedge to guide the cut. Again use a sharp chisel to square the ends of stopped dadoes **(Fig. 2)**.

Cut the bottom and top shelf to size, then lay out and cut the notches at the front corners of both pieces. Then lay out

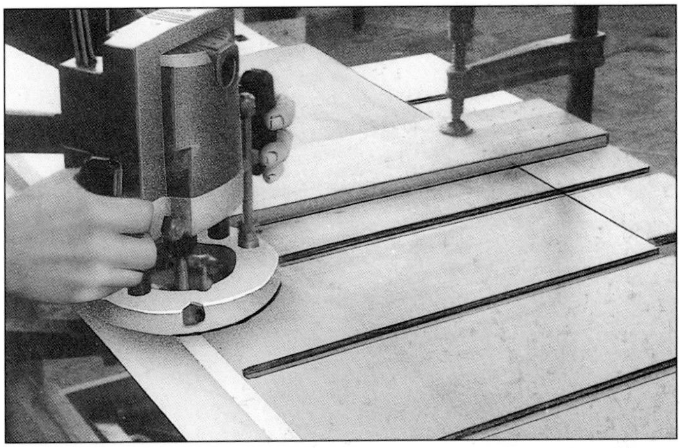

Fig. 1 ***Cut the case partitions to size, then lay out the shelf locations on both. Cut the shelf dadoes using the router and a straightedge guide.***

Materials List

Key	No.	Size and description (use)
A	1	$1\frac{13}{16} \times 2\frac{1}{2} \times 32\frac{1}{2}$" poplar (edge band)
B	1	$\frac{3}{4} \times 21\frac{1}{2} \times 32\frac{1}{2}$" MDF (top)
C	2	$\frac{3}{4} \times 24 \times 78$" MDF (side)
D	1	$\frac{3}{4} \times 4 \times 34$" MDF (toeboard)
E	1	$\frac{1}{4} \times 33\frac{1}{2} \times 77\frac{3}{4}$" hardboard (back)
F1	1	$\frac{3}{4} \times 22\frac{7}{8} \times 33\frac{1}{4}$" MDF (bottom)
F2	1	$\frac{3}{4} \times 22\frac{7}{8} \times 33\frac{1}{4}$" MDF (top shelf)
G	1	$\frac{3}{4} \times 4 \times 32\frac{1}{2}$" MDF (cleat)
H	1	$\frac{3}{4} \times 1\frac{5}{8} \times 32\frac{1}{2}$" MDF (doorstop)
I	2	$\frac{3}{4} \times 16\frac{5}{32} \times 72\frac{1}{8}$" MDF (door)
J	1	$\frac{3}{4} \times 19\frac{7}{8} \times 60$" MDF (center partition)
K	1	$\frac{3}{4} \times 19\frac{1}{8} \times 60$" MDF (right partition)
L	1	$\frac{3}{4} \times 3\frac{3}{8} \times 60$" MDF (facing)
M	7	$\frac{3}{4} \times 13\frac{5}{8} \times 19\frac{7}{8}$" MDF (shelf)
N	5	$\frac{3}{4} \times 5\frac{15}{16} \times 12\frac{13}{16}$" MDF (drawer front)
O	10	$\frac{1}{2} \times 5\frac{15}{16} \times 19\frac{5}{8}$" Baltic Birch plywood (drawer side)
P	5	$\frac{1}{2} \times 5\frac{7}{16} \times 12\frac{5}{16}$" Baltic Birch plywood (drawer back)
Q	5	$\frac{1}{4} \times 12\frac{5}{16} \times 18\frac{7}{8}$" birch plywood (drawer bottom)
R1	1	$\frac{1}{4} \times 1 \times 31\frac{1}{2}$" hardboard (spline)
R2	2	$\frac{1}{4} \times \frac{7}{8} \times 22\frac{1}{4}$" hardboard (spline)
S	1	$1\frac{3}{8}$"-dia. x $15\frac{3}{4}$" fir closet pole
T	1 pr.	$1\frac{3}{8}$"-dia. closet pole sockets
U1	3	176° self-closing hinge, with inset plate (right door only)
U2	3	95° self-closing hinge (left door only)
V1	2	176° free swing hinge, with inset plate (right door only)
V2	2	95° free swing hinge (left door only)
W	4	self-sticking plastic door cushions
X	2	3" gray nylon wire pulls
Y	4	$\frac{5}{8}$"-dia. steel furniture glides
Z	3	$1\frac{1}{4}$" No. 8 fh screws
AA	as reqd.	$\frac{5}{8}$" No. 5 rh screws
BB	as reqd.	$\frac{3}{4}$" brads
CC	1	$1\frac{3}{4} \times 2 \times 74$" poplar (post)
DD	1	$1\frac{3}{4} \times 3\frac{3}{4} \times 74$" poplar (post)
EE	1	$\frac{3}{4} \times 4 \times 8$" MDF (toeboard)
FF	1	$\frac{3}{4} \times 4\frac{3}{4} \times 8$" MDF (toeboard)
GG	1	$\frac{1}{4} \times 3\frac{3}{4} \times 4$" hardboard (spacer)
HH	1	$\frac{1}{4} \times 4 \times 4$" hardboard (spacer)
II	4	$1\frac{1}{2}$" No. 8 fh screws

Misc.: Glue; 120-, 220-, and 320-grit sandpaper; mineral spirits; wax; interior enamel undercoat primer; gloss enamel paint.

* MDF stands for medium-density fiberboard.

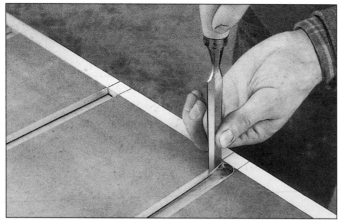

Fig. 2 *Using a sharp chisel, carefully square the ends of all the stopped shelf dadoes. Then cut the case bottom and the top shelf to size.*

Fig. 3 *Again using a router and straightedge guide, cut dadoes in the case bottom and top shelf to house the case partitions.*

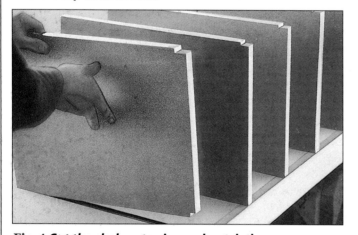

Fig. 4 *Cut the shelves to size and notch the corners. Then begin assembly by gluing the shelves into the dadoes cut in both interior partitions.*

Fig. 5 *Quickly clamp the assembly together before glue starts to dry. Be sure to check for square and readjust the clamps if necessary.*

TECH *Tips*

Drawer Design
A drawer can be as simple as four pieces of wood, butted together and fastened with screws or nails (don't bother with glue, which adds very little strength in an endgrain butt joint). From there you move up to the slightly more complex drawer that we show here, in which the parts are fastened with rabbets at the front and a dado at the back. Purists will sneer at this, of course, since it's not the quintessential dovetail joint, but we've seen kitchen drawers built this way that are still going strong after 50 or a 100 years! Translation: It's a perfectly acceptable and simple way to build a rugged drawer.

The bottom can be as simple as a piece of plywood slid in a groove or a thin piece of solid wood held in a frame. If you look at many very old drawers (from the early 1800s, before woodworking machinery was in wide use) that's exactly what you'll see. If you choose a solid wood bottom, be sure to fasten it only at the front so it's free to expand and contract.

the dadoes in the bottom and top shelf for the false side and center partition. Rout these stopped dadoes using a ¾-in. straight bit (**Fig. 3**). Cut the partition, false side, and facing strip to size, then glue and clamp the strip to the false side.

After the glue dries, lay out the dadoes in the partition and false side, and route the dadoes, using a straightedge guide. Square all stopped dado ends with a sharp chisel.

Assembly

Next, cut the short shelves to size and, again, using either a band saw or jigsaw, cut notches in the front corners. Then glue and clamp together the false side, partition, and shelves (**Fig. 4**). Use a clamp over each shelf joint to make sure that all joints are brought tight (**Fig. 5**), then check for square.

Continue assembly by gluing and clamping the bottom and top shelf to the false side and partition (**Fig. 6**). Use cauls across the joints to evenly distribute the clamping pressure. Finally, glue and clamp the case sides to the existing assembly (**Fig. 7**). When the glue dries, cut and install the toeboard at the bottom of the case. Then cut the case back to size, but do not attach it yet. Also, locate and temporarily install the closet pole sockets as shown in the drawing. Then cut and install the closet pole.

Next, cut the doors to finished size, and using a 35-mm bit, bore hinge-mounting holes on the back side of the doors. Then temporarily mount the hinges on the doors. By using three self-closing and two free-swinging hinges on each door, you won't need door catches. Also keep in mind that if you want to position this wardrobe next to the wall units, you must install 95° hinges on the door that swings against the wall units. These hinges will prevent the wardrobe door from hitting the wall units.

Next, lay out the center location of hinge-mounting plates on the case sides. Use the template shown in the wall units drawing to bore these holes. Attach the mounting plates, then hang the doors on the cabinet, and check for proper fit. Adjust the doors, using the screws on the hinges and mounting plates, for uniform margins on all edges. Bore the holes for door pulls at this time.

Drawer Assembly

Cut the drawer fronts to size (**Fig. 8**). Then lay out the finger-pull cutout on a piece of scrap MDF and use a jigsaw to make the cut (**Fig. 9**). Sand the profile smooth, then use this template to trace the cutout onto each of the drawer fronts. Cut each and sand smooth.

Next, cut the drawer sides, backs, and bottoms to size. Use dado blades in a table saw to cut the rabbets on the ends of the drawer fronts and to cut the dadoes in sides for the drawer backs (**Fig. 10**). Then cut the grooves for the drawer bottoms in the fronts and sides, and sand all drawer surfaces smooth. Assemble the drawers with glue and brads, as shown (**Figs. 11 and 12**).

Fig. 6 *Glue and clamp the top shelf and case bottom to the partition assembly. Use cauls under the clamp jaws to distribute clamping pressure.*

Fig. 7 *Join the case sides to the existing assembly using glue and clamps. Again, use cauls to evenly distribute clamping pressure.*

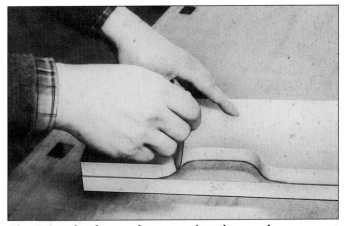

Fig. 8 *Cut the drawer fronts to size, then make a template for the finger-pull cutout on scrap board. Trace the template onto each drawer front.*

Fig. 9 *Use a jigsaw or band saw to make the finger-pull cutouts. Sand the edge smooth with a drum sander to remove any saw marks.*

Fig. 10 *Cut rabbets on the drawer fronts and dadoes in sides using dado blades. A stop block clamped to the miter gauge speeds the cuts.*

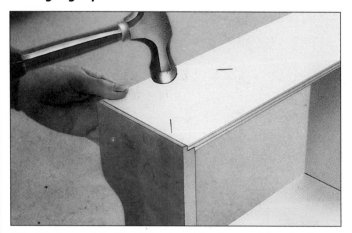

Fig. 11 *Assemble the drawer with glue and brads. Set and fill the brad heads, then check for square before setting the drawers aside to dry.*

To prepare for finishing, remove the drawers, doors, and all hardware from the case. Sand all surfaces with 120- followed by 220-grit sandpaper. Dust off thoroughly and wipe clean with a tack cloth.

Finishing

In choosing a finish for these pieces we had to balance our desire for a high-gloss look with the relative toxicity of many gloss finishes. While the toughest and glossiest finishes are either epoxies or polyurethane enamels, these materials yield fumes which are best left to an industrial, not a home environment. We did, however, find a gloss enamel that is safe for home use. It is Devoe Paint's Bar-Ox Alkyd Quick Dry Gloss Enamel. This is a full-gloss enamel that dries so rapidly that we found no evidence of dust contamination—a common problem with gloss finishes.

This finish can be applied by either brush or spray. The best results will come from spray application. It is extremely important when applying this, or any solvent-based finish, that a proper respirator be worn and a fan used to exhaust fumes to the outside.

Begin the finishing process by priming all surfaces with the enamel undercoat. One coat of primer is sufficient on the flat surfaces, while two coats are necessary on the panel edges. Sand lightly with 320-grit open-coat sandpaper between coats and dust off thoroughly. After priming, examine all surfaces by shining a bright light across each. This technique will aid in spotting any scratches or irregularities that will need further work before top coating.

For application of the topcoat, thin the enamel with up to ½ pint of mineral spirits per gallon of paint. Always coat the interior surfaces of cases first, followed by the exterior surfaces: edges first, then flat surfaces. When spraying, keep the gun approximately 8 in. from the work, with your arm moving in a line parallel to the work surface (**Fig. 13**).

Let the first coat dry thoroughly—at least 12 hours at 70°F, longer if the temperature is lower. Scuff lightly with 320-grit paper and wipe with a tack cloth. Apply the second coat as you did the first and let it dry thoroughly. Finally, examine the finish carefully to see if there are areas that might require a third coat.

This finish will dry to the touch in 12 hours. But you should allow it to cure for at least a week before putting the pieces into service. After a week, install the case back, drawers, door, and closet pole. Apply a small amount of wax to shelves where drawers will slide to ease the action and protect the painted surfaces from scratching (**Fig. 14**).

To stabilize this wardrobe, it's a good idea to screw it to a wall. To do this, simply locate the wall studs, transfer these locations to the wall cleat in the back of the case, bore clearance holes, and drive the screws into place.

If you want to attach the wardrobe to the wall units, build the filler strip shown in the drawing (**Fig. 15**).

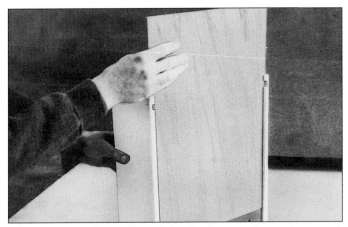

Fig. 12 *Once glue is dry, slide the bottom into place and attach to the bottom edge of the drawer back with screws. Be sure to bore pilot holes.*

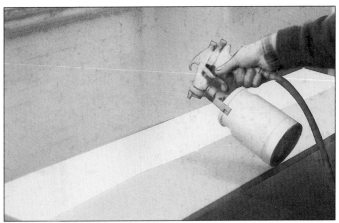

Fig. 13 *When spraying enamel, hold the gun about 8 in. away from the work. Keep the gun moving and overlap the previous spray about 50 percent.*

Fig. 14 *Once the finish is completely dry, apply a light coat of wax to the drawer shelves to prevent scratching and ease drawer movement.*

Fig. 15 *If the wardrobe is to be joined to the wall units, build a filler post out of poplar boards. Rout the same radius on the top edge of assembly.*

MATERIAL *Matters*

Know Your Paint

Our project calls for alkyd paint, which is often referred to by its outmoded name, oil paint. Alkyd resin—the stuff that holds the pigment particles together and glues them to the surface—has some unique characteristics that you should to be aware of before you start painting. Once you know what these traits are, you'll know how to achieve optimum results: a smooth, hard film that will protect the wardrobe and continue to look great for many years.

Alkyd paint usually has a stronger odor than waterborne products. It's a bit stickier to apply and needs to be very carefully stirred to get all the pigment off the bottom of the can. Like all paints, it works best in moderate temperature and humidity, and can be downright difficult to work with in cold or hot temperatures.

Alkyd paint can be applied over waterborne coatings, so don't be afraid to use a latex primer. Just make sure you buy a primer that's compatible. Alkyd coatings sometimes take a bit longer to cure than latex. Take this into account before sanding one coat to prepare for the second.

Living Room
and
Home Office

 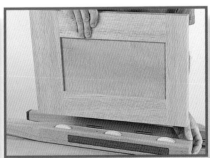 

Book Keeper

This traditional solid oak barrister's bookcase features lift-up, slide-back doors.

At one time, a barrister's bookcase was considered standard equipment in law offices throughout old England—and in the States, as well. Today, the bookcases enjoy even greater popularity outside the office, and have become very sought-after—and pricey—items at antique shops, flea markets, and garage sales everywhere. A barrister's bookcase provides an attractive, practical way to store and display books—particularly encyclopedia sets and rare, antique book collections. Here, we present step-by-step instructions and plans to build a faithful reproduction oak barrister's bookcase, including easy-to-follow details for making the lift-up, slide-back doors.

*Key*POINTS

TIME
Prep Time	6 hours
Shop Time	8 hours
Assembly Time	16 hours

EFFORT
Skill Level	intermediate

COST / BENEFITS
Expense: moderate
- A beautiful display case for your most treasured books.
- Lift-up, slide-back doors make it easy to grab what you want when you want it.

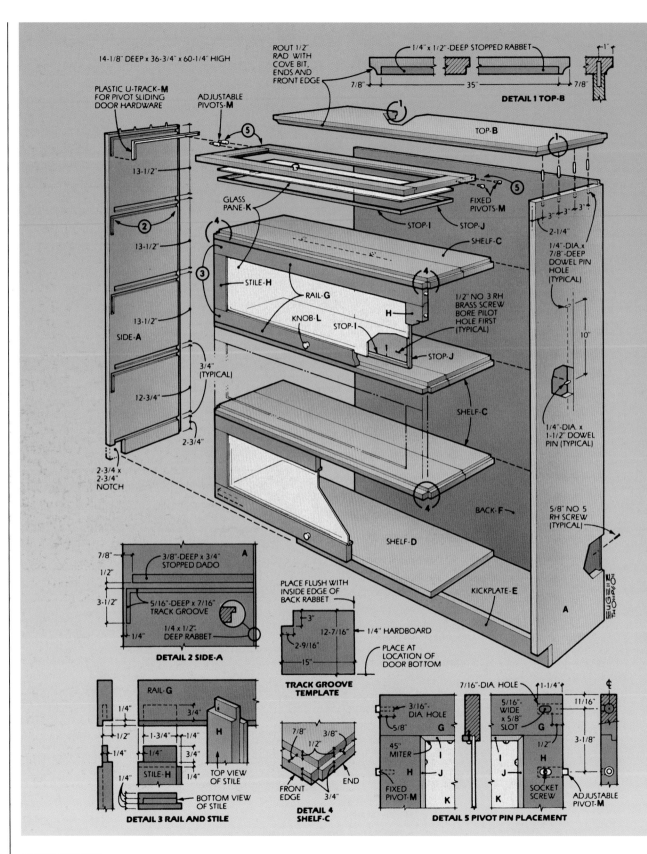

14-1/8" DEEP x 36-3/4" x 60-1/4" HIGH

ROUT 1/2" RAD WITH COVE BIT, ENDS AND FRONT EDGE

1/4" x 1/2"-DEEP STOPPED RABBET

1"

7/8"   35"   7/8"

DETAIL 1 TOP-B

PLASTIC U-TRACK-M FOR PIVOT SLIDING DOOR HARDWARE

ADJUSTABLE PIVOTS-M

TOP-B

5

13-1/2"

2

13-1/2"

GLASS PANE-K

STOP-I   STOP-J

FIXED PIVOTS-M

5

3" 3" 3"

SHELF-C

2-1/4"

1/4"-DIA. x 7/8"-DEEP DOWEL PIN HOLE (TYPICAL)

4

3

STILE-H

RAIL-G

H

1/2" NO 3 RH BRASS SCREW BORE PILOT HOLE FIRST (TYPICAL)

13-1/2"

KNOB-L   STOP-I

STOP-J

SIDE-A

10"

3/4" (TYPICAL)

12-3/4"

SHELF-C

2-3/4"

1/4"-DIA. x 1-1/2" DOWEL PIN (TYPICAL)

2-3/4 x 2-3/4" NOTCH

BACK-F

SHELF-C

4

5/8" NO 5 RH SCREW (TYPICAL)

SHELF-D

KICKPLATE-E

A

EUGENE THOMPSON

7/8"

3/8"-DEEP x 3/4" STOPPED DADO

A

1/2"

3-1/2"

5/16"-DEEP x 7/16" TRACK GROOVE

1/4"

1/4" x 1/2" DEEP RABBET

DETAIL 2 SIDE-A

PLACE FLUSH WITH INSIDE EDGE OF BACK RABBET

3"

12-7/16"   1/4" HARDBOARD

2-9/16"

15"

PLACE AT LOCATION OF DOOR BOTTOM

TRACK GROOVE TEMPLATE

RAIL-G

1/4"

3/4"

H

1/2"   1-3/4" 1/4"

1/4"

1/4"   3/4"

STILE-H

1/4"

TOP VIEW OF STILE

1/4"

BOTTOM VIEW OF STILE

DETAIL 3 RAIL AND STILE

7/8"   3/8"

1/2"

FRONT EDGE

END

3/4"

DETAIL 4 SHELF-C

7/16"-DIA. HOLE   1-1/4"

3/16"-DIA. HOLE

5/8"

G

45° MITER

H

FIXED PIVOT-M

I   J

K

5/16"-WIDE x 5/8" SLOT

G

I

J

1/2"

H

SOCKET SCREW

K

11/16"

3-1/8"

ADJUSTABLE PIVOT-M

DETAIL 5 PIVOT PIN PLACEMENT

The bookcase is constructed of 4/4 and 6/4 red oak, surface planed to the thicknesses given in the materials list. Of course, it wouldn't be a barrister's bookcase without the four pivot sliding doors. You can find the door hardware online or at your local home-improvement center. Use ⅛-in. clear glass for the door panes and ¼-in. oak-veneer plywood for the cabinet back.

Stock Preparation

Start by edge-joining boards together to form the cabinet top, sides, and shelves. Rough cut the boards slightly oversize and then smooth the mating edges on a jointer. Next, edge-join the boards together with glue and ¼-in.-dia. x 1½-in. hardwood dowel pins spaced about 10 in. apart. Be sure to mark dowel pin locations on the board faces so that you don't accidentally cut through a dowel when trimming the panels to their finished dimensions. Leave the panels clamped together until the glue dries thoroughly.

Once the glue has dried, use a hand scraper to smooth the panel surfaces. Now crosscut the panels to the finished length using a portable circular saw and a straightedge guide (**Fig. 1**). Rip the panels to the finished width on a table saw.

Routing Procedures

Next, using a ¾-in.-dia. straight bit and a straightedge guide, route ⅜-in.-deep stopped dadoes in the inside surface of the cabinet sides. The dadoes, which will house the four shelves, are stopped ⅞ in. from the front edge of the cabinet sides (see Drawing Detail 2). Square up the ends of each stopped dado with a sharp chisel. Then use an edge-guide attachment on the router to rout a ¼ x ½-in.-deep rabbet in the inside rear edge of the cabinet sides (**Fig. 2**). Also, rout a stopped rabbet in the inside rear edge of the cabinet top. Again, square the ends of the stopped rabbet with a sharp chisel. These rabbets will accept the ¼-in. plywood cabinet back. Now readjust the router's edge guide to cut a ⅜ x ½-in.-deep rabbet on both ends of each of the three middle shelves. Readjust the edge

Fig. 1 *Crosscut edge-joined panels to length with a portable circular saw. Clamp a straightedge guide to ensure square cuts.*

Fig. 2 *Rabbet the rear inside edge of cabinet sides and top to accept the plywood back. Note the edge-guide attachment on the router.*

Materials List

Key	No.	Size and description (use)
A	2	¾ x 13½ x 59" oak (side)
B	1	1¼ x 14⅛ x 36¾" oak (top)
C	3	1¼ x 13¼ x 34¾" oak (shelf)
D	1	¾ x 12⅜ x 34¾" oak (bottom shelf)
E	1	¾ x 2¾ x 35½" oak (kickplate)
F	1	¼ x 35 x 56¾" oak plywood (back)
G	8	¾ x 2¼ x 33⅞" oak (rail)
H	8	¾ x 2¼ x 11⅜" oak (stile)
I	8	¼ x ½ x 29⅞" oak (glass stop)
J	8	¼ x ½ x 9⅜" oak (glass stop)
K	4	⅛ x 9¼ x 29¾" glass (pane)
L	4	1"-dia. brass knobs
M	4 pr.	pivot sliding door hardware

Misc.: Carpenter's glue; ¼"-dia. x 1½" hardwood dowel pins; ½-in. No. 3 brass rh screws; ⅝-in. No. 5 rh screws; 120- and 220-grit sandpaper; cherry and walnut stain; varnish; 4/0 steel wool.

Fig. 3 *After rabbeting the ends and front edge of shelves, use a dovetail saw or backsaw to notch the front corners of each shelf.*

Fig. 4 *Rout the door track dadoes with the aid of a template clamped to cabinet side and a guide bushing on the router base.*

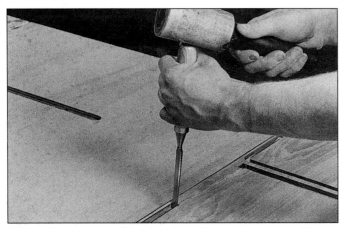

Fig. 5 *Use a sharp chisel and mallet to square up the ends of the door track dadoes. Be careful not to cut beyond the routed dado.*

guide once again, and rout a ½-in.-deep x ⅞-in. rabbet along the front edge of the middle shelves. These rabbets provide a step for the doors to close against while creating a ¾-in.-thick reveal of shelving between the closed doors. Use a dovetail saw or backsaw to notch the front corners of each shelf (**Fig. 3**).

Prepare to rout the four matching pairs of L-shaped dadoes in the cabinet sides for installing the door track hardware. To ensure consistent accuracy in routing the dadoes, make a template from ¼-in. hardboard or plywood as shown in the drawing. Remove the edge-guide from the router, install a ⁷⁄₁₆-in.-dia. bit and attach a ⅝-in.-dia. guide bushing to the router base. Set the router's depth of cut to ⁵⁄₁₆ in.

To rout the dadoes, first clamp the template to the cabinet side flush with the inside edge of the back rabbet (**Fig. 4**). Position the template's bottom edge at the height of the corresponding door bottom. Rout the dadoes while holding the guide bushing firmly against the template edge. Advance the router slowly across the cabinet side and then down to form the 3½-in.-long leg of the L-shaped dadoes.

Repeat this procedure for the remaining dadoes—four per cabinet side. Keep in mind that the matching dado pairs are mirror images of each other. Therefore, the template must be flipped over (bottom side up) when routing the second cabinet side.

Use a sharp chisel to square up the ends of the door track dadoes (**Fig. 5**). Also, use a sabre saw to cut a 2¾ x 2¾-in. notch in the bottom front corner of each cabinet side for installing the kickplate.

SKILL*Builder*

Cut It Out
This bookcase project calls for a woodworking technique called template routing. The procedure isn't hard, but it does take some practice to get it down pat. If this is your first time routing a template, these pointers can help you get it right:

The finished cutout is only as good as the template, so the most important step in creating your template is the first step. Make sure you measure and mark your lines carefully before you cut.

The template opening must have parallel sides that are straight and smooth. Any irregularity in the template opening will be transferred directly to the router and the cutout that it makes. Suffice to say that even if a template does not require painstaking accuracy, it still needs to be well made.

Next, clamp the cabinet top to the workbench with its bottom side facing up. Then use a ½-in.-rad. cove bit to rout the decorative detail along the front and two end edges only (**Fig. 6**). Lay out and bore ¼-in.-dia. x ⅞-in.-deep dowel pinholes in the top edges of the cabinet sides using a doweling jig and portable drill (**Fig. 7**).

Bore matching dowel pinholes in the underside surface of the cabinet top (**Fig. 8**). Finish sand the cabinet members and shelves with 120- and 220-grit sandpaper.

Assemble the bookcase cabinet by applying glue to the ¾-in.-wide dadoes in the cabinet sides and to both ends of each shelf. Clamp the cabinet parts together with eight bar clamps (**Fig. 9**). Place cauls under the clamp jaws to distribute clamping pressure evenly across the joints.

Check the cabinet for squareness and make any necessary adjustments before the glue starts to set. After the glue has dried thoroughly, remove the clamps. Then attach the top to the cabinet sides with glue and ¼-in.-dia. x 1½-in. hardwood dowel pins. Glue and clamp the kickplate to the bottom front of the cabinet.

Door Construction

Cut all the door parts to size. Next, install a dado blade in the table saw and cut the tenon cheek on the outside face of each door stile. Use a miter gauge with a stop clamped in place to make accurate repetitive cuts. Readjust the stop on the miter gauge and cut the cheeks on the inside face of each stile (**Fig. 10**). Use this same setup to cut the tenon shoulder on the

There are a number of tools that can be helpful in creating templates. A sabre saw, a file, a sanding block—even a Dremel rotary tool can be used to cut and shape a template. The router itself can also be used to make its own template. In fact, some woodworkers prefer to make the straight cuts on the template with the router. Then again, some other woodworkers find the router's size and bulk make it too difficult for this use. It's a matter of personal preference.

Obviously the depth of the cutout affects the finished dimension of the case. That is, if you make the cutouts deeper than they should be, the case will be narrower than the plans indicate. Set the router for what you think is the proper depth then make a test cut on a piece of scrap wood. Carefully measure the depth of cut and adjust the router accordingly. Bear in mind, though, that if you decide to route the cutout area in two passes, you need to remember to double check the router's depth of cut before making the final pass.

Fig. 6 With the cabinet top clamped upside down, rout a decorative profile only in the front and end edges with a ½-in.-rad. cove bit.

Fig. 7 Bore ¼-in.-dia. x ⅞-in. dowel pinholes in the top edge of each cabinet side. Use a doweling jig to ensure accuracy.

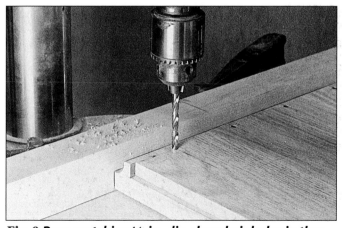

Fig. 8 Bore matching ¼-in.-dia. dowel pinholes in the underside of the cabinet top. Here, a drill press is used with an auxiliary fence.

Fig. 9 *Assemble the cabinet with eight bar clamps. Place cauls under the clamp jaws to distribute even clamping pressure.*

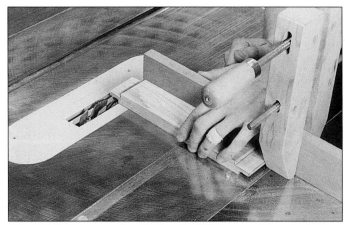

Fig. 10 *Cut tenon cheeks on a table saw with a dado blade. A handscrew clamped to the miter gauge fence acts as a stop.*

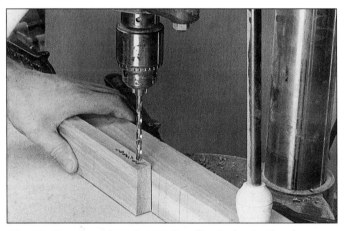

Fig. 11 *Bore overlapping ¼-in.-dia. holes in the door rails to form mortises. Clamp an auxiliary fence to the drill press table to position the work.*

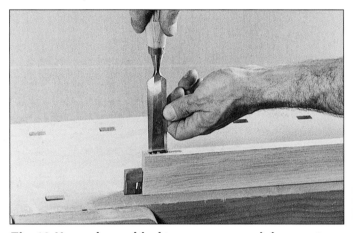

Fig. 12 *Use a sharp chisel to remove remaining waste from the mortises. Chisel the mortise walls smooth and square up the ends.*

outside edge of each stile. Cut a ¼ x ¾-in.-deep x 1¼-in. mortise in each end of every door rail. Form the mortises on a drill press by boring a series of overlapping ¼-in.-dia. holes (**Fig. 11**). Use a sharp chisel to square up and finish the mortises (**Fig. 12**). Move over to the table saw and cut a ¼ x ½-in.-deep rabbet in the rear inside edge of all the stiles and rails to accept the glass and stops (**Fig. 13**). Dry assemble each door to be sure that the mortise-and-tenon joints fit together properly.

You should correct a too-tight fit by paring the parts with a sharp chisel. Apply glue to the joints and assemble the doors with bar or pipe clamps. Be sure that the door frames are square before the glue sets.

After the glue dries, check the fit of each door in the cabinet. The doors should have a uniform ⅟₁₆-in. space at each edge. You should make any necessary adjustments with a hand plane or sanding block.

Next, bore holes in the door edges to accept the pivot pins. Note that each door receives four pivots—two fixed pivots (³⁄₁₆-in.-dia. holes) and two adjustable pivots (⁷⁄₁₆-in.-dia. holes). Also, bore and chisel two ⁵⁄₁₆-in.-wide x ⅝-in. slots through the back of each door and into the adjustable pivot holes (see Drawing Detail 5). The slots allow access to the hex-socket adjusting screws. Tap the pivot pins into the holes with a hammer. Thread the hex-socket screws into the adjustable pivots with a hex-key wrench (**Fig. 14**).

Cut the U-shaped plastic door tracks to length and press them into the grooves that were routed in the cabinet sides. If the tracks fit loosely, apply a few spots of hot-melt glue to hold them fast. Then slide each door into the tracks from the rear of the cabinet.

Position the adjustable pivots as necessary to obtain proper tension for smooth door travel. Remove the doors from the cabinet after making the final adjustments.

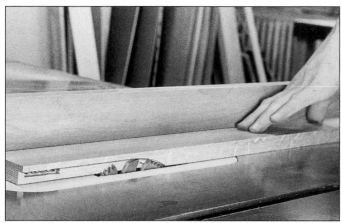

Fig. 13 *Use a dado blade and table saw to cut a ¼ x ½-in. deep rabbet in each door rail and stile to accept the glass pane and stop.*

Fig. 14 *Insert adjustable pivot pins in holes bored in the door ends. Then use a hex-key wrench to tighten the adjusting screw.*

Fig. 15 *After finishing the doors, insert the glass panes and attach the oak glass stops with ½-in. No. 3 brass roundhead screws.*

Now cut ¼ x ½-in. oak glass stops for the doors, but don't install them yet. Bore holes for the doorknobs. Cut the cabinet back from ¼-in. oak-veneer plywood. Sand all parts with 120- and 220-grit sandpaper. Wipe away any sanding dust with a tack cloth.

To create a faithful reproduction finish, we mixed equal parts of cherry and walnut stain. Simply wipe the stain onto the wood and let it dry overnight. Then apply two coats of varnish. Let the piece dry and sand it lightly between coats. After the varnish has dried, rub the final coat with 4/0 steel wool to achieve a satin sheen.

Install the glass panes and mount the glass stops to the door frames with ½-in. No. 3 brass roundhead screws (**Fig. 15**). Bore pilot holes to avoid splitting the stops. Slide the doors into their tracks from the cabinet rear, attach the knobs, and check the doors' operation. Finally, attach the cabinet back with ⅝-in. No. 5 roundhead screws.

MATERIAL*Matters*

The Clear Choice
Varnish is a common finish and is often used on woodworking projects. Like any commonly used tool, material, or technique, it's good to know all you can about this part of the project.

Varnish is a general term that means a clear, somewhat shiny coating. It can be made with natural oils and resins or synthetic materials. Varnish is sometimes double termed with polyurethane (technically a synthetic chemical, not a finish) as in "polyurethane varnish." It gets even more confusing when you see it double termed with shellac, a finish unto itself, as in "shellac varnish." Normally, you would just say that the project is finished with shellac, but some older woodworking references use the term "shellac varnish," as do a few old-timers.

Varnish can be applied as a gel (gel varnish), straight from the can or thinned with the appropriate solvent—which is usually paint thinner. (This is where the term "'shellac varnish" is particularly misleading because shellac itself is only thinned with alcohol).

When applying varnish, the first coat, or even two coats, are not applied at full thickness. For these coats you'll want to use varnish mixed with thinner. The amount of thinner in the varnish will vary depending on your own experience and preferences and what the manufacturer recommends.

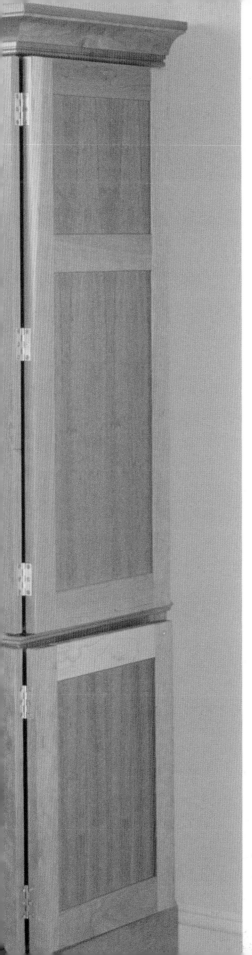

Cyber Secretary

A handsome cherry cabinet that eliminates clutter in your home office.

There's no question our electronic tools and toys have changed our lives. Though all this new equipment makes life easier and more enjoyable, it also takes up a lot of space in our homes. But the fact is that big TV, the new sound system, and the family computer can blend right in—it just takes a fresh look at the kind of furniture we build and use.

It wasn't so long ago that the well-equipped family library was centered around a couple dozen volumes of an up-to-date encyclopedia. In those days, bookcases and shelves kept the desks and tables clear, while adding a touch of sophistication to the home.

*Key*POINTS

TIME
Prep Time	6 hours
Shop Time	16 hours
Assembly Time	20 hours

EFFORT
Skill Level	intermediate

COST / BENEFITS
Expense: **expensive**
- The **locking pullout work surface** is perfect for a keyboard and mouse pad.
- You can easily substitute wood type to **suit your decor.**

119

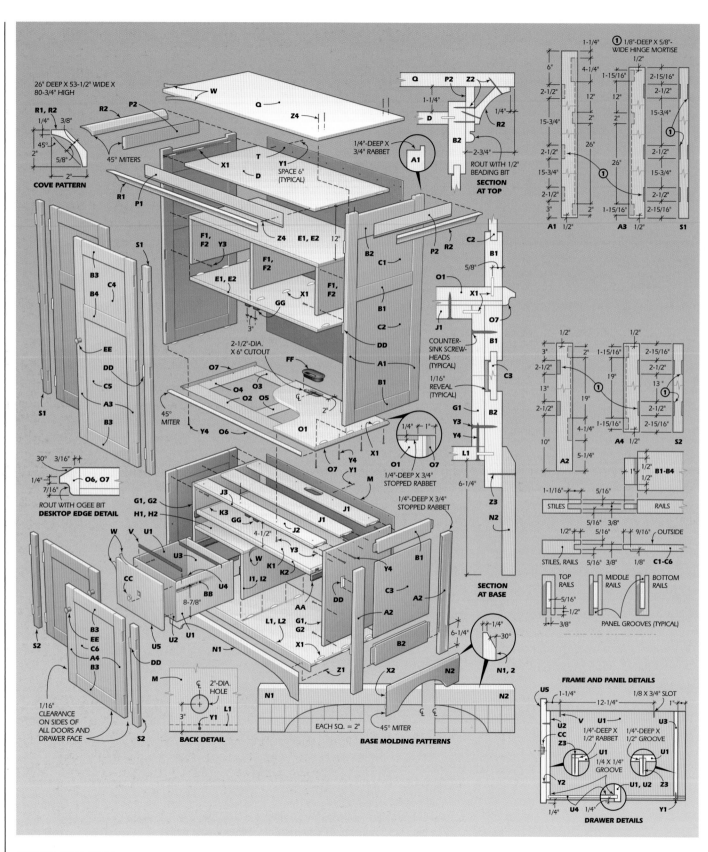

26" DEEP X 53-1/2" WIDE X 80-3/4" HIGH

R1, R2
1/4" 3/8"
45°
2"
5/8"
2"
COVE PATTERN

45° MITERS

R2 P2

W

Q

Z4

Q P2 Z2
D
1-1/4"
1/4"
R2
B2
2-3/4"
SECTION AT TOP
ROUT WITH 1/2" BEADING BIT

1/4"-DEEP X 3/4" RABBET A1

X1
T
D
Y1
SPACE 6" (TYPICAL)

R1 P1

S1

F1, F2 Y3
E1, E2

F1, F2

Z4 E1, E2 12"

B2 C1
P2 R2

C2
B1
5/8"
O1
X1
O7
J1
B1
C2
DD
A1
B1

B3
B4 C4

EE
DD
C5
A3
B3

S1

45° MITER
Y4 O6

O7 O3
O4
O2 O5
O1

2-1/2"-DIA. X 6" CUTOUT

X1
GG
3"

FF

2"

COUNTER-SINK SCREW-HEADS (TYPICAL)

1/16" REVEAL (TYPICAL)

C3
G1
B2
Y3
Y4
L1

30° 3/16"
1/4"
7/16"
O6, O7
ROUT WITH OGEE BIT
DESKTOP EDGE DETAIL

Y4
Y1 O7
O7
M
1/4"-DEEP X 3/4" STOPPED RABBET

X1
O1 O7
1/4" 1"
1/4"-DEEP X 3/4" STOPPED RABBET

Z3
N2
6-1/4"

J3
G1, G2
H1, H2
GG
J1
J1
J2
4-1/2"
Y3

W V U1
U3
CC
U4
I1, I2
BB
8-7/8"
U2 U1
N1

K3
K1
K2
W

Y3
K1
Y4
B1

DD
C3
A2
A2
AA
L1, L2 G1, G2
X1
B2

S2
B3
EE
C6
A4
B3
DD
U5
M

2"-DIA. HOLE
3" Y1
L1
BACK DETAIL

1/16" CLEARANCE ON SIDES OF ALL DOORS AND DRAWER FACE

S2

Z1 X2 N2 N1, 2
6-1/4" 1/4" 30°

N1
EACH SQ. = 2"
45° MITER
BASE MOLDING PATTERNS

N2

① 1/8"-DEEP X 5/8"-WIDE HINGE MORTISE
1-1/4"
1/2"
6" 4-1/4" 1-15/16" 2-15/16"
2-1/2" 12" 2-1/2"
15-3/4" 2" 15-3/4"
26"
2-1/2" 26" 2-1/2"
15-3/4" 15-3/4"
2-1/2" 2-1/2"
3" 2" 1-15/16" 2-15/16"
A1 1/2" **A3** 1/2" **S1**

1/2" 1/2"
3" 2" 1-15/16" 2-15/16"
2-1/2" 2-1/2"
13" 19" 13"
2-1/2" 2-1/2"
10" 19" 1-15/16" 2-15/16"
4-1/4"
5-1/4"
A2 **A4** 1/2" **S2**

1" 1/2"
B1-B4
1/2"

1-1/16" 5/16"
STILES **RAILS**
5/16" 3/8"

1/2" 5/16" 9/16" OUTSIDE
STILES, RAILS 5/16" 3/8" 1/8" **C1-C6**

TOP RAILS MIDDLE RAILS BOTTOM RAILS
5/16"
1/2"
3/8"
PANEL GROOVES (TYPICAL)

FRAME AND PANEL DETAILS
U5 1-1/4" 1/8 X 3/4" SLOT
12-1/4" 1"
U2 V U1 U3
CC 1/4"-DEEP X 1/2" RABBET 1/4"-DEEP X 1/2" GROOVE
Z3 U1
1/4 X 1/4" GROOVE
Y2 U1, U2 Z3
1/4" U4 1/4" Y1
DRAWER DETAILS

Today it may seem as though we've progressed, as entire encyclopedias are now contained on a single CD. Maybe so, in terms of information access. On the other hand, our new computers, printers, monitors, and mice demand space of their own. And unless you're happy giving up your dining room table to a humming and glowing network of wires and boxes, it's time to give all this gear a more practical place to call home.

Materials List

Key	No.	Size and description (use)
A1	4	1 x 3 x 48" cherry (upper case stile)
A2	4	1 x 3 x 31" cherry (lower case stile)
A3	4	1 x 3 x 44$7/8$" cherry (upper door stile)
A4	4	1 x 3 x 23$7/8$" cherry (lower door stile)
B1	6	1 x 3 x 19$1/4$" cherry (case rail)
B2	4	1 x 5$1/4$ x 19$1/4$" cherry (case rail)
B3	8	1 x 2$15/16$ x 17$3/32$" cherry (door rail)
B4	2	1 x 3 x 17$3/32$" cherry (door rail)
C1	2	$1/2$ x 12 x 18$1/4$" plywood (side panel)
C2	2	$1/2$ x 18$1/4$ x 26" plywood (side panel)
C3	2	$1/2$ x 18$1/4$ x 19" plywood (side panel)
C4	2	$1/2$ x 12 x 16$3/32$" plywood (door panel)
C5	2	$1/2$ x 16$3/32$ x 26" plywood (door panel)
C6	2	$1/2$ x 16$3/32$ x 19" plywood (door panel)
D	1	$3/4$ x 23 x 46" plywood (upper top)
E1	2	$3/4$ x 21$1/2$ x 46" plywood (shelf)
E2	2	$3/8$ x $3/4$ x 46" cherry (edge band)
F1	3	$3/4$ x 11 x 21$1/2$" plywood (upright)
F2	3	$3/8$ x $3/4$ x 11" cherry (edge band)
G1	2	$3/4$ x 21$1/2$ x 24" plywood (inner side)
G2	2	$3/8$ x $3/4$ x 24" cherry (edge band)
H1*	1	$3/4$ x 18$3/4$ x 21$1/2$" plywood (drawer box top)
H2*	1	$3/8$ x $3/4$ x 18$3/4$" cherry (edge band)
I1	1	$3/4$ x 12 x 21$1/2$" plywood (drawer box side)
I2	1	$3/8$ x $3/4$ x 12" cherry (edge band)
J1	2	$3/4$ x 4$1/2$ x 44$1/2$" plywood (stretcher)
J2	1	$3/4$ x 4$1/8$ x 44$1/2$" plywood (stretcher)
J3	1	$3/8$ x $3/4$ x 44$1/2$" cherry (edge band)
K1	1	$3/4$ x 16$1/2$ x 41$3/8$" plywood (work surface)
K2	2	$3/4$ x 1 x 42$7/8$" cherry (edge band)
K3	2	$3/4$ x 1 x 16$1/2$" cherry (edge band)
L1	1	$3/4$ x 22$5/8$ x 46" plywood (lower bottom)
L2	1	$3/8$ x 2 x 46" cherry (edge band)
M	1	$1/4$ x 24$3/4$ x 47$1/2$" plywood (lower back)
N1	1	$3/4$ x 7 x 49$1/2$" cherry (base)
N2	2	$3/4$ x 7 x 24" cherry (base)
O1	1	$3/4$ x 23$1/4$ x 48" plywood (desktop)
O2	1	$1/4$ x 4 x 48" plywood (spacer)
O3	1	$1/4$ x 4 x 40" plywood (spacer)
O4	2	$1/4$ x 4 x 19$1/4$" plywood (spacer)
O5	1	$1/4$ x 4 x 15$1/4$" plywood (spacer)
O6	1	$3/4$ x 1 x 49$1/2$" cherry (edge molding)
O7	2	$3/4$ x 1 x 24" cherry (edge molding)
P1	1	$1/2$ x 3 x 49" cherry (molding)
P2	2	$1/2$ x 3 x 23$3/4$" cherry (molding)
Q*	1	$3/4$ x 26 x 53$1/2$" plywood (case top)
R1	1	2 x 2 x 53" cherry (cove molding)
R2	2	2 x 2 x 25$3/4$" cherry (cove molding)
S1	2	1 x 1$3/4$ x 44$7/8$" cherry (hinged stile)
S2	2	1 x 1$3/4$ x 23$7/8$" cherry (hinged stile)
T	1	$1/4$ x 47$1/2$ x 48$3/4$" plywood (upper back)
U1	2	$1/2$ x 10$1/4$ x 18" plywood (drawer side)
U2	1	$1/2$ x 10$1/4$ x 16$7/16$" plywood (drawer front)
U3	1	$1/2$ x 9$3/4$ x 16$7/16$" plywood (drawer back)
U4	1	$1/4$ x 16$7/16$ x 16$3/4$" plywood (bottom)
U5*	1	$3/4$ x 11$7/8$ x 17$7/8$" plywood (drawer face)
V	2	$1/8$ x $3/4$ x 16$15/16$" aluminum (file hanger)
W	as reqd.	veneer tape
X1	as reqd.	No. 20 plates
X2	as reqd.	No. 0 plates
Y1	as reqd.	$3/4$" No. 6 rh wood screws
Y2	as reqd.	1" No. 8 rh wood screws
Y3	as reqd.	1$1/2$" No. 8 fh wood screws
Y4	as reqd.	2" No. 8 fh wood screws
Z1	as reqd.	1" brads
Z2	as reqd.	3d finish nails
Z3	as reqd.	4d finish nails
Z4	as reqd.	6d finish nails
AA	1 pr.	18" shelf slides
BB	1 pr.	18" drawer slides
CC	1	ring pull
DD	20	1$1/2$ x 2$1/2$" hinges
EE	4	1$3/8$"-dia. cherry knobs
FF	1	grommet
GG	4	magnetic catch

Misc.: Ogee bit; 30° chamfer bit; glue; 120-, 150-, 180-, and 220-grit sandpaper; tack cloth; 4/0 steel wool; Waterlox Original Sealer/Finish.
* Dimension includes veneer tape.
Note: All plywood cherry veneer. MDF-core stock preferred for door and side panels.

Fig. 1 *After cutting door and side-frame pieces to size, clamp together stiles of the same size and lay out the mortise locations.*

We've designed a dedicated computer cabinet with plenty of space for all the essentials, plus shelves for books, office accessories, and things you just like to have around. To handle the paperwork, our case features a file drawer on full extension slides, and we've incorporated a locking pullout work surface that's perfect for a keyboard and mouse pad. The cabinet doors open 270° so you have full access to the interior of the case. We constructed our updated secretary out of a combination of solid cherry and cherry-veneered panels, but you can substitute another wood if it better suits your decor.

Making the Doors and Panels

Begin by ripping and crosscutting 1-in.-thick cherry to size for the stiles and rails of the doors and case sides. Lay out the rail and mortise locations on the stiles, clamping stiles of the same length together to ensure accuracy (**Fig. 1**). Next, use a router edge guide and spiral bit to rout the mortises. To support the router, clamp two or three stiles together face-to-face. Register the guide on the outside face of each stile for consistent mortise locations. Then rout the panel grooves in the edges of the stiles and rails (**Fig. 2**) and square the mortises with a sharp ⅜-in. chisel (**Fig. 3**).

Equip your table saw with a dado blade to cut the rail tenons, then use a stop block clamped to the miter gauge to position the rails (**Fig. 4**). For the best glue joint, cut the tenons about ½₂ in. thicker than specified. After holding the rails on edge to cut the tenon shoulders, use a sharp chisel to pare the tenons to exact size.

We used ½-in. cherry-veneer MDF (medium-density fiberboard) for the panels. Although you can use cherry-veneer plywood instead, the stability and flatness of MDF make it a better choice. Cut the panels to size, and use a router table to shape the rabbet around the inside surface of each one (**Fig. 5**). Sand each panel with 120-, 150-, 180-, and 220-grit paper.

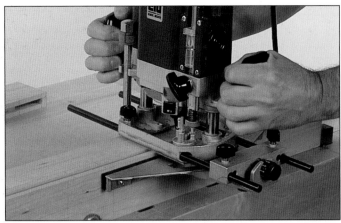

Fig. 2 *Use a router and edge guide to cut mortises and panel grooves. Clamp together stock to provide a firm base for the router.*

Fig. 3 *After the grooves are cut, use a sharp ⅜-in.-wide chisel to square the ends of each mortise in the side and door stiles.*

Fig. 4 *Use a dado blade in the table saw to cut the tenons slightly oversize. Then pare them to the exact size with a sharp chisel.*

TECH *Tips*

Tenons Anyone?

Many a beginning woodworker finds fitting mortise and tenons to be an unnecessarily tricky job. But like anything else, time and experience will render the job as easy as pie. In the meantime, you may find these basics useful:

Shave Time

If you find the tenon is a bit oversize, pare it to fit. It is always easier to shave down the tenon than to expand the width of the mortise with a chisel.

Bullnose

A tenon can be reduced using one of three tools. A razor-sharp chisel, a cabinetmaker's rasp, or a specialized type of plane known as a shoulder plane (or bullnose shoulder plane). All three tools are worked across the width of the tenon, shaving off excess material a bit at a time.

Glue the Cheeks

If much to your chagrin, you find that the tenon is much too small, don't panic. Make sure that its sides (formally known as cheeks) are flat and straight, and glue a thin strip of wood to them. Then try again.

To assemble a frame, spread glue in the mortises and on all tenon surfaces. Then join the rails to one of the stiles and slide the panel into position (**Fig. 6**). Place the opposite stile in place and clamp the frame to pull the joints tight. Compare opposite diagonal measurements to be sure that the assembly is square, and let the glue cure. Proceed with the rest of the frames and doors in the same manner.

Inside the Cabinet

The inner case parts are constructed of veneer-core cherry panels. Rip and crosscut these parts about 1 in. oversize, and cut edge-banding strips from solid cherry to cover the exposed edges. Cut the strips about $\frac{1}{16}$ in. wider than the thickness of the panels. Next, spread glue on a panel edge and clamp the strip so that it overhangs both faces of the panel. After about 20 minutes, scrape off any glue that has squeezed out. When the glue has fully cured, plane the edge-banding strip flush. Then cut the panels to finished dimension. Lay out the joining-plate locations for the upper case shelf assembly and cut the slots (**Fig. 7**). Apply glue, join the uprights to the shelves, and clamp.

To construct the lower case insert, first apply veneer tape to the exposed edge of the drawer enclosure top as shown in the

drawing. Use a household iron to apply the tape and trim the excess with a chisel. Lay out and cut the plate slots, then glue the drawer-box top and side together. Cut plate slots for joining the drawer box to the left side of the inner case and install plates without glue to align the parts. Secure the subassembly with screws (**Fig. 8**). Assemble both inner sides with the stretchers using dry joining plates and screws (**Fig. 9**).

Outer Case Work

It's easiest to cut the hinge mortises in the case side frames before assembling the cases. Use a marking gauge and square to mark the outline of each mortise. Then make a series of parallel chisel cuts along the mortise just shy of the finished depth (**Fig. 10**). Hold the chisel horizontally to pare away the waste (**Fig. 11**), and test fit each hinge to see that it sits flush.

Use your router and edge guide to cut the rabbet along the back edges of the side frames. Note that each lower case side

Fig. 5 *Mount a straight bit in the router table and cut the rabbets on the back sides of the side and door panels. Then sand the panels.*

Fig. 6 *Apply glue to the mortises and tenons and join rails to one stile. Slide the panel in place, add the remaining stile, and clamp until the glue sets.*

has a stopped rabbet. Stop the cut about ⅛ in. short and square the end with a chisel.

Next, cut the joining-plate slots in the lower case side frames and lower bottom panel. Apply glue to these joints and assemble the sides to the panel. Clamp the parts and set the assembly aside for the glue to cure.

Lower Case Assembly

Place the lower case insert between the sides, using joining plates to hold the drawer-box side in position on the case bottom. Install clamps to keep the insert from shifting. Bore and countersink pilot holes and fasten the insert subassembly to the sides and bottom with screws (**Fig. 12**). Cut the back panel to size and bore a 2-in.-dia. hole for power cord access. Next, screw the back in place.

Rip ¾-in.-thick stock to width for the base and cut it to length with 45° miter joints at the front corners. Cut No. 0

joining-plate slots in the miter joints (**Fig. 13**). Lay out the curved profiles and use a sabre saw to make the cuts.

Mount a chamfer bit in the router table to shape the top edge of the base pieces. Then glue together the three base pieces using clamps to pull the miters tight. Fasten the base to the lower case with 6d finishing nails and 1-in. brads. Bore pilot holes for the nails.

Upper Case Assembly

Cut a panel to size for the desk surface and glue ¼-in. spacers to the underside as shown in the drawing (**Fig. 14**).

Glue mitered edge-banding strips to the desktop front and side edges (**Fig. 15**). Plane the edging flush, and rout the edge profile. Cut the bottom part of the molding with an ogee bit, and bevel the top of the profile with a 30° chamfer bit.

Mark the position of the wire grommet in the desktop, bore holes, and use a sabre saw to make the cutout. Then rout the

Fig. 7 *Cut the plate slots in case parts. Clamp a straightedge to each upper case shelf to position slots for center partition.*

Fig. 8 *Use plates and glue to build the L-shaped section of the drawer box. Use dry plates and screws to attach it to the inner case side.*

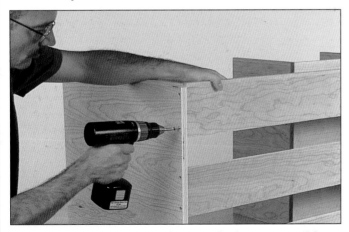

Fig. 9 *Secure the top stretchers to the lower case sides with screws. Joining plates hold parts in alignment while fastening.*

Fig. 10 *Use a chisel to outline each mortise. Then make a series of cuts across the grain and about ⅛ in. apart within the waste area.*

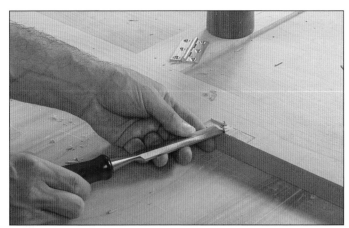

Fig. 11 *Hold the chisel horizontally to pare away the waste in each hinge mortise. Test the fit of each hinge and adjust as required.*

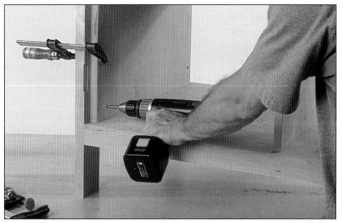

Fig. 12 *Slide the inner case into position between the lower case outside frames and clamp. Screw the inner sides to the outer frames.*

Fig. 13 *Cut the base pieces to finished length with mitered ends. Use joining plates in the miters to help hold the joints tight.*

Fig. 14 *Build up the bottom edges of the desktop by gluing ¼-in.-thick spacers to the panel. Keep the strips flush with the panel edges.*

stopped rabbet along the back edge of the desktop and square the ends with a sharp chisel.

Lay out and cut the joining-plate slots for the upper case assembly and bore pilot holes for screwing the desktop to the sides. Apply glue to the plates and slots to join the case top and sides and assemble these parts with clamps. Place dry plates in the desktop slots and join the desktop to the sides with screws (**Fig. 16**).

Use a beading bit to rout strips of ½-in.-thick cherry for the upper case molding. Miter the strips to length and install them with 3d finishing nails. Cut the case upper top to size and apply veneer tape to the exposed edges. Fasten the upper top panel to the side-frame stiles and beaded molding with 6d finishing nails.

We shaped the cove molding on a table saw with a standard 10-in.-dia. blade. While not unusual, this technique requires special care and the operation must be carried out cautiously.

If you are not comfortable with the procedure, purchase appropriate molding from your lumber dealer.

To make the cove molding, first rip 1-in. stock to a width of 4 in., and cut each piece several inches longer than finished length. Next, set your miter gauge to 38° and use it to position a long wooden fence across the saw table at that angle. With the blade height at ⅜ in., move the fence so that it's ¹³⁄₁₆ in. from the front edge of the blade and clamp it to the table. Mount a featherboard to the table to hold the work against the fence. Set the saw blade to a height of ¹⁄₁₆ in. and use pushsticks to move the stock across the spinning blade (**Fig. 17**). Raise the blade ¹⁄₁₆ in. for the next pass, and continue until the cove depth is reached. Then remove the wooden fence and set the blade to 45° to rip the face and back angles of the molding. Finish by smoothing with a gooseneck scraper and 220-grit sandpaper (**Fig. 18**). Use a miter saw to cut the cove molding to length and nail it to the top of the upper case as shown.

Final Steps

Mount the hinges in the case sides and cut the hinged stiles to size. Clamp a hinged stile against one of the case sides with a ¹⁄₁₆-in. shim under its bottom end. Use a knife to transfer the hinge locations to the edge of the stile. Then lay out the hinge mortises along both edges of the hinged stile. Repeat the process for each stile, cut the mortises, and mount the stiles to the sides.

Install the back panel of the top case with ¾-in. No. 6 screws. After fastening hinges to the open side of the hinged stiles, transfer the mortise locations to the cabinet doors. Mount the doors to the case and trim them as necessary to achieve a uniform margin of ¹⁄₁₆ in. Install the doorknobs and magnetic catches.

Cut the drawer stock to finished sizes. Use a dado blade in the table saw to cut the rabbet and dado in each side. Cut the grooves for the drawer bottom. Make slots in the top edge of

Fig. 15 *Glue solid edging to the desktop panel. Let the edging overhang the panel faces and plane it flush after the glue sets.*

Fig. 16 *After using glue and plates to join the top to the side frames, position the desktop at the bottom of the sides and screw it in place.*

the sides for the hanging-file rails. Use glue and 6d finishing nails to assemble the drawer box (**Fig. 19**). Slide the bottom into place and screw it to the drawer back.

Cut the drawer face from ¾-in. cherry plywood and apply veneer tape to the four edges. Mark the location of the flush pull on the drawer face and cut a recess to house the pull. Mount the pull to the face with screws (**Fig. 20**), and screw the drawer face to the front of the drawer. Cut pieces of ⅛ x ¾-in. aluminum bar for the hanging-file rails and use a dab of epoxy to secure them to the drawer.

Mount the drawer slides on the case and drawer. For initial installation, use only the slotted holes to allow for adjustment. After testing that the drawer is operating smoothly, install the rest of the screws.

Cut a panel for the pullout work surface and apply edge banding. Mount the slide to the inner case sides and mount the clips to the work surface ends (**Fig. 21**). Install the work surface in the case, checking for smooth operation.

Cut the wire-grommet hole in the lower case rear stretcher, and position the upper case on the lower case. Bore and countersink pilot holes through the lower case stretchers into the bottom of the desktop, and drive screws to fasten the sections together.

Disassemble the case and remove the hardware for finishing. Set all nail heads and fill the holes. Sand all surfaces with 120-, 150-, 180-, and 220-grit paper. Remove all sanding dust before moving to the next, finer grit of sandpaper. Use a tack cloth to wipe all surfaces before applying your first coat of finish.

We finished our cabinet with three coats of Waterlox Original Sealer/Finish. Use a brush or rag to spread a liberal coat, let it sit for 10 to 15 minutes, and wipe off the excess. Let the finish dry overnight and repeat the process for each coat. When the final coat is dry, burnish the surface with 4/0 steel wool and polish it with a soft cloth.

Fig. 17 *Use a wooden fence angled across the saw table to guide the stock for a cove cut. Increase the blade height in ¹⁄₁₆-in. increments.*

Fig. 18 *Use a gooseneck scraper to remove saw marks from the face of the cove molding. Then sand with 220-grit sandpaper.*

Fig. 19 *Assemble the drawer box using glue and 6d finishing nails. Note $1/8$ x $3/4$-in. slots in the drawer sides for hanging-file guides.*

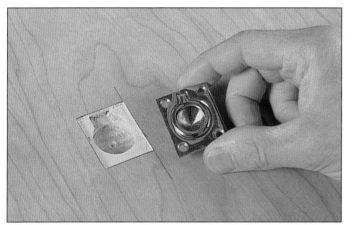

Fig. 20 *Cut a mortise in the drawer face for the ring pull. A 1-in.-dia. recess in the center of the mortise fits the body of the pull.*

Fig. 21 *To install the pullout work surface, install support clips on the panel edges and attach the panel to the side-mounted slides.*

Safety Sense

BE SAFE WHILE YOU RIP

When using a table saw to rip lumber, adjust the blade height so it barely clears the lumber. The more of the blade that is exposed above the stock, the more likely an accident will occur. (This assumes you have an older saw without the blade guard common on newer models or that you are one of the many woodworkers who remove the guards because of their clunkiness.) Now, some old-timers will tell you that more blade height is better when ripping because it produces more down force on the stock, and less force back toward the operator. This is true, to a certain extent. If you are ripping lumber on the table saw, and you feel what you think is an excessive amount of back force, raise the blade up just a bit and then try it. Still, the basic safety rule of "the less blade the better" will always hold true. All other table saw basics apply: Keep your pushstick handy, wear safety glasses, and have a splitter installed behind the blade to eliminate the lumber pinching on the saw blade.

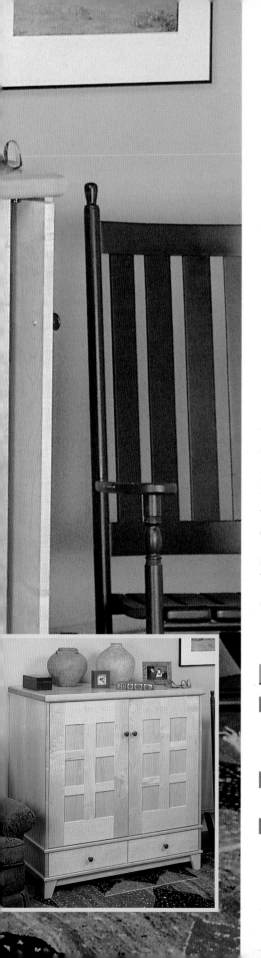

Open For Viewing

This television cabinet makes a handsome home for your TV and VCR.

Remember the old console TVs? Mounted in wooden cabinets, those early sets were as much furniture as new technology. The designers knew, or at least thought, that no one would want the naked machine in their home. After all, it just didn't match anything. In fact, many TV cabinets had doors to keep the tube tastefully under wraps until the family's favorite show came on. Well, everything old is really new again—only with a twist. The days of plastic TVs and vestigial wood-grain accents are over. This modern TV cabinet helps reincorporate "the box" into the design scheme of your home and has plenty of room for your home theater components.

*Key*POINTS

TIME
Prep Time . . . . 8 hours
Shop Time . . . . 20 hours
Assembly Time . . . . 20 hours

EFFORT
Skill Level . . . . intermediate

COST / BENEFITS
Expense: expensive
• A place for the TV, VCR, cable box—even two drawers for video tapes and DVDs.
• The twin doors fully retract for unobstructed viewing.

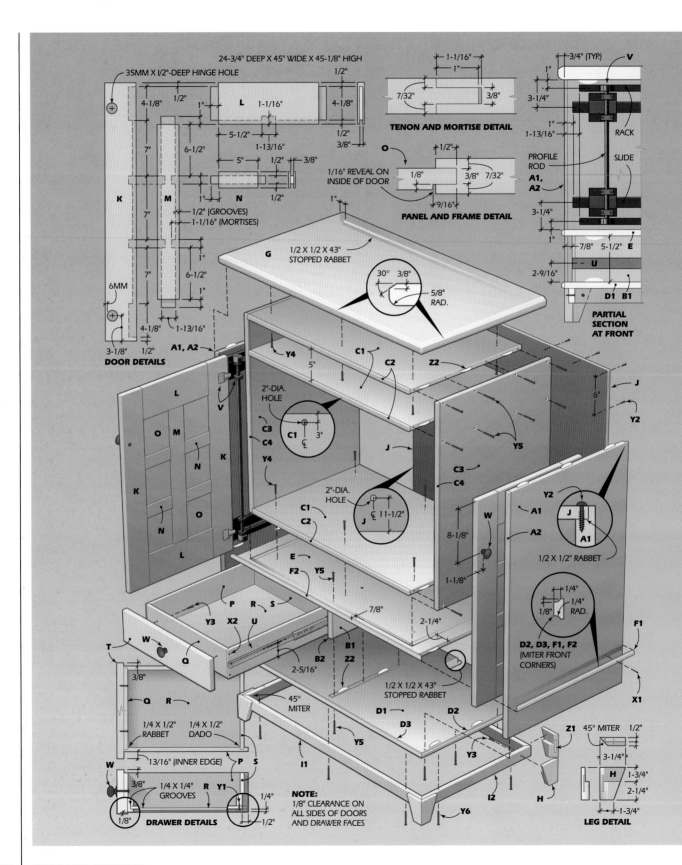

24-3/4" DEEP X 45" WIDE X 45-1/8" HIGH

35MM X I/2"-DEEP HINGE HOLE

4-1/8" 1/2" 1" 1/2" L 1-1/16" 4-1/8"

7" 6-1/2" 5-1/2" 1-13/16"

5" 1/2" 3/8"

K M N 1" 1/2"

7" 1/2" (GROOVES) 1-1/16" (MORTISES)

1"

7" 1"

6MM 6-1/2" 1"

4-1/8" 1-13/16"

3-1/8" 1/2"

A1, A2

DOOR DETAILS

1-1/16" 1" 7/32" 3/8"

TENON AND MORTISE DETAIL

O

1/16" REVEAL ON INSIDE OF DOOR

1/2" 1/8" 3/8" 7/32"

9/16"

PANEL AND FRAME DETAIL

3/4" (TYP.) V

1" 3-1/4" RACK

1" 1-13/16" SLIDE

PROFILE ROD A1, A2

3-1/4"

1" 7/8" 5-1/2" E

U 2-9/16"

D1 B1

PARTIAL SECTION AT FRONT

G 1/2 X 1/2 X 43" STOPPED RABBET

30° 3/8" 5/8" RAD.

Y4 C1 C2 Z2

5"

2"-DIA. HOLE

C3 C4

C1 3" C
L

Y4

2"-DIA. HOLE

C1 C2 J C 11-1/2"

J

Y5

C3 C4

J A1

A2 Y2

J A1

W

1/2 X 1/2" RABBET

8-1/8"

1-1/8"

E F2 Y5

P R S

Y3 X2 U

7/8" 2-1/4"

1/4" 1/4" RAD. 1/8"

D2, D3, F1, F2 (MITER FRONT CORNERS)

T W Q

3/8"

B1 B2 Z2

2-5/16"

1/2 X 1/2 X 43" STOPPED RABBET

F1

Q R

1/4 X 1/2" RABBET 1/4 X 1/2" DADO

13/16" (INNER EDGE) P S

45° MITER

D1 D2

D3 Y5

Y3

I1

X1

Z1 45° MITER 1/2"

3-1/4"

H 1-3/4" 2-1/4"

1-3/4"

LEG DETAIL

W 3/8" 1/4 X 1/4" GROOVES R Y1

1/4"

1/8" 1/2"

DRAWER DETAILS

NOTE: 1/8" CLEARANCE ON ALL SIDES OF DOORS AND DRAWER FACES

I2 H

Y6

Y2

J 6"

Y5

A good television cabinet, though, does more than just keep the interior decorator of the house happy. With most sets wired at least to a VCR and cable box, the modern household needs a central location for everything—including a place to hide those ugly wires and store your growing movie collection. Plus, an independent cabinet means we're not wedded to this year's TV when next year's model looks too good to pass up.

We designed our television cabinet with enough room for a typical 27-in. set. We've included a shelf that's wide enough to accommodate a VCR or DVD player and cable or satellite box, and two roomy drawers for tapes and DVDs. The full-width front doors on the cabinet are mounted on retractable slides that allow the doors to slip back into the case sides for unobstructed viewing.

We constructed our cabinet out of a combination of solid maple and maple-veneer panels. The case sides, shelves, and back are made from veneer-core panels, while we used flat, stable MDF (medium-density fiberboard) stock with maple veneers for the door panels. We used solid maple stock for the door frames and the 1 5/8-in.-thick case top.

The Case Panels

Begin by cutting 3/4-in. panels to rough size for the case sides, shelves, drawer partition, and insert-case parts. Rip maple edge-banding strips from 13/16-in. maple, and glue the strips to the front edges of the case sides, drawer partition, and insert panels. Center the strips so they protrude beyond the panel faces an equal amount on both sides. Let the glue set for

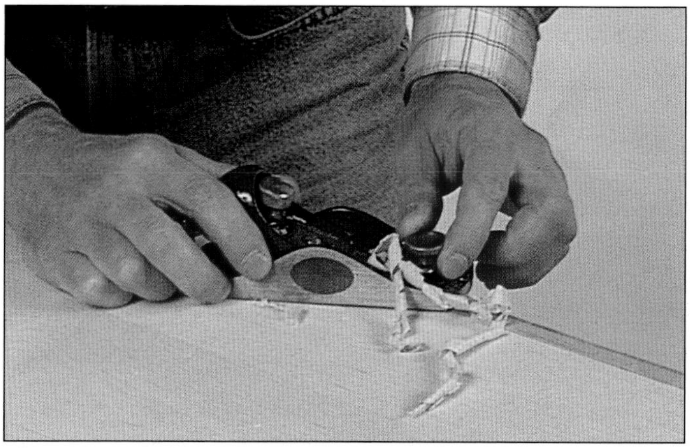

Fig. 1 ***Use a plane to trim the edge banding flush with the panel surfaces. If the wood tears, try planing in the opposite direction.***

Materials List

Key	No.	Size and description (use)
A1	2	3/4 x 25 5/8 x 38 3/4" plywood (case side)
A2	2	3/8 x 3/4 x 25 5/8" maple (edge band)
B1	1	3/4 x 5 1/2 x 22 1/4" plywood (partition)
B2	1	3/8 x 3/4 x 5 1/2" maple (edge band)
C1	3	3/4 x 22 1/4 x 36" plywood (insert shelf)
C2	3	3/8 x 3/4 x 36" maple (edge band)
C3	2	3/4 x 22 1/4 x 32 1/2" plywood (insert side)
C4	2	3/8 x 3/4 x 32 1/2" maple (edge band)
D1	1	3/4 x 24 x 43 1/2" plywood (case bottom)
D2	2	3/8 x 3/4 x 24 3/8" maple (edge band)
D3	1	3/8 x 3/4 x 44 1/4" maple (edge band)
E	1	3/4 x 23 1/2 x 42" plywood (middle shelf)
F1	2	3/8 x 3/4 x 24 3/8" maple (molding)
F2	1	3/8 x 3/4 x 44 1/4" maple (molding)
G*	1	1 5/8 x 24 3/4 x 45" maple (top)
H	8	1 x 3 1/4 x 4" plywood (leg)
I1	2	3/4 x 1 3/4 x 42 1/2" maple (base rail)
I2	2	3/4 x 1 3/4 x 23" maple (base rail)
J	1	1/2 x 39 3/4 x 43" plywood (back)
K	4	13/16 x 4 x 32 1/4" maple (stile)
L	4	13/16 x 5 1/8 x 14 13/16" maple (rail)
M	2	13/16 x 2 13/16 x 24" maple (mullion)
N	8	13/16 x 2 x 7" maple (short rail)
O	12	1/2 x 6 x 7" plywood (door panel)
P	4	1/2 x 4 3/4 x 22 1/2" maple (drawer side)
Q	2	1/2 x 4 3/4 x 19 1/8" maple (drawer front)
R	2	1/4 x 19 1/8 x 21 3/4" plywood (bottom)
S	2	1/2 x 4 1/4 x 19 1/8" maple (drawer back)
T	2	13/16 x 5 1/4 x 20 13/16" maple (drawer face)
U	2 pr.	22" drawer slides
V	2	pocket door hardware
W	4	knobs
X1	as reqd.	1" brads
X2	as reqd.	4d finish nails
Y1	as reqd.	1/2" No. 6 rh wood screws
Y2	as reqd.	1" No. 6 rh wood screws
Y3	as reqd.	1" No. 8 fh wood screws
Y4	as reqd.	1 1/4" No. 8 fh wood screws
Y5	as reqd.	2" No. 8 fh wood screws
Y6	as reqd.	2 1/4" No. 8 fh wood screws
Z1	as reqd.	No. 0 joining plates
Z2	as reqd.	No. 20 joining plates

Misc.: 30° chamfer bit; glue; 120-, 150-, 180-, and 220-grit sandpaper; tack cloth; 4/0 steel wool; white restoration varnish.

* Laminate from narrower stock.

Note: MDF-core stock preferred for door panels.

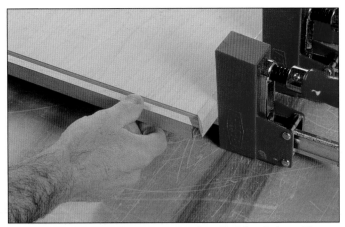

Fig. 2 *Cut the case bottom panel to finished size. Glue mitered edge-banding strips to the front and both ends of the panel.*

Fig. 3 *Glue up solid maple stock to form the case top. Joining plates in mating surfaces help keep pieces aligned during assembly.*

about 20 minutes, then scrape off any excess. When the glue is dry, use a block plane to trim the strips flush with the faces (**Fig. 1**). Then cut the panels to exact size.

Install edge banding on the case bottom ends and front edge, using miter joints at the corners (**Fig. 2**), and plane the strips flush. Do not edge band the middle shelf at this time. The edge molding for that shelf will be applied after you've assembled the case.

Make the 24¾-in.-wide maple top by gluing up several narrow pieces of stock. Cut each piece an inch or two longer than finished dimension and joint the mating edges. While simple glued butt joints are fine, joining plates help align the pieces during assembly. After cutting the slots (**Fig. 3**), spread glue, install the plates, and clamp the boards. Scrape off any excess glue after about 20 minutes. When the glue has fully cured, use a circular saw and straightedge guide to cut the panel to size.

Case Assembly

Lay out the joining plate positions for the case panels and cut the slots. For slots in a panel face, use a straightedge guide to position the plate joiner (**Fig. 4**).

Use a router with a straight bit and edge guide to cut the rabbets along the back edges of the case sides (**Fig. 5**). Note that the rabbets for the top and bottom panels stop short of the panel ends. Use a sharp chisel to square the rabbet ends after they've been routed.

Rout the edge profile on the case top in two steps. First, use a ⅝-in.-rad. rounding-over bit to cut the profile along the bottom edge of the top panel (**Fig. 6**). Then turn the panel over and use a 30° chamfer bit to cut the top profile.

Use a ¼-in. cove bit to rout the edge band on the case bottom edge. Adjust the depth of the bit so it makes only a ⅛-in.-deep cut, and test the cut on a piece of scrap stock before moving on to the actual piece. Use the same bit in the

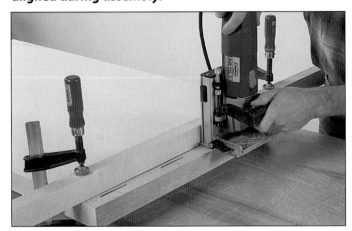

Fig. 4 *Cut joining-plate slots in case parts. Clamp a guide across the panels to help position the joiner for slots in the panel faces.*

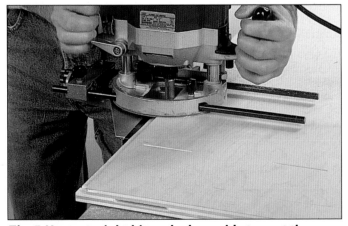

Fig. 5 *Use a straight bit and edge guide to rout the rabbets along the back edges of the case sides and the top and bottom panels.*

router table to cut the molding for the middle shelf and case sides. Start with a maple blank about 48 in. long, 4 in. wide, and ¾ in. thick. Rout both corners of one edge of the blank and use a table saw to rip the molding from the blank.

Join the drawer partition to the middle shelf with joining plates and screws. Because this joint is hidden, use plates to align the parts and use screws instead of glue. Clamp the parts together while you bore pilot holes for 2-in. No. 8 screws and drive the screws.

Next, spread glue in the plate slots to join the case sides with the middle shelf and assemble. Use cauls to distribute the clamping pressure (**Fig. 7**). Apply glue to the slots to join the top and sides, position the top, and use clamps to pull the joints tight.

Bore and countersink screw holes in the case bottom and pilot holes in the case sides and drawer partition. Then install joining plates and screw together the parts.

Miter the molding to length for the middle shelf and case sides. Spread glue on the shelf strip and clamp it in place. Install the side strips using glue and 1-in. brads (**Fig. 8**). Now you're ready to set the nail heads and fill.

Making the Base

Cut 4-in.-sq. leg blocks of 1-in. maple, with one edge of each parallel to the grain beveled to 45°. Cut a No. 0 plate joint slot in the beveled edge. Next, use a dado blade in the table saw to shape the rabbet at the top inside edge of each leg block (**Fig. 9**).

Spread glue on the beveled edges and plate slots, insert the plates, and assemble the legs. When the glue has dried, make the angled cuts to taper each leg.

Cut the base rails to size with mitered ends. Glue and screw the rails to the legs (**Fig. 10**). Bore and countersink pilot holes for attaching the rails to the case, and then install the base.

Cut the case back from a sheet of ½-in.-thick plywood. Mark the location of the 2-in.-dia. cord-access hole in the back panel and bore the hole with a multispur or Forstner bit. Then mount the back to the case with 1-in. No. 6 screws.

Door Construction

For all door parts, rip and crosscut ¹³⁄₁₆-in.-thick maple to size. Lay out the joints and use a router with a spiral up-cutting bit and edge guide to cut the mortises. Clamp the stiles together to form a wide, stable base for the router, and cut the four mortises in each stile (**Fig. 11**).

Next, cut the mortises in the top and bottom rails and mullions. Use a sharp chisel to square the rounded ends of each mortise (**Fig. 12**). Adjust the bit cutting depth and then rout the panel grooves in the edges of stiles, rails, and mullions (**Fig. 13**).

Use a dado blade in the table saw to cut the tenons on the rails and mullions. Cut the tenon cheeks first (**Fig. 14**), then readjust the blade height to cut the shoulder at the outside

Fig. 6 *Use a ⅝-in.-rad. rounding-over bit to shape the bottom edge of the case top. Rout a 30° chamfer around the top edge.*

Fig. 7 *Glue the case sides to the middle shelf. A caul with a thin veneer shim at the center distributes pressure across the panel.*

Fig. 8 *Use glue and 1-in. brads to fasten molding to the case sides. Set the nail heads and fill with a matching, sandable wood filler.*

Fig. 9 *Use a clamp to hold the leg blanks to the table saw miter gauge when cutting the rabbet along the top inside surface.*

Fig. 10 *After cutting the base rails to size with mitered ends, use screws and glue to fasten the rails to the mitered legs.*

Fig. 11 *Rout the mortises in the door-frame components. Clamping stiles together provides an extra-wide base for the router.*

Fig. 12 *When the routing is done, use a sharp chisel to square the rounded ends of the mortises in stiles, mullions, and rails.*

Fig. 13 *Adjust the router bit cutting depth and shape the panel grooves in the edges of the door stiles, rails, and mullions.*

Fig. 14 *Use a dado blade in the table saw to cut the rail and mullion tenons. A stop clamped to the miter gauge positions the work.*

Fig. 15 *After joining the short rails to the mullion, apply glue and clamp the rails in place. Then install the panels and stiles.*

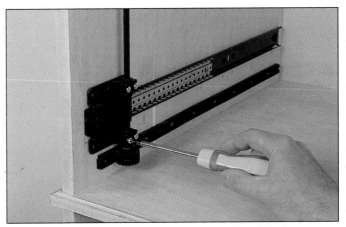

Fig. 16 *Screw the pinion-wheel/mounting-block assembly to the door slide. Detailed instructions are included with the hardware.*

edge of the top and bottom rails. Clamp the short rails to the miter gauge so your hands stay safely away from the blade.

Cut the door panels to size and use a straight bit in the router table to shape the rabbet around the inside edges of each panel. Sand the panels with 120-, 150-, 180-, and 220-grit paper before beginning the door assembly.

Spread glue in mullion mortises and corresponding short rail tenons, assemble these parts, and clamp. Next, spread glue on the mullion tenons and top and bottom rail mortises and join (**Fig. 15**). When the glue has set, slide the panels into the grooves. Then spread glue on the rest of the joints, add the stiles, and clamp.

Study the instructions included with the door hardware so that you understand the operation of the slide before beginning the installation. Secure the door slides to the inside of the cabinet sides. Cut small spacer blocks to help position the slides accurately between the case top and bottom so they are parallel to each other. Next, attach the rack drives to the case sides. Secure the pinion wheels and mounting hardware to the profile rods as shown in the slide instructions. Mount the rod assembly on the slides (**Fig. 16**) and fasten the mounting plates.

Use a Forstner or multispur bit in a drill press to bore a 35mm-dia. x ½-in.-deep recess in the doors for each hinge. Install the hinges (**Fig. 17**) and mount the doors on the slides. Use the mounting-plate screws to adjust the doors for proper operation and a uniform ⅛-in. margin.

Final Steps

Bore the 2-in.-dia. wire-access hole in the insert shelf. After assembling the case insert with joining plates and screws, slide the insert into the cabinet, bore and countersink pilot holes, and screw the insert to the cabinet top and middle shelf.

Cut ½-in. maple to size for the drawer parts. Use a dado blade to make the rabbet and dado joints in the drawer sides

and the grooves for drawer bottoms. Use glue and 4d finishing nails to assemble the drawer boxes.

Cut bottom panels from ¼-in. maple plywood, slide them in place, and screw each to a drawer back. Cut drawer faces from ¹³⁄₁₆-in. stock and screw them to the drawers. Mount the drawer slides following the manufacturers instructions. Bore pilot holes for the door and drawer knobs, but don't install them until the case is finished.

Disassemble the case and remove the hardware to prepare for finishing. Sand all case parts to 220 grit, dusting carefully between grits. Wipe all surfaces with a tack cloth before applying the first coat of finish.

We applied three coats of Behlen's Water White Restoration Varnish, following the manufacturer's instructions. When the last coat is dry, buff the finish with 4/0 steel wool and polish it with a soft cloth. Finally, reassemble the case and install the doors, drawers, and hardware.

Fig. 17 *Bore 35mm-dia. recesses in the door stiles for the hinge cups. Then install the hinges to the doors and adjust for proper operation.*

Bookworm's Bookcase

Traditional glass-pane and wood-muntin doors highlight this freestanding piece.

A s the saying goes, there's nothing like good books. But they can present some storage problems—especially if you like to keep them after you've read them. Wall-mounted shelves are a common solution for all this bound wisdom. But they're not easily portable if you want to rearrange the furniture or if you're moving to a new house. Because of this, modular units that combine storage for books with audio and video equipment have become a popular solution. Unfortunately, many of these pieces can be a bit overpowering, making you feel like you're in a NASA control room instead of the comfort and privacy of your own home.

*Key*POINTS

TIME
Prep Time	10 hours
Shop Time	12 hours
Assembly Time	24 hours

EFFORT
Skill Level	intermediate

COST / BENEFITS
Expense: **moderate**
- This bookcase is a step above traditional open shelving—it provides an elegant setting for your favorite literary works.

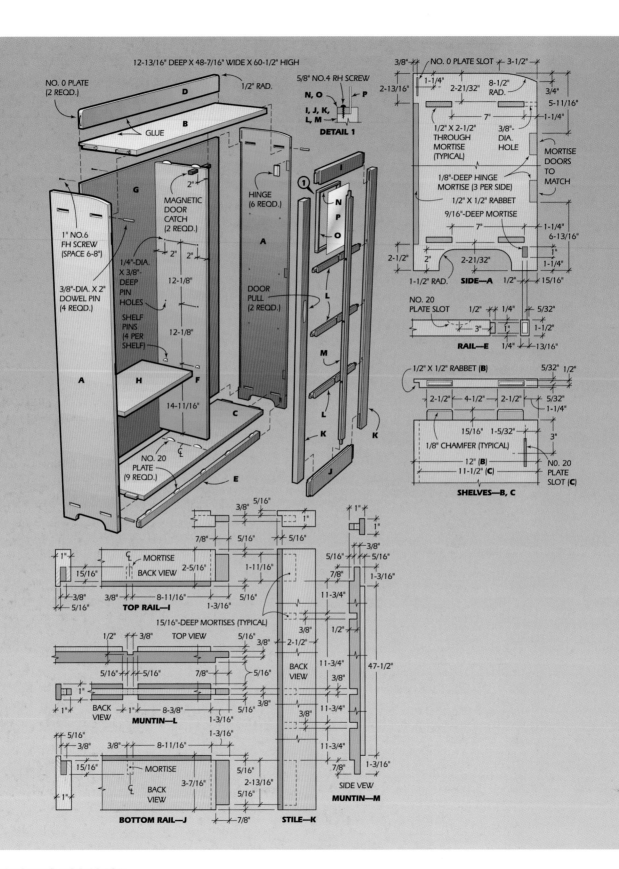

12-13/16" DEEP X 48-7/16" WIDE X 60-1/2" HIGH

NO. 0 PLATE (2 REQD.)

D

1/2" RAD.

GLUE

B

5/8" NO.4 RH SCREW

N, O

P

I, J, K, L, M

DETAIL 1

3/8"

NO. 0 PLATE SLOT

3-1/2"

2-13/16"

1-1/4"

2-21/32"

8-1/2" RAD.

3/4"

5-11/16"

7"

1-1/4"

1/2" X 2-1/2" THROUGH MORTISE (TYPICAL)

3/8"-DIA. HOLE

MORTISE DOORS TO MATCH

1/8"-DEEP HINGE MORTISE (3 PER SIDE)

1/2" X 1/2" RABBET

9/16"-DEEP MORTISE

7"

1-1/4"

6-13/16"

2-1/2"

2"

2-21/32"

1"

1-1/4"

1-1/2" RAD.

SIDE—A

1/2"

15/16"

2"

MAGNETIC DOOR CATCH (2 REQD.)

HINGE (6 REQD.)

A

1" NO.6 FH SCREW (SPACE 6-8")

G

3/8"-DIA. X 2" DOWEL PIN (4 REQD.)

1/4"-DIA. X 3/8"-DEEP PIN HOLES

2" 2"

12-1/8"

12-1/8"

DOOR PULL (2 REQD.)

SHELF PINS (4 PER SHELF)

A

H

F

14-11/16"

C

NO. 20 PLATE (9 REQD.)

E

I

N

P

O

1

L

M

L

K

K

J

NO. 20 PLATE SLOT

1/2"

1/4"

5/32"

3"

1"

1-1/2"

RAIL—E

1/4"

13/16"

1/2" X 1/2" RABBET (B)

5/32"

1/2"

2-1/2"

4-1/2"

2-1/2"

5/32"

1-1/4"

15/16"

1-5/32"

3"

1/8" CHAMFER (TYPICAL)

12" (B)

11-1/2" (C)

NO. 20 PLATE SLOT (C)

SHELVES—B, C

3/8"

5/16"

1"

1"

1"

7/8"

5/16"

5/16"

3/8"

5/16"

5/16"

7/8"

1-3/16"

1"

MORTISE

2-5/16"

BACK VIEW

1-11/16"

11-3/4"

15/16"

3/8"

3/8"

8-11/16"

5/16"

3/8"

5/16"

TOP RAIL—I

1-3/16"

15/16"-DEEP MORTISES (TYPICAL)

1/2"

3/8"

TOP VIEW

5/16"

3/8"

2-1/2"

3/8"

1/2"

11-3/4"

5/16"

5/16"

7/8"

5/16"

BACK VIEW

47-1/2"

1"

1"

BACK VIEW

1"

8-3/8"

5/16"

MUNTIN—L

1-3/16"

11-3/4"

3/8"

3/8"

11-3/4"

5/16"

3/8"

3/8"

8-11/16"

1-3/16"

15/16"

MORTISE

3-7/16"

BACK VIEW

2-13/16"

5/16"

5/16"

1"

BOTTOM RAIL—J

7/8"

STILE—K

7/8"

11-3/4"

1-3/16"

SIDE VEW

MUNTIN—M

This bookcase is meant to be a tasteful alternative to those other approaches. Its multipaned glass doors, exposed tenons, and quarter-sawn oak construction work together to create a sense of seriousness and an air of solidity, which are unusual these days. This overall design is a synthesis of several traditional Arts & Crafts pieces. But we did scale down the size of the case slightly so it could be easily placed in a family room, den, living room, or bedroom without dominating the space.

Case Joinery and Assembly

Since most of the case parts are all 11 to 12 in. wide, and quarter-sawn stock is generally quite narrow, you'll have to glue up panels for the case sides, partition, top, bottom, and shelves. Begin by ripping and crosscutting slightly oversize boards for your glued-up panels. Edge join the mating boards, then lay out No. 20 joining plate slots, 6 to 8 in. on center, along the joints. Cut the slots using a flat tabletop as a registration surface (**Fig. 1**). Apply glue to the slots, edges, and plates and assemble each panel, clamping the joints tight until the glue sets. When all the panels are dry, rip and crosscut the parts to finished size.

Lay out the arched cutout at the bottom and the curved profile at the top front edge of each case side. Use a sabre saw to make these cuts (**Fig. 2**).

Mark the end limits of the rabbets on the case sides that will house the back panel. Use a router with a ¾-in.-dia. straight bit and edge guide to make the cuts (**Fig. 3**). Square the ends of the rabbet with a chisel. Then use the same setup to cut the rabbet along the back edge of the top shelf.

The through tenons that join the top and bottom panels to the case sides are cut in several stages. Begin by cutting a continuous tenon on the ends of the top and bottom panels, using a dado blade in your table saw (**Fig. 4**). Use the same blade setup to cut the tenons on the ends of the bottom front rail. You'll have to move the stop block for these rail cuts, since these tenons are shorter than the through tenons.

Use a band saw to make the end cuts that define the width of each tenon. Clamp a rip fence and stop block to the band

Fig. 1 *Cut and joint stock for the sides, top, bottom, partition, and shelves. Then, cut slots in mating edges with a plate joiner.*

saw table to make the repeat cuts (**Fig. 5**). Then use a chisel to chop out the waste between the through tenons (**Fig. 6**).

Lay out the exact locations of the through mortises on the case sides. A plunge router with an up-cut spiral bit is the ideal tool for cutting these joints. And be sure to use a straightedge, clamped to the case side, to guide the router (**Fig. 7**). Make the cuts in several passes and finish each mortise by squaring the ends of the cut with a sharp chisel.

Use a router and straightedge guide to cut the mortises in the case sides for the bottom rail. Again, square the mortise cuts with a sharp chisel. Test fit all these joints, and when

Materials List

Key	No.	Size and description (use)
A	2	¹³⁄₁₆ x 12 x 60" oak (side)
B	1	¹³⁄₁₆ x 12 x 48⁷⁄₁₆" oak (top)
C	1	¹³⁄₁₆ x 11½ x 48⁷⁄₁₆" oak (bottom)
D	1	¹³⁄₁₆ x 3 x 46⁹⁄₁₆" oak (rail)
E	1	¹³⁄₁₆ x 1½ x 47⁷⁄₁₆" oak (rail)
F	1	¹³⁄₁₆ x 11½ x 53³⁄₈" oak (partition)
G	1	½ x 47⁹⁄₁₆ x 54¹¹⁄₁₆" oak plywood (back)
H	6	¹³⁄₁₆ x 10³⁄₈ x 22³⁄₄" oak (shelf)
I	2	1 x 2⁵⁄₁₆ x 20¹⁄₈" oak (door rail)
J	2	1 x 3⁷⁄₁₆ x 20¹⁄₈" oak (door rail)
K	4	1 x 2½ x 53¼" oak (door stile)
L	6	1 x 1 x 20⁷⁄₈" oak (muntin)
M	2	1 x 1 x 49⁷⁄₈" oak (muntin)
N	32	⁵⁄₁₆ x ⁹⁄₁₆ x 9" oak (glass stop)
O	32	⁵⁄₁₆ x ⁹⁄₁₆ x 11¹⁄₈" oak (glass stop)
P	16	⅛ x 8¹⁵⁄₁₆ x 11¹¹⁄₁₆" glass (pane)

Misc.: Yellow glue; 120- and 220-grit sandpaper; 0000 steel wool; aniline stain; tung oil varnish; No. 0 and No. 20 joining plates; 1½" brass butt hinges; magnetic door catches; brass shelf pins; No. 4 rh screws.

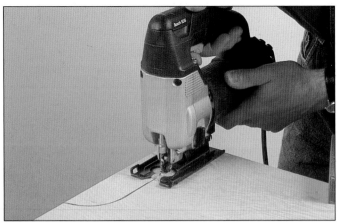

Fig. 2 *Mark the cutouts at the bottom of both sides and make the cuts with a sabre saw. Smooth the cuts with a spokeshave.*

Fig. 4 *Use a table saw with a dado blade installed to make the tenon cuts on the ends of the case bottom and top.*

Fig. 5 *Use a band saw and stop block to make the shoulder cuts on the through tenons for the top and bottom panels.*

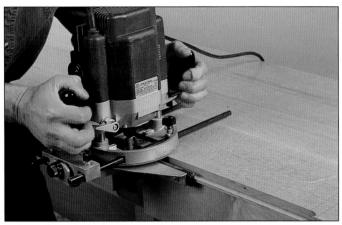

Fig. 3 *Cut the rabbets for the back panel in the case sides and top using a router with a ¾-in.-dia. straight bit and edge guide.*

satisfied, use a chisel to cut a ⅛-in. chamfer on the ends of each through tenon.

Lay out the locations of the plate slots for the joints between the center partition and the top and bottom panels. Then clamp a straightedge guide to the panels to help position the plate joiner and cut the slots (**Fig. 8**). Next, lay out and cut the slots for the joint between the bottom rail and the case bottom. Apply glue to this joint and clamp the rail to the bottom (**Fig. 9**).

Lay out the rounded profile at each end of the top rail and use the sabre saw to make the cut. Cut a No. 0 joining plate slot in each end of the rail, and a matching slot in each case side. Apply glue to the bottom edge of the rail and clamp it along the back edge of the case top (**Fig. 10**).

Sand the top and bottom assemblies and the partition with 120- and 220-grit paper, then dust off thoroughly. Next, apply glue to the plate slots and plates and clamp the partition to the case top and bottom. While the glue sets on this assembly, lay out the hinge locations on the case sides. We used solid brass 1½ x 2-in. butt hinges. Use a sharp knife to outline each mortise. Then make a series of parallel chisel cuts ⅛ in. apart down the length of the mortise and pare away the waste (**Fig. 11**).

Apply glue sparingly to the mortise-and-tenon joints and joining plate slots, then clamp the sides to the top-partition-bottom assembly. Compare opposite diagonal measurements to be sure that the case is square, adjust the clamps if necessary, and let the glue dry. Then bore a ⅜-in.-dia. dowel-pin hole into each through tenon from the front edge of each case side. Apply glue to these holes and tap in a white oak dowel to lock the joints and provide a decorative accent. Finish the case assembly by cutting a piece of ½-in.-thick white oak plywood to size for the case back. Sand the panel smooth with 220-grit sandpaper, then attach it to the case with screws.

Door Construction

Mill 5/4 stock to finished dimension for the door parts. Lay out the mortise locations in the door stiles and at the center of each door rail for the vertical muntins. Remove most of the waste from each mortise by boring overlapping holes using a drill press with a ⅜-in.-dia. bit. Use a sharp chisel to square the ends and walls of each mortise (**Fig. 12**).

Set up the table saw to cut the glass rabbet on door parts. Cut the rabbets in two steps, making the first cut, then readjusting the saw and fence to make the perpendicular cut. Begin with door rails and stiles (**Fig. 13**) to perfect your technique, then finish up with the smaller muntins (**Fig. 14**).

Use a dado blade in the table saw to cut the tenons on the rail and muntin ends. Cut the back side of each tenon with one setup, then move the stop block on the saw table to make the face cuts.

Study the plan to understand the configuration of the half-lap joints at the intersection points of vertical and horizontal muntins. Then use a dado blade to cut these joints (**Fig. 15**).

Test fit each joint and use a razor-sharp chisel to make any necessary adjustments. Then apply glue and clamp the muntin assembly together (**Fig. 16**). Next, glue and clamp the top and bottom rails to the vertical muntin and compare diagonal measurements to ensure that the assembly is square (**Fig. 17**). To avoid a frantic glue-up process, join only one stile at a time to the muntin-rail assembly.

Cut strips of stock to form the glass stops, then crosscut them to size to fit around each pane of glass. Test the fit of all stops (**Fig. 18**), but do not fasten the glass in place until after the doors are finished.

Check the fit of each door in its opening in the bookcase.

Cut the shelves to finished size and check for proper fit. Then remove the shelves, doors, stops, and hardware and finish sand all the pieces with 220-grit sandpaper. Remove all the dust.

Fig. 6 *Use a chisel to remove waste between the through tenons. Work from both sides of the board to prevent tearout.*

Fig. 7 *Cut the through tenon mortises in the case sides using a router with an up-cut spiral bit. Square the cuts with a chisel.*

Fig. 8 *Cut plate slots in the case top and bottom for the partition. Clamp a guide board in place to align the plate joiner.*

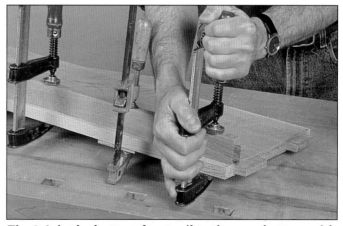

Fig. 9 *Join the bottom front rail to the case bottom with joining plates and glue. Clamp them together until the glue sets.*

Fig. 10 *Cut the top rail to size and shape cut a plate slot in each end. Apply glue and clamp together until the glue sets.*

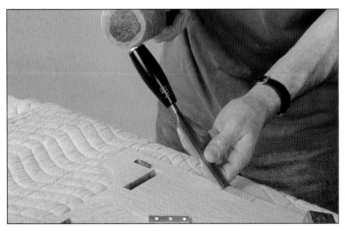

Fig. 11 *Use a sharp chisel to cut recesses in the case sides for the flush-mounted hinges. Work carefully for a precise fit.*

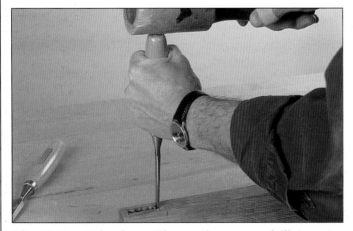

Fig. 12 *To cut the door stile mortises, use a drill press to bore overlapping holes. Then square up the holes with a sharp chisel.*

MATERIAL*Matters*

Wood Wise
Almost everyone has counted the rings of wood in a stump, known as growth rings. And most people know that each ring represents one year of growth. For all of us woodworkers who always want to know more, here are some lesser-known facts.

The dark-colored part of the ring is the late growth, that which is formed in late spring and summer. The light-colored part of the ring is early growth, that which forms in the spring.

The growth rings can take any one of three positions relative to the board's face. They can run perpendicular to the board's face, in which case the board is said to be quartersawn; the rings can be nearly parallel to the board's face, in which case the board is called flat-sawn; or the rings can be somewhere between the two.

This project uses quartersawn lumber because boards with this grain pattern have distinctive cross flecks. Quartersawn oak lumber was highly favored by Arts & Crafts (or Craftsman) furniture builders.

Finishing

To stain the case, we used a water-soluble aniline dye. The color we chose is brown mahogany. Water-soluble dyes yield excellent color and clarity and are relatively easy to use, but they do raise the grain of the wood after application. To prevent this, before staining, wipe the entire bookcase with a slightly damp sponge and let it dry thoroughly. The surface should become extremely rough to the touch. Lightly sand with 220-grit sandpaper, then dust off the case before staining.

We finished our bookcase with three coats of a tung oil varnish. Simply wipe on each coat with a brush or rag, let it set for about 10 minutes, and wipe off the excess. After overnight drying, repeat the process. When the final coat is dry, you can burnish the surface with 0000 steel wool and apply a coat of paste wax.

When the finish is done, install the glass panes in the doors and fasten the stops with ⅜-in. No. 4 rh screws. Since the door pulls we chose have an antique bronze finish, we wanted our brass hinges to match. Whitechapel offers a solution that darkens the finish on brass hinges. Just be sure to carefully follow the application instructions on the package—this solution is poisonous.

Fig. 13 *Cut the rabbets for the door rails and stiles on a table saw. Make the first cut on the board edge and the second on the face.*

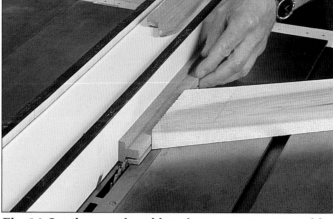

Fig. 14 *Cut the muntin rabbets in two passes on a table saw. Be sure to use a fingerboard and pushstick to make the cuts.*

Fig. 15 *Use a table saw and dado blade to cut the half-lap joints where the muntins cross. Check the blade setup on scrap stock first.*

Fig. 16 *Check the fit of each muntin half-lap joint before applying glue. Use a sharp chisel to make any minor adjustments.*

Fig. 17 *Glue the muntins together, then clamp the door rails in place. Check for square by comparing diagonal measurements.*

Fig. 18 *Cut the glass stops to size and attach with screws. Do not install the glass panes until after the finish has been applied.*

Grand Display

This impressive bookcase is the ideal showcase for your home library.

A good bookcase is more than just a set of shelves. It's a home for your most treasured volumes—a place to not only store and protect, but, more importantly, to display. In fact, while it may be designed to hold books, it's also the perfect place to show off photographs and collectibles.

The problem is, a bookcase with such a daunting responsibility won't make the grade if it's built of plywood or pine. What you need is something that lives up to the objects it holds. With this in mind, our bookcase is constructed of solid mahogany and features details of pomele sapele veneer and wenge.

Key POINTS

TIME
Prep Time	8 hours
Shop Time	10 hours
Assembly Time	18 hours

EFFORT
Skill Level	intermediate

COST / BENEFITS
Expense: **expensive**
- The case's **finished back** allows it to be used either against a wall or in the center of a room as a partition.

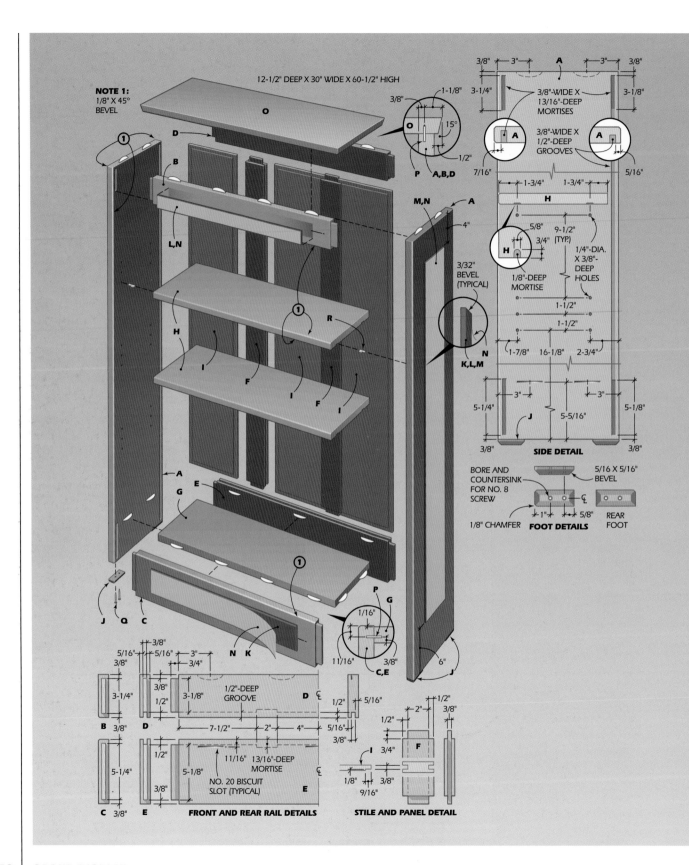

12-1/2" DEEP X 30" WIDE X 60-1/2" HIGH

NOTE 1:
1/8" X 45°
BEVEL

3/8"
1-1/8"
15°
1/2"

O
P
A,B,D

3/32"
BEVEL
(TYPICAL)

M,N
A
4"

K,L,M

L,N
B
D
H
I
F
I
F
I
A
G
E
R
N

J Q C

P
G
1/16"
11/16"
3/8"
C,E

N K

6"
J

SIDE DETAIL

3/8" 3" A 3" 3/8"
3-1/4" 3-1/8"
3/8"-WIDE X
13/16"-DEEP
MORTISES
A A
3/8"-WIDE X
1/2"-DEEP
GROOVES
7/16" 5/16"

1-3/4" 1-3/4"
H
5/8" 9-1/2"
(TYP)
3/4"
H 1/4"-DIA.
X 3/8"-
DEEP
HOLES
1/8"-DEEP
MORTISE
1-1/2"
1-1/2"
1-7/8" 16-1/8" 2-3/4"

3" 3"
5-1/4" 5-5/16" 5-1/8"
J
3/8" 3/8"

BORE AND
COUNTERSINK
FOR NO. 8
SCREW
5/16 X 5/16"
BEVEL

1/8" CHAMFER **FOOT DETAILS**
1" 5/8"
REAR
FOOT

3/8"
5/16" 5/16" 3"
3/8" 3/4"
3-1/4" 3-1/8"
1/2"-DEEP
GROOVE
D
B 3/8" D
7-1/2" 2" 4"

1/2"
5-1/4" 5-1/8"
11/16" 13/16"-DEEP
MORTISE
NO. 20 BISCUIT
SLOT (TYPICAL)
C 3/8" E
3/8"

1/2" 5/16"
5/16"
3/8"

1/2"
2" 3/8"
I 3/4"
F
1/8" 3/8"
9/16"

FRONT AND REAR RAIL DETAILS   **STILE AND PANEL DETAIL**

To accent our bookcase, we've used wenge, a dense, dark wood and pomele sapele veneer, a mahogany-like wood with a heavily quilted grain figure. These attractive exotic woods are not likely to be stocked by your local lumberyard, but they are available through mail-order sources.

Building the Case

Begin by cutting the case parts to finished dimension. Try to match the color and grain of the pieces for a uniform appearance. Mark the locations of the front and back rails on each side. Note that the front rails are set back ⅛ in., while the back rails are flush. Use a marking gauge and square to lay out the mortises for each joint.

Rout the rail mortises with a spiral up-cutting bit (**Fig. 1**). Make two or three passes to reach the full mortise depth to avoid breaking the bit or overloading the router. Then rout the back-panel grooves (**Fig. 2**).

Lay out the mortises in the edges of the top and bottom back rails. Maintain the router's previous edge-guide setting and readjust the depth to cut these mortises. Clamp two rails together to provide a wider, more stable base for the router, but be sure to register the edge guide against the outer face of the rail being cut. Readjust the bit depth again to cut the panel grooves in the rails, and then rout the panel grooves in the back stiles. Square the mortises with a chisel (**Fig. 3**).

Use a dado blade in your table saw to cut the tenon cheeks on the rails and stiles (**Fig. 4**). A stop block clamped to the saw table ensures that all tenons will be the same length. Since most dado blades leave small ridges on the surface of the stock, cut the tenons about ½ in. heavy and pare them to size with a sharp chisel. Readjust the blade height to cut the shoulders at the edges of the tenons (**Fig. 5**).

Mark the locations of the joining-plate slots on the inner surfaces of the bottom rails and cut the slots (**Fig. 6**). Adjust

Fig. 1 *Use a spiral up-cutting bit to rout the mortises in the case sides. Reach the full mortise depth in two or three passes.*

Fig. 2 *Rout the grooves for rear panels in the case sides. The grooves extend between the mortises for top and bottom rails.*

Materials List

Key	No.	Size and description (use)
A	2	1 x 11½ x 59" mahogany (side)
B	1	1 x 4 x 28½" mahogany (front top rail)
C	1	1 x 6 x 28½" mahogany (front bottom rail)
D	1	1 x 4 x 28½" mahogany (rear top rail)
E	1	1 x 6 x 28½" mahogany (rear bottom rail)
F	2	1 x 3 x 50½" mahogany (stile)
G	1	1 x 9⅜ x 27" mahogany (bottom)
H	3	1 x 10⅜ x 26¹⁵⁄₁₆" mahogany (shelf)
I	3	½ x 8 x 50" mahogany (rear panel)
J	4	½ x 1 x 2½" wenge (foot)
K	1	³⁄₁₆ x 3½ x 22" wenge (panel core)
L	1	³⁄₁₆ x 2 x 22" wenge (panel core)
M	2	³⁄₁₆ x 5½ x 49" wenge (panel core)
N	as reqd.	pomele sapele (panel veneer)
O	1	1 x 12½ x 30" mahogany (top)
P	23	No. 20 joining plates
Q	8	1½" No. 8 fh wood screws
R	12	shelf pins

Misc.: Glue; wax paper; 120-, 220-, and 320-grit sandpaper; 4/0 steel wool; Waterlox Original Sealer/Finish.

Fig. 3 *After routing the mortises in the back rails for the stiles, use a sharp chisel and mallet to square the ends of all mortises.*

Fig. 4 *Use a dado blade in the table saw to cut the tenons. A stop block clamped to the table ensures uniform tenon lengths.*

Fig. 5 *After paring the tenons to size, readjust the dado blade height and hold the rails and stiles on edge to cut the tenon shoulders.*

Fig. 6 *Mark the plate centers on the front and back bottom rails and cut the slots. Use the joiner fence to locate slot heights.*

the joiner fence so that the slots are set back the proper distance from the rail edge. Note that the front rail has four slots while the back rail has three slots.

Next, lay out the slots on the edges and ends of the bottom shelf and cut them. Use a flat tabletop as a registration surface for locating the slots. Be sure that you hold both the joiner and workpiece tight to the table when cutting. Use the same technique to cut the slots in the top ends of the case sides as well as the top edges of front and back upper rails. Mark the case sides to indicate the positions of the slots for the bottom shelf joint, then cut those slots (**Fig. 7**). Clamp a guide block to the case side to aid in locating the joiner for these cuts.

Make a template out of plywood or hardboard for the shelf-pin hole locations. Note that the edge-to-hole distance is different for the front and back holes. Position the template on each case side and use a depth stop on the drill bit to bore the shelf-pin holes (**Fig. 8**).

Install a chamfer bit in the router table and cut the ⅛-in. chamfer on the front edges and outside back edges of the case sides. Then chamfer the front rails and front edges of the adjustable shelves. Install a straight bit in your router and cut the rabbet around the edges of the back panels (**Fig. 9**).

To make the wenge feet, first rip a strip of 1-in.-thick wenge to 2½ in. wide. Adjust the table saw blade to 45° and chamfer the end of the strip (**Fig. 10**). Readjust the blade to 90° to cut a ½-in.-high foot off the strip. Repeat the procedure for the remaining feet. Bore and countersink screw holes in the case feet. Spread a bit of glue on each foot and fasten them to the bottom ends of the sides with 1½-in. No. 8 screws (**Fig. 11**).

Decorative Panels

Cut the wenge panel cores larger than finished dimension—they'll be trimmed to exact size after the veneer is glued in place. After cutting the wenge stock to width, clamp a fence to your band saw and resaw the thin panel cores. Cut the pieces about ½ in. thicker than indicated and plane them smooth.

To cut the veneer, first place a scrap plywood or particleboard panel on your worktable and lay a sheet of veneer over it. Lay out the outlines of the veneer pieces to match the wenge cores. Place a straightedge guide over each cutline and hold a veneer saw against the guide while lightly scoring the veneer (**Fig. 12**). It will take several passes with the saw to cut through the veneer.

You can easily press the veneer onto both side panels at the same time. Use a roller to spread glue onto the wenge cores (**Fig. 13**). Place a veneer sheet over each core, then cover each with wax paper.

Stack the two panels with edges and ends aligned and sandwich them between ¾-in.-thick cauls. It's best to use double cauls on both sides of the stack to evenly distribute the clamping pressure. Apply clamps, beginning at the center and working toward both ends (**Fig. 14**). Space the clamps 3 to 4 in. apart. Allow the panels to sit in the clamps for at least 2 hours. Then remove the clamps and let the panels dry overnight.

Follow the same procedure for assembling the front-rail panels. Don't be alarmed if the panels show a slight warp. Usually, veneer is applied to both sides of the core to avoid this. When the thin panels are glued and clamped to the bookcase, they'll flatten out.

After the glue has cured, cut the panels to finished size and chamfer the edges. Sand the panel edges and outer surfaces of the front rails and sides to 220 grit. Mark the location of each panel on its case part.

Spread glue on the back of the top-rail panel, place it on the rail, and clamp it in position (**Fig. 15**). Use plenty of clamps to ensure a good bond between the panel and rail. Repeat the procedure for the bottom rail and side panels.

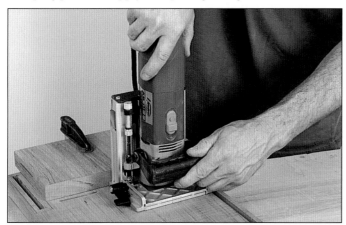

Fig. 7 *After cutting slots in shelf ends, cut matching slots in case sides. A block clamped to the side locates the joiner.*

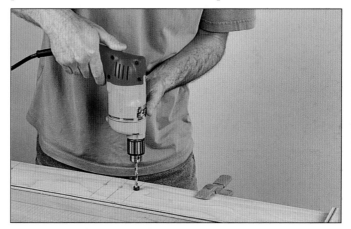

Fig. 8 *Make a template of the shelf-pin hole locations. Then use the template to position the holes in each of the case sides.*

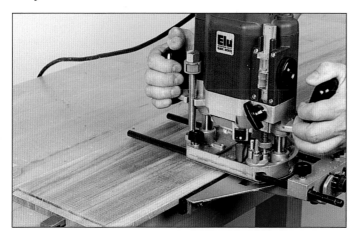

Fig. 9 *Cut back panels to size from ½-in.-thick stock and use a straight bit in the router to shape the rabbet around the panel edges.*

Fig. 10 *Cut a 45° chamfer at the end of a 1 x 2½-in. wenge blank. Set the blade to 90° and saw across the end to make a foot.*

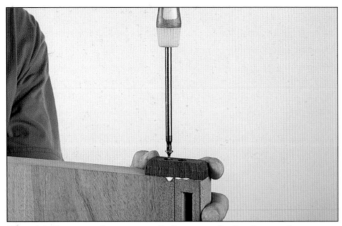

Fig. 11 *Bore and countersink screw holes in each case foot. Apply glue and screw the feet to the bottom ends of the case sides.*

Fig. 12 *Hold the veneer saw tight against a straight guide and run it lightly over the veneer several times to make the cut.*

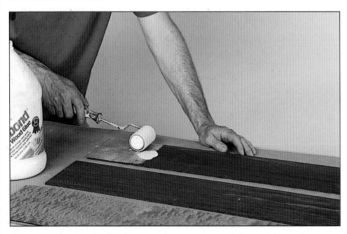

Fig. 13 *Spread glue onto the wenge strips using a foam roller. Then place a sheet of veneer over each core panel.*

Assembly

Dry fit the front and back bottom rails to the bottom shelf (**Fig. 16**). Then glue and clamp the assembly.

Slide the two back stiles over the edges of the center back panel. Next, apply glue to the mortise-and-tenon joints for the stiles and upper and lower back rails, and assemble the parts (**Fig. 17**). Take care to keep glue off the panel edges. Use long bar clamps to pull the back rail/stile joints tight and let the glue set.

Slide the two remaining back panels into the rail and stile grooves. Next, apply glue to the joints for one of the two case sides. Assemble the side to the back subassembly and front rail and apply clamps (**Fig. 18**). When the glue is dry, add the other side.

Mark the locations of the joining-plate slots in the case top and cut the slots. Clamp a straightedge guide to the top to aid in positioning the joiner.

Set the table saw blade to a 15° angle and bevel the case top edges (**Fig. 19**). Use the miter gauge when trimming the ends, and the fence when cutting the front and back edges. Sand the case and top to 220 grit, spread glue in the slots and on the joining plates, and clamp the top in place.

Mark the locations of the shelf-pin notches in the bottom faces of the adjustable shelves. Use a router with an edge guide and straight bit to cut the notches, and sand the shelves.

Finishing

We finished our case with Waterlox Original Sealer/Finish. Apply the finish liberally with a brush or rag and allow it to penetrate for about 30 minutes. Use a lint-free rag to wipe off the excess, leaving only a damp surface. After overnight drying, lightly scuff the surface with 320-grit paper and dust off. Repeat the application using the same method for two or three more coats. When the last coat has cured, rub the surface with 4/0 steel wool followed by a soft cloth.

Safety Sense

LEANING TOWER
Many of today's floors are covered with wall-to-wall carpeting, which may look great, but it can create problems when you're installing a bookcase. Many bookcases lean forward because the back of the case rests on the carpet tack strip at the corner of the wall and floor, while the front of the case rests solely on the carpet. To prevent your bookcase from tipping forward, shim the front of the case back, and if need be, also fasten the case to a wall stud.

Fig. 14 *Stack the side panels with wax paper between each piece and plywood cauls on top and bottom. Then apply clamps.*

Fig. 15 *Spread glue on the back of a panel and clamp it to a rail. Use plenty of clamps to ensure a good bond between the panel and rail.*

Fig. 16 *Spread glue in the joining-plate slots and on mating edges and plates, then assemble the bottom shelf and rails.*

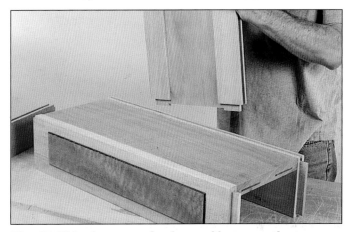

Fig. 17 *Slide the center back panel between the two stiles. Apply glue and join the stiles to the top and bottom back rails.*

Fig. 18 *Join one case side to the bottom/back subassembly, then add the front top rail followed by the second side.*

Fig. 19 *Cut the case top to finished dimension. Reset the table saw blade to 15° and cut the beveled edge around the top.*

Desk of Distinction

This mahogany desk makes a handsome centerpiece for your home office.

With all the business involved in running a home, it's no wonder most of us run out of space to handle the paperwork. We do the monthly bills at the kitchen table and use the counter for everything from sorting mail to balancing the checkbook. But if you're tired of coffee cup rings on your important papers, it may be time to bring your woodworking skills to bear on the problem—it may be time to build a desk.

A good desk does more than provide a central work surface for paperwork. With a full complement of drawers, it handles all your home-office storage needs—from stationery to tape dispensers to file folders.

*Key*POINTS

TIME
Prep Time .... 10 hours
Shop Time .... 18 hours
Assembly Time .... 20 hours

EFFORT
Skill Level .... intermediate

COST / BENEFITS
Expense: **expensive**
- The **stylish, practical design** allows you to get out from under piles of paperwork.
- The **tooled leather top** adds **a touch of sophistication**.

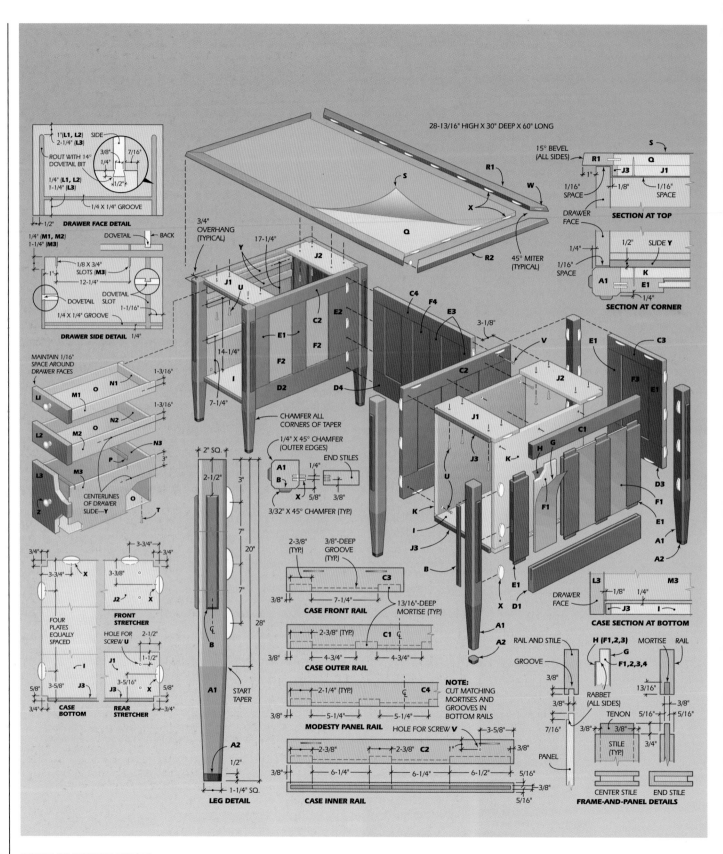

Our creation features the same design elements and materials found in our matching bookcase (page 144). It's constructed of solid mahogany with decorative panels of pomele sapele veneer and accents of wenge. And for a real touch of class, we've given our desk an elegant tooled leather top. To simplify making the top, we ordered a ready-to-install leather panel from an online supplier. The pomele sapele veneer and wenge are available from mail-order lumber and veneer suppliers.

Making the Legs and Rails

The desk is made up of two pedestal units with drawers. The pedestals are joined at the front by an assembly called the modesty panel. Cut 2-in.-square stock for the desk legs to exact length. Then use your band saw to cut the tapered profiles at the bottom of each leg (**Fig. 1**). Smooth the sawn surfaces with a sharp hand plane (**Fig. 2**).

Make the rails and stiles from 1-in. stock and lay out the mortise-and-tenon joints. Rout the mortises using extra rails clamped to the side of each workpiece to provide solid router support (**Fig. 3**). Then square the mortise ends with a sharp chisel. Readjust the router bit depth and rout the panel grooves in both the rails and stiles (**Fig. 4**). Use a dado blade

in your table saw to cut the stile tenons (**Fig. 5**), and then test fit the joints.

Veneering the Panels

It's best to make the panels oversize and trim them after veneering. To cut the veneer, use a veneer saw guided by a straightedge. Make a series of light passes while holding the saw tight to the guide (**Fig. 6**). It's most efficient to stack a few sheets and cut them together.

Note that most of the panels have sapele veneer on the face and plain mahogany on the back. Only the modesty panel requires sapele on both faces. Cut the MDF (medium-density fiberboard) panel cores to match the size of the veneer sheets.

Materials List

Key	No.	Size and description (use)
A1	8	2 x 2 x 27$\frac{1}{2}$" mahogany (leg)
A2	8	$\frac{1}{2}$ x 2 x 2" wenge (foot)
B	16	$\frac{3}{16}$ x $\frac{7}{8}$ x 13$\frac{1}{2}$" wenge (trim)
C1	2	1 x 2$\frac{1}{2}$ x 24$\frac{1}{2}$" mahogany (outer rail)
C2	2	1 x 2$\frac{1}{2}$ x 24$\frac{1}{2}$" mahogany (inner rail)
C3	2	1 x 2$\frac{1}{2}$ x 12$\frac{3}{4}$" mahogany (front rail)
C4	1	1 x 2$\frac{1}{2}$ x 25$\frac{1}{2}$" mahogany (modesty rail)
D1	2	1 x 4 x 24$\frac{1}{2}$" mahogany (outer rail)
D2	2	1 x 4 x 24$\frac{1}{2}$" mahogany (inner rail)
D3	2	1 x 4 x 12$\frac{3}{4}$" mahogany (front rail)
D4	1	1 x 4 x 25$\frac{1}{2}$" mahogany (modesty rail)
E1	16	1 x 3$\frac{1}{8}$ x 15" mahogany (stile)
E2	2	1 x 7$\frac{1}{4}$ x 15" mahogany (inner stile)
E3	4	1 x 3 x 15" mahogany (modesty stile)
F1	6	$\frac{1}{2}$ x 4$\frac{3}{4}$ x 14$\frac{1}{4}$" MDF (outer panel)
F2	4	$\frac{1}{2}$ x 6$\frac{1}{4}$ x 14$\frac{1}{4}$" MDF (inner panel)
F3	2	$\frac{1}{2}$ x 7$\frac{1}{4}$ x 14$\frac{1}{4}$" MDF (front panel)
F4	3	$\frac{1}{2}$ x 5$\frac{1}{4}$ x 14$\frac{1}{4}$" MDF (modesty panel)
G	as reqd.	pomele sapele veneer
H	as reqd.	mahogany veneer
I	2	$\frac{3}{4}$ x 14$\frac{1}{4}$ x 25$\frac{1}{2}$" plywood (case bottom)
J1	2	$\frac{3}{4}$ x 5$\frac{5}{8}$ x 14$\frac{1}{4}$" plywood (case stretcher)
J2	2	$\frac{3}{4}$ x 6 x 14$\frac{1}{4}$" plywood (case stretcher)
J3	4	$\frac{3}{8}$ x $\frac{3}{4}$ x 12$\frac{3}{4}$" mahogany (edge band)
K	4	$\frac{3}{4}$ x 18$\frac{1}{2}$ x 20" plywood (drawer casing)
L1	2	1 x 2$\frac{15}{16}$ x 12$\frac{5}{8}$" mahogany (drawer face)
L2	2	1 x 4$\frac{7}{8}$ x 12$\frac{5}{8}$" mahogany (drawer face)
L3	2	1 x 12 x 12$\frac{5}{8}$" mahogany (drawer face)
M1	4	$\frac{1}{2}$ x 2$\frac{3}{16}$ x 20$\frac{1}{4}$" maple (drawer side)
M2	4	$\frac{1}{2}$ x 4$\frac{1}{8}$ x 20$\frac{1}{4}$" maple (drawer side)
M3	4	$\frac{1}{2}$ x 10 x 20$\frac{1}{4}$" maple (drawer side)
N1	2	$\frac{1}{2}$ x 1$\frac{11}{16}$ x 11$\frac{1}{4}$" maple (drawer back)
N2	2	$\frac{1}{2}$ x 3$\frac{5}{8}$ x 11$\frac{1}{4}$" maple (drawer back)
N3	2	$\frac{1}{2}$ x 9$\frac{1}{2}$ x 11$\frac{1}{4}$" maple (drawer back)
O	6	$\frac{1}{4}$ x 11$\frac{1}{4}$ x 19$\frac{1}{4}$" plywood (drawer bottom)
P	4	$\frac{1}{8}$ x $\frac{3}{4}$ x 11$\frac{3}{4}$" aluminum bar (hanger)
Q	1	$\frac{3}{4}$ x 25$\frac{1}{2}$ x 55$\frac{1}{2}$" lauan plywood (top)
R1	2	$\frac{13}{16}$ x 2$\frac{1}{4}$ x 60" mahogany (top edge)
R2	2	$\frac{13}{16}$ x 2$\frac{1}{4}$ x 30" mahogany (top edge)
S	1	25$\frac{1}{2}$ x 55$\frac{1}{2}$" leather
T	12	$\frac{1}{2}$" No. 8 rh wood screws
U	28	1$\frac{1}{4}$" No. 8 fh wood screws
V	8	2$\frac{1}{2}$" No. 8 fh wood screws
W	as reqd.	No. 0 plates
X	as reqd.	No. 20 plates
Y	6 pr.	drawer slides
Z	6	1$\frac{1}{4}$"-dia. brass drawer pulls

Misc.: 120-, 150-, 180-, 220-, and 320-grit sandpaper; 4/0 steel wool; glue; vinyl wallpaper paste; wax paper; foam roller; Waterlox Original Sealer/Finisher.

Fig. 1 *Mark the tapers on one face of each leg and cut with a band saw. Then mark and cut the tapers on the adjoining faces.*

Fig. 3 *Lay out the rail mortises in 1-in. stock. Use a spiral up-cutting bit and edge guide to rout the mortises. Square the mortise ends with a sharp chisel.*

Fig. 4 *Readjust the bit depth and rout the panel grooves. Spare pieces clamped to the work help support the router.*

Fig. 2 *Use a sharp plane to smooth the tapers. Reverse the direction of the plane at the bottom to avoid splintering the foot.*

If you wish, you can use veneer-core hardwood panels, but make sure to align the face grain of the panel with the grain of the sapele and mahogany veneers.

Because the panels are small, you can easily veneer all like-size pieces at the same time. Use a foam roller to spread glue on one face of a panel core (**Fig. 7**). Place the glued surface on a veneer sheet, then roll glue on the opposite face. Place the second veneer sheet in place and cover both faces with wax paper. Repeat this procedure for each panel of the same size, and then stack the panels together with all edges aligned. Place ¾-in.-thick plywood cauls on the top and bottom of the stack and apply clamps (**Fig. 8**). Position the first clamp at the center of the stack, and work your way toward the edges.

Let the glue cure overnight. Then rip and crosscut the panels to finished dimension, and use your router table to cut the rabbet around the inside edges of each panel. Sand the panels with 120-, 150-, 180- and 220-grit sandpaper, dusting off thoroughly between grits.

Assembly

Starting with the modesty panel, spread glue in the rail mortises and on stile tenons, join the stiles to the bottom rail, and slide the panels into place (**Fig. 9**). Next, add the top rail, clamp, and compare opposite diagonal measurements to ensure that the assembly is square. Repeat the process for each of the pedestal side and front panels.

Cut blanks for the pedestal bottoms and stretchers from ¾-in. mahogany-veneer plywood, MDF core, or similar panel stock. Cut edge-banding strips from solid mahogany, and glue them to the exposed edges of the bottom panels and top stretchers as shown in the drawing (**Fig. 10**). Allow the ¹³⁄₁₆-in.-wide edging strip to overhang the panel on both the top and bottom faces. After the glue sets, use a sharp plane to trim the edging flush. Mark the notches in the bottom and stretcher panels, and make the cuts on your band saw.

Fig. 5 *Use a dado blade and table saw to cut the stile-tenon cheeks. Readjust the blade height to cut the shoulders.*

Fig. 6 *Cut veneer with a veneer saw guided by a wooden straightedge. Make light passes to avoid tearing the wood.*

Fig. 7 *Spread glue onto the panel core using a foam roller. Flip the panel onto a veneer sheet and repeat on the opposite side.*

Lay out the joining-plate slots in the desk legs, modesty panel, and pedestal parts. Use spacer blocks underneath your plate joiner to locate the slots in the legs and panel edges (**Fig. 11**). Clamp a straightedge guide to the inner pedestal sides to locate the plate joiner when cutting the slots for the modesty panel joints. Bore and countersink screw holes in the inner pedestal sides for fastening the modesty panel.

Use a chamfer bit in the router table to shape the edges of the desk legs (**Fig. 12**). Note that the inside corner of each leg should be left square from the top end to a height of 8 in.

Cut wenge trim strips to size, and chamfer the edges with a sharp block plane or sanding block. Sand the leg surfaces and wenge strips to 220 grit, then mark the outline of each strip on the legs with light pencil marks. Spread a light coat of glue on the back of a strip, and clamp it in place on a leg. After about 20 minutes, carefully remove any excess glue. Repeat for each wenge strip.

Begin each pedestal assembly by gluing the front legs to the front panel (**Fig. 13**). Then join the pedestal bottom and stretchers to one of the pedestal sides (**Fig. 14**). After the glue sets, add the opposite side to the assembly. Next, join the front leg/panel assembly to the sides (**Fig. 15**). Cut the inner plywood blocking panels to size and screw them in place.

TECH *Tips*

Flat as a Board
Sometimes fluctuations in humidity can cause cupping in a panel that has been glued together from solid pieces. To keep a panel flat, lay it on a flat surface, cover it and weigh it down, or clamp it down until you are ready to install it.

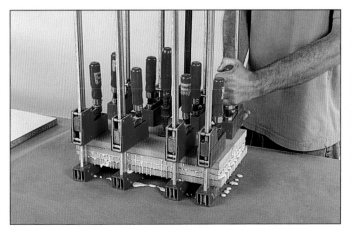

Fig. 8 *Clamp like-size veneered panels together and separate with wax paper. Use ³/₄-in.-thick cauls to evenly distribute pressure.*

Fig. 9 *Apply glue and join the pedestal stiles to a rail. Slide the veneered panels into place and add the second rail.*

Fig. 10 *Cut mahogany edge-banding strips and glue them to plywood blanks for the pedestal bottoms and top stretchers.*

Fig. 11 *Mark the position of the slots in the legs, and use spacer blocks under the plate joiner to properly locate the cuts.*

Fig. 12 *Use a router table to chamfer the leg corners. At the inside corner of each leg, chamfer only the tapered section.*

TECH *Tips*

The Eyes Have It

Ever notice how difficult it can be to cut, plane, or pare with a chisel down to a straight line? No matter how straight your tool appears to be, your lines keep coming out crooked. Well, the problem might not be with your tools or wood.

You may not realize it, but we all have a dominant eye—that is, the eye that guides the motion and response of our dominant hand. If you are right-handed but your left eye is dominant (or vice versa) then you have to compensate when working with hand tools.

Here's a quick test to help you determine which eye is dominant: Extend either arm with your thumb raised, then place your thumb over an object on a wall. Keeping your focus on your thumb, close one eye, then open it and close the other. The thumb will appear to move considerably when sighted with one eye. The eye that produces the least amount of apparent movement is the dominant eye.

When using handsaws, chisels and planes, a person who's right-handed but "left-eyed" will need to compensate by tipping the tool toward them slightly to produce a straight cut. Not trusting your own eyes will seem strange at first, but with practice, it will become second nature.

Fig. 13 *Begin assembling both pedestals by gluing each front panel to a leg. Apply clamps and let the glue cure before continuing.*

Install joining plates in the modesty panel slots, and use screws to fasten the panel to both pedestals. It's not necessary to use glue on these joints since the screws provide plenty of holding power. Bore and countersink screw holes in the top stretchers for fastening the desktop.

Drawer Details

Cut drawer parts to size. Install a ½-in. x 14° dovetail bit in your router, and use it to cut the slots in the drawer faces and drawer sides (**Fig. 16**). Then use a ¼-in. straight bit and edge guide to rout the drawer-bottom grooves. Install the dovetail bit in your router table and use a tall fence to cut the dovetails on the ends of drawer sides and backs. Clamp a backup board to each workpiece to provide additional stability and to keep the ends of the cuts from splitting out (**Fig. 17**). Cut the notches at the top front ends of the drawer sides.

Use a small brush to spread glue in the dovetail joints and assemble the sides to the faces and the backs to the sides. Check that each drawer box is square, and set it aside for the glue to set. Cut the drawer bottoms to size, slide them in place and fasten with screws.

Install drawer slides to both the pedestal and drawer sides following the manufacturer's instructions. Note the centerlines of the slides as shown in the drawing. Use only the slotted holes for initial fastening so you can adjust the slides as required. You should have a uniform margin of ¹⁄₁₆ in. around each drawer when it's closed. Bore holes for the knobs in each drawer face, but don't install the hardware until after you've applied the finish.

Finishing Touches

Cut the plywood desktop panel and mitered mahogany edging to size, and add the joining-plate slots. Apply glue and clamp the edging in place (**Fig. 18**). Mark guidelines for the angled top edge, and use a sharp block plane to shape the edge. Use

Fig. 14 *Join a case bottom and pair of stretchers to each pedestal side. Clamp and check the assembly for square.*

Fig. 15 *Apply glue and clamp together the front leg/ panel subassembly and the side-panel subassembly. Let the glue set before continuing.*

Fig. 16 *After routing the dovetail slots in the drawer fronts and sides, use a ¼-in. straight bit to rout the bottom groove.*

Old Reliable

Mahogany is a tropical hardwood, and there are many types of this tree. In other words, mahogany is no different than calling a wood "oak"—there is no single type of mahogany. Having said that, mahogany is moderately hard and heavy and works relatively easily. In case you've never worked with it, here are some things you should be aware of.

If you've noticed that working with tropical hardwoods like mahogany dulls the cutting edges on your tools faster than domestic hardwoods do, it's not your imagination. Tropical trees grow on a very thin strata of top soil. In tropical climates, the biosphere tends to exist from this shallow layer upward. As a result of soil conditions and weather patterns, tropical hardwood trees often carry minerals from the soil right into their wood and trap them there. The presence of these minerals, and the reasonably hard nature of the wood itself, makes life tough for cutting edges. Tropical hardwoods can also be hard on your hands—they may actually discolor your hands as you work with them.

For the most part, though, most of the challenges associated with working with mahogany are about the same as they are for working with other woods. And there are many more rewards than drawbacks.

Mahogany is somewhat porous. Unless you apply a filler to the wood before applying the finish, the finish will dimple. Instead of using a grain filler, you can apply two or more coats of thinned finish. You may find it easier when working with mahogany to apply rubbing finishes (at least until your finishing skills become more advanced). Once the porosity is taken care of, mahogany surfaces shine beautifully with both clear and slightly amber finishes.

One clear benefit to choosing mahogany is that it is incredibly stable. When properly cut and dried, the wood maintains its shape and dimension nearly indefinitely—a characteristic that furniture builders have prized for hundreds of years. It's not a coincidence that many fine antiques are built out of mahogany. Well built and well finished, with a rich maroon glow, these pieces have survived hundreds of years—much of which was spent in daily service.

220-grit paper to sand the top edging and bottom face of the desktop panel.

For best results, finish the desk before installing the leather. Because it's important to keep the finish from the top plywood surface, carefully apply masking tape around the perimeter of the plywood panel against the edging.

We finished our desk with Waterlox Original Sealer/Finish. Apply the finish with a brush or rag and let it sit for about 30 minutes. Wipe away the excess and let the surface dry overnight. Next, lightly sand with 320-grit paper and dust off before applying the next coat, using the same technique. After several coats, use 4/0 steel wool to burnish the surface and remove any dust.

Remove the masking tape from the desktop panel, and inspect the plywood to make sure that there are no raised areas or depressions. Fill any holes with wood filler and carefully sand the panel. Remove any dust, and use a

Fig. 17 *Install the dovetail bit in your router table and cut the dovetails on the sides and backs. Then test fit the joints.*

Fig. 18 *Use plate joints to assemble the top panel and mitered mahogany edging. The panel top is $1/16$ in. below the top of edging.*

paintbrush to spread a coat of vinyl wallpaper paste (**Fig. 19**). Be sure to coat the entire surface, especially along the edges and in the corners of the panel. Allow the paste to dry at least 1½ hours and then apply a second coat.

Roll up the leather panel with the finished surface inside. Align one of the short edges against the desktop edging. Then unroll the leather a few inches at a time, using your hands to smooth it out (**Fig. 20**). The leather will stretch if necessary, so take the time to produce a tight fit against the mahogany edging. Work out any air bubbles and apply firm pressure to ensure a good bond. After 10 minutes, smooth the top again. If you find any paste on either the leather or wood, wipe it off with a soft, moist cloth. Let the paste dry overnight.

Place the top on the pedestal base and adjust it so there is an equal overhang on all sides. Bore holes and screw the top to the pedestals. Finally, install the drawer knobs and slide the drawers into the pedestals.

Fig. 19 Brush two coats of wallpaper adhesive onto the desktop panel, paying extra attention to the edges and corners. After the paste dries, apply another coat.

Fig. 20 Position the end of the leather on the top. Unroll a few inches at a time while pressing it in place. Then smooth the top.

MATERIAL *Matters*

Primary School

Most complex woodworking projects—this one included—utilize both primary and secondary woods. As you will see, each type of wood serves a unique purpose.

As the name implies, a primary wood is the wood that you see on a finished piece—the doors, the top, the side panels, and drawer fronts. The two most important things to consider when choosing your primary wood is that the wood is attractive and the grain patterns on the individual pieces can be arranged in a manner that is pleasing to the eye. For example, we've all seen an antique where the two halves of a top or door panel have grain patterns that are mirror images of one another. There's no mechanical reason to do this, it just looks nice. There's no arguing with the fact that, although primary wood can be difficult to work, its beauty makes up for any hassle.

The function of secondary wood is to act as the underlying structural material. This wood doesn't have to be pretty—its most important attribute is that it is stable. Solid poplar and just about any type of plywood that is a reasonable grade (and is flat when you buy it) are good choices for secondary wood. Just cruise the plywood aisle of a home center to find what you need. There are a lot to choose from—birch plywood, lumber and solid-core plywoods, fir plywood—it's all fair game.

We're not talking modern cost-cutting or shoddy craftsmanship when we point out this "anything goes" approach. Many fine antiques, especially those built in thrifty New England, are so rough and ready on the inside, bottom, and back, you won't believe your eyes when you take a drawer out and shine a flashlight inside the piece or turn it around so you can see the back. Believe it or not, there are pieces of furniture that are worth a fortune— some sitting in museums—with back boards that have knots as big as your fist.

This isn't always the case, of course, but the simple truth is that secondary wood performs an entirely different function than primary wood. This holds true whether it's a drawer bottom, a drawer frame, a reinforcing block, or a back panel. If you can save money on secondary wood, do so without regret. Just make sure the wood is stable and meets the mechanical requirements of the piece.

Surround Sound

It's furniture for your home stereo system, exactly what every audiophile needs.

There is a staggering variety of stereo systems today, and depending on your finances and level of enthusiasm, you can spend hundreds or thousands of dollars on equipment. For serious music fans, the sleek, black cases of stacked stereo components are the only way to go. But most of us would rather shut all this equipment behind closed doors and concentrate on the music.

With this in mind, we built this Arts & Crafts style cabinet. It easily accommodates all your high-tech audio components, including a receiver, cassette deck, and CD player. The cabinet also has two drawers—one for cassettes and one for CDs.

*Key*POINTS

TIME
Prep Time	4 hours
Shop Time	10 hours
Assembly Time	10 hours

EFFORT
Skill Level	intermediate

COST / BENEFITS
Expense: moderate
- Functional, yet attractive piece adds style to your living room.
- The cabinet even includes a spot for your turntable and vinyl albums.

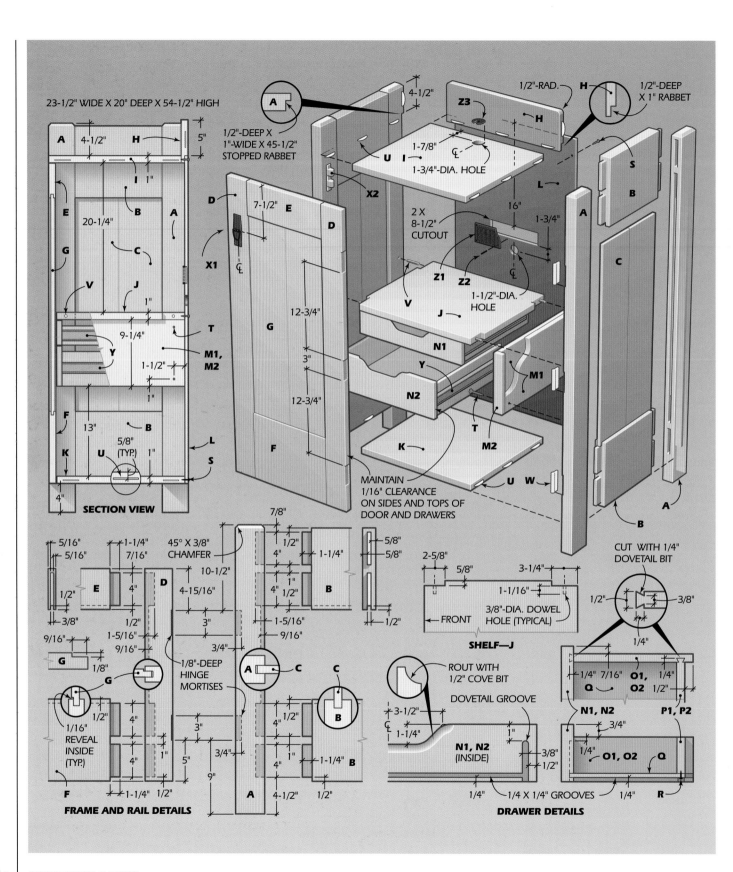

23-1/2" WIDE X 20" DEEP X 54-1/2" HIGH

1/2"-DEEP X 1"-WIDE X 45-1/2" STOPPED RABBET

1/2"-DEEP X 1" RABBET

1/2"-RAD.

4-1/2"

Z3

H

S

B

U I

1-7/8"

1-3/4"-DIA. HOLE

16"

L

A

C

2 X 8-1/2" CUTOUT

1-3/4"

X2

Z1 Z2

V

J

1-1/2"-DIA. HOLE

N1

Y

M1

N2

T

M2

K

U W

MAINTAIN 1/16" CLEARANCE ON SIDES AND TOPS OF DOOR AND DRAWERS

A

B

SECTION VIEW

A 4-1/2" H 5"

I 1"

E B A

20-1/4"

G C

V J

1"

T

Y 9-1/4"

M1, M2

1-1/2"

1"

F B 13"

K L

U 5/8" (TYP.) 1"

S

4"

D E 7-1/2"

X1 CL

D

G 12-3/4"

3"

12-3/4"

F

FRAME AND RAIL DETAILS

5/16"
5/16"

1-1/4"
7/16"

45° X 3/8" CHAMFER

7/8"

1/2"

5/8"
5/8"

E D 4"

4"

1-1/4"

B

1/2" 4" 1/2"

1/2"

3/8"

1/2"

4-15/16"

4" 1/2"

1/2"

9/16"

G

1/8"

1-5/16"

9/16"

3/4"

1-5/16"

9/16"

3"

1/8"-DEEP HINGE MORTISES

A C C B

G

1/2"

4"

4"

1/16" REVEAL INSIDE (TYP.)

3/4"

3"

4" 1/2"

4"

4"

1-1/4" B

A 4-1/2" 1/2"

5"

9"

F 1-1/4" 1/2"

2-5/8"

5/8"

3-1/4"

1-1/16"

3/8"-DIA. DOWEL HOLE (TYPICAL)

FRONT

SHELF—J

ROUT WITH 1/2" COVE BIT

3-1/2"

CL 1-1/4"

1"

N1, N2 (INSIDE)

3/8"

1/2"

1/4"

1/4 X 1/4" GROOVES

1/4"

DOVETAIL GROOVE

CUT WITH 1/4" DOVETAIL BIT

1/2"

3/8"

1/4"

1/4" 7/16" O1, O2

Q

1/4"

1/2"

N1, N2

P1, P2

3/4"

1/4"

O1, O2 Q

R

DRAWER DETAILS

Though most people prefer high-tech audio components, we recognize that many others just can't part with their vinyl collections. For these lovers of nostalgia we have provided space for a turntable on top and a shelf for a modest LP collection down below.

In keeping with traditional Arts & Crafts pieces, we used quartersawn white oak for the cabinet. If you have trouble locating quartersawn oak where you live, look online for a mail-order supplier.

Building the Case

Rip and crosscut stock for the case rails and shelves, leaving each piece a bit oversize, so you can trim the glued-together panels to finished dimension after the glue has set. Joint the edge of each workpiece straight and square, then lay out the joining-plate slots spaced approximately 6 in. on center.

Hold the plate joiner and the workpiece tightly to the surface of the workbench and cut the slots (**Fig. 1**). Spread glue in the slots along the edges of the workpieces and on the joining plates (**Fig. 2**). Position the plates and assemble a panel. Clamp the panel to pull the joints tight, then check that the panel is flat.

Next, glue up the 1/2-in.-thick stock for the side and door panels. It's not a good idea to use joining plates to align the joints on these thinner panels because the plate joint may be visible after the panel is finished.

Prepare the rest of the stock for the case parts. Rip, crosscut and joint all parts to finished dimension, including the previously glued-up panels. Label each part to indicate the face side and orientation in the case.

Lay out the mortises in the case side stiles by clamping the stiles together, then mark across their edges using a square (**Fig. 3**). Use a plunge router with a 1/2-in.-dia. up-cutting bit and an edge guide to cut the stile mortises (**Fig. 4**). Before you begin cutting, clamp two stiles together to provide a stable surface for the plunge router, and cut the mortise in two or three passes.

Fig. 1 ***Cut joining-plate slots in the boards' edges. The plates keep the boards aligned while they are being glued and clamped.***

Materials List

Key	No.	Size and description (use)
A	4	1 3/4 x 3 3/4 x 54" white oak (stile)
B	4	1 3/4 x 10 x 15" white oak (rail)
C	2	1/2 x 13 1/2 x 30 5/8" white oak (panel)
D	2	1 x 3 7/16 x 44 7/16" white oak (stile)
E	1	1 x 4 15/16 x 15 1/2" white oak (rail)
F	1	1 x 10 x 15 1/2" white oak (rail)
G	1	1/2 x 14 x 30 5/8" white oak (panel)
H	1	1 x 6 x 20" white oak (rail)
I	1	1 x 19 x 20" white oak (shelf)
J	1	1 x 18 3/8 x 21 1/4" white oak (shelf)
K	1	1 x 18 3/8 x 20" white oak (shelf)
L	1	1/2 x 22 x 45 1/2" plywood (back)
M1	2	3/4 x 9 1/4 x 17 5/8" plywood (blocking)
M2	2	3/4 x 1 x 9 1/4" white oak (edge band)
N1	1	3/4 x 3 1/2 x 18 3/8" oak (drawer face)
N2	1	3/4 x 5 5/8 x 18 3/8" oak (drawer face)
O1	2	1/2 x 2 3/4 x 16 3/4" maple (drawer side)
O2	2	1/2 x 4 7/8 x 16 3/4" maple (drawer side)
P1	1	1/2 x 2 1/4 x 17" maple (drawer back)
P2	1	1/2 x 4 3/8 x 17" maple (drawer back)
Q	2	1/4 x 16 1/4 x 17" plywood (drawer bottom)
R	2	3/4" No. 6 rh wood screws
S	as reqd.	1" No. 6 rh wood screws
T	4	2 1/2" No. 8 fh wood screws
U	as reqd.	No. 20 plates
V	as reqd.	3/8"-dia. x 2" wood dowels
W	3	1 5/8 x 3" butt hinges
X1	1	door pull
X2	1	door catch
Y	2 pr.	16-in. drawer slides
Z1	1	vent grille
Z2	as reqd.	1/2" escutcheon pins
Z3	1	oak grommet

Misc.: 120-, 150-, 180-, and 220-grit sandpaper; glue; aniline dye-based brown mahogany stain; Waterlox Original Sealer/Finish; 4/0 steel wool.
Note: All plywood to be veneer- or MDF-core with oak face veneers.

Fig. 2 *To ensure a properly bonded joint, apply glue to the joining-plate slots, the board edges, and the joining plates.*

Fig. 3 *Lay out the mortises in the case stiles by clamping the workpieces together, and mark across them using a square.*

Fig. 4 *Clamp two stiles together to form a base for a plunge router, then cut the stile mortises using a spiral up-cutting bit.*

Fig. 5 *With a stile held securely to the bench, use a chisel and mallet to cut the rounded ends of each mortise square.*

While you have the router out, readjust its depth of cut, and cut the panel grooves in the stile edges. Readjust the router again to cut the panel grooves in the side rails, and then chop the ends of the mortises square using a mallet and chisel (**Fig. 5**).

Install dado blades in the table saw and cut the tenons on the side rails. Since the rails are quite wide, the tenons are divided into two separate pieces. Begin by cutting one wide tenon on each end of the rails (**Fig. 6**). Cut the tenons slightly oversize, and then pare them smooth with a razor-sharp chisel. Divide each tenon into two sections by making a rectangular cutout in the center using a handsaw and chisel.

Next, set the table saw blade to cut a 45° bevel, and cut the chamfered ends on the side stiles (**Fig. 7**). Use the miter gauge to guide the work. Test fit the joints for each case side and make adjustments as necessary. Sand the side panels with 120-, 150-, 180-, and 220-grit paper before assembly.

To assemble a cabinet side, spread glue in the stile mortises and on the rail tenons, then join the rails to one stile. Slide the panel into position (**Fig. 8**), but be sure not to get any glue on the panel's edge or its groove. Now you can place the second stile in position and clamp the assembly.

Cut the rounded top corners on the back rail using a sabre saw. Mark the locations of the joining-plate slots in the rail and top shelf, and then cut the slots. Dry assemble the two pieces (**Fig. 9**). Next, spread glue in the slots, on the plates, and on the edge of the glue joint, and clamp the parts together.

Cut out the notches in the middle shelf, mark the position of the shelf dowel holes, and then use a doweling jig to bore the holes (**Fig. 10**). When you've completed this step, bore matching holes in the case side stiles.

Finish laying out the joining-plate slots in the bottom shelf and case sides, then cut the slots. Clamp a straightedge to the sides to position the plate joiner. Next, use the router and edge guide to cut the rabbet along the back edge of the top rail/shelf assembly (**Fig. 11**) and along the back edges of the case sides. Use a chisel to square the rabbet ends.

Mark the hinge mortise outlines on the case, and cut the outline using a chisel and a marking gauge. Pare the mortise to depth with a chisel.

If you plan to set a turntable on the top shelf of the case, you should bore a hole through the shelf for a wire grommet. The grommet we used requires a 1¾-in.-dia. hole.

To assemble the case, spread glue in the plate slots, dowel holes, and on the dowels and plates, then join the shelves to one of the case sides (**Fig. 12**). Take care not to get any glue on the portion of the middle shelf that abuts the side panels. The panels must be free to expand and contract seasonally, and a glue bond will cause a panel to crack when this happens. With a helper, position the other side over the ends of the shelves, and then clamp the assembly. Compare opposite

diagonal measurements on the case to check for square, then let the glue cure.

Glue together two pieces of ¾-in.-thick plywood to form the drawer blocking, then glue a solid oak strip to the block as a facing. Note that the grain on the facing should run horizontally to match the drawer faces. Screw the blocking to the case side (**Fig. 13**).

Cut a piece of ½-in.-thick oak plywood to size for the case back, then lay out the position of the vent-grille cutout. Drill clearance holes at the corners of the cutout, and use a sabre saw to remove the waste. Fasten the grille to the back with escutcheon pins, and bore a 1½-in.-dia. hole in the back for power cord access. Finally, screw the back to the case.

Making the Drawers

Rip and crosscut the drawer parts. Install a dovetail bit in the router, and set the router to make a ¼-in.-deep cut. Cut the

Fig. 6 *With a clamp on the miter gauge serving as a workpiece stop, cut the side rail tenons with dado blades in the table saw.*

Fig. 7 *Set the table saw blade to 45°, place a stile against the miter gauge, and cut the chamfer on each edge of the stile.*

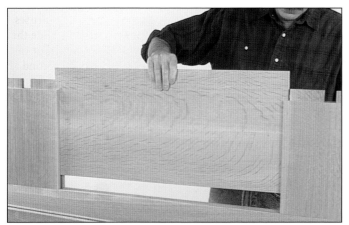
Fig. 8 *Assemble the case sides by applying glue only to the mortises and tenons, not in the panel groove or on the panel edge.*

Fig. 9 *After you have cut the joining-plate slots in the top shelf and back rail, test fit the pieces, then glue and clamp them together.*

dovetail dado in the drawer sides and the stopped dado in the drawer face (**Fig. 14**).

Clamp a tall fence to the router table, and clamp a backup block to each drawer side and back when you cut the dovetail on these parts (**Fig. 15**). The backup block—rather than the workpiece—tears out when it exits the bit.

Next, use a router and edge guide to cut the drawer bottom grooves in the drawer sides and the stopped groove in the drawer face.

After marking the curved cutout on the drawer faces, make the cuts with a sabre saw. Use a router and cove bit to shape the edge of the cutout (**Fig. 16**).

Next, apply glue to the mating parts of the drawer joints, and then slide the parts together—you should not need to clamp the assembly. Now rip and crosscut the plywood bottom panels and screw each bottom to the drawer back.

Install drawer slides in the case and drawer rails on the drawers, using screws only in the slides' positioning slots. Adjust the slides so the drawers move smoothly and the drawer faces have a ¹⁄₁₆-in.-wide margin on all edges. Install the remaining screws.

The cabinet door is built in essentially the same way as the rest of the cabinet. Keep in mind, however, that the panel groove is only ⅜ in. wide, so you must cut a shallow rabbet around the inside edge of the panel. To do this, use a straight bit in the router table, and push the panel slowly over the bit (**Fig. 17**). Cut the crossgrain rabbets first, then cut the rabbets along the grain. Any small amount of grain that is torn out while cutting across the grain will then be removed.

Like the drawers, the door is installed on the case with a ¹⁄₁₆-in.-wide space on all four sides. Transfer the locations of hinge mortises to the door edge, and then cut the mortises using the same techniques used on the case. Mount the door pull and catch. The pull in the photo has been discontinued, but you can find similar pulls at your local hardware store.

Fig. 10 *Make the center case shelf, cut the notches in its ends, and bore the holes in the notches using a doweling jig.*

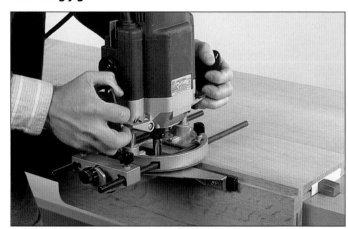

Fig. 11 *Using the router with an edge guide, make two or three passes, and cut the rabbet on the back edge of the top rail/shelf assembly.*

Fig. 12 *Apply glue to the slots, dowel holes, joining plates, and dowels, then assemble the shelves to one case side.*

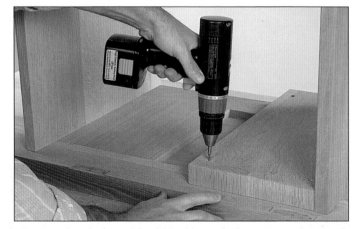

Fig. 13 *The drawer blocking is made from two pieces of plywood with solid oak facing. Screw the blocking to the case side.*

Fig. 14 *Clamp each drawer front to the workbench, and then use a router and dovetail bit to cut the dovetail dadoes in the drawer front.*

For staining, remove the door, drawers, back, and all hardware. Sand all parts as you did the side panels. We stained our cabinet with water-soluble aniline dye-based brown mahogany stain. This water-soluble stain is more resistant to sunlight fading than other aniline stains, but it will raise the grain—the water in the stain makes wood fibers on the surface stand up, giving the surface a fuzzy texture. To prevent this, wipe the wood surfaces with a lightly dampened sponge, and let all the pieces dry—this will raise the surface fibers. Next, gently sand off the raised fibers using 220-grit sandpaper, then apply the stain.

To finish the cabinet, apply three coats of Waterlox Original Sealer/Finish (formerly Waterlox Transparent) according to the manufacturer's directions. When the last coat is dry, burnish the surface with 4/0 steel wool, and polish it with a soft cloth. Complete the project by reassembling all the pieces and installing the cabinet hardware.

Safety Sense

GOT A SLOT?

Though a plate joiner seems like a harmless machine (since its blade is rarely exposed when cutting), you should still follow some basic rules when using one. First, when cutting a slot in a small workpiece, always clamp the workpiece firmly to the bench. Be especially wary of kick back when cutting plate slots in hardwood or endgrain. Finally, keep your hands positioned in such a way that they won't be anywhere near the blade if something goes wrong.

Fig. 15 *Cut the drawer side's dovetail in the router table. Clamp a backup block to the side, then move the side over the bit.*

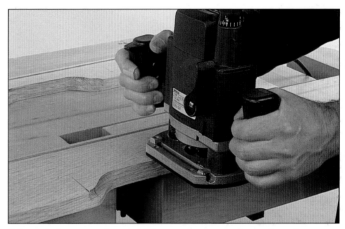

Fig. 16 *Cut out the profile on the top edge of each drawer front. Next, use the router to cut the cove along the edge.*

Fig. 17 *Install a straight bit in the router table, and then slide the door panel over the bit to cut the rabbet on the inside panel edges.*

Shelf Life

This attractive bookcase provides a showplace for your favorite books and collectibles.

Many of us love books and magazines. Whether our passion is classical literature, science fiction, Victorian romance or a collection of *Popular Mechanics* that spans the decades, we need a place to keep our valuable reading material.

Often these treasured possessions are stuffed away in boxes for lack of adequate space. To help solve this common problem, we present this handsome bookcase, constructed of solid curly maple. It has adjustable shelves, a solid, paneled back that allows it to be used against a wall or as a room divider, and is finished with a rub-on oil that's easy to apply.

*Key*POINTS

TIME
Prep Time	6 hours
Shop Time	10 hours
Assembly Time	14 hours

EFFORT
Skill Level	intermediate

COST / BENEFITS
Expense: **moderate**

• Adjustable shelves are deep enough to not only accommodate standard and large format books, but also to provide **display space for art and photographs.**

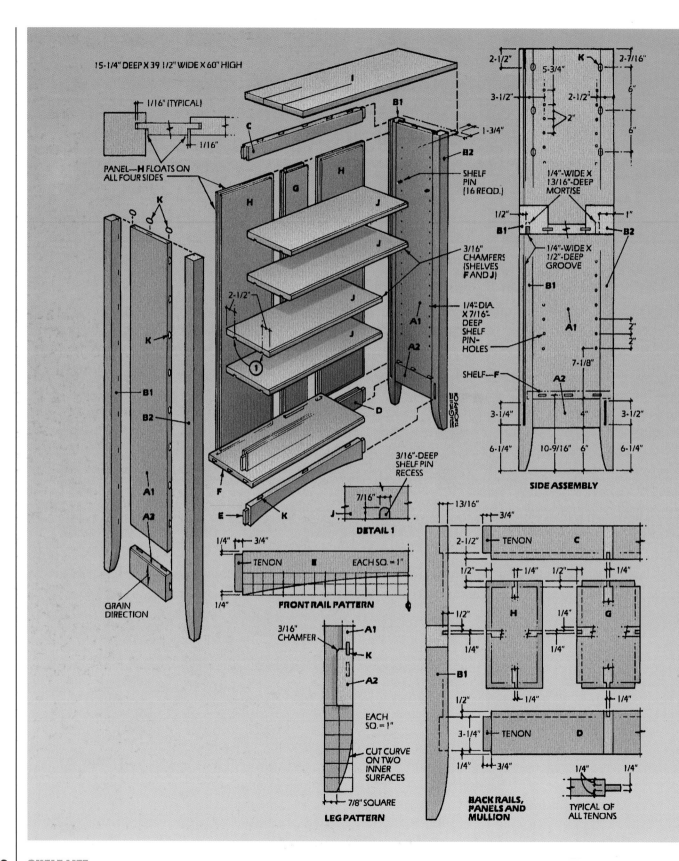

15-1/4" DEEP X 39 1/2" WIDE X 60" HIGH

1/16" (TYPICAL)

1/16"

PANEL—H FLOATS ON
ALL FOUR SIDES

GRAIN
DIRECTION

B1

C

B2

H G H

H

J

J

J

J

K

K

B1

B2

A1

A2

F

E K

1

D

A1

A2

SHELF
PIN
(16 REQD.)

3/16"
CHAMFERS
(SHELVES
F AND J)

1/4" DIA.
X 7/16"
DEEP
SHELF
PIN
HOLES

2-1/2"

3/16"-DEEP
SHELF PIN
RECESS

DETAIL 1

J

7/16"

1/4" 3/4"

TENON

EACH SQ. = 1"

FRONT RAIL PATTERN

3/16"
CHAMFER

A1

K

A2

EACH
SQ. = 1"

CUT CURVE
ON TWO
INNER
SURFACES

7/8" SQUARE

LEG PATTERN

SIDE ASSEMBLY

2-1/2"

5-3/4"

3-1/2"

2-1/2"

2"

1/2"

B1

B1

A1

SHELF—F

A2

3-1/4"

6-1/4"

10-9/16"

6"

6-1/4"

K

2-7/16"

6"

6"

1/4"-WIDE X
13/16"-DEEP
MORTISE

1"

B2

1/4"-WIDE X
1/2"-DEEP
GROOVE

2"

2"

7-1/8"

4"

3-1/2"

13/16"

3/4"

2-1/2" TENON C

1/2" 1/4" 1/2" 1/4"

1/2" H 1/4" G

1/4" 1/4"

B1

1/2" 1/4" 1/4"

3-1/4" TENON D

1/4" 3/4"

1/4" 1/4"

BACK RAILS,
PANELS AND
MULLION

TYPICAL OF
ALL TENONS

Making the Sides

Begin construction by selecting the lumber to be used for each part of the bookcase. Rip and crosscut to rough size the stock for the case side panels. Keep in mind that the side panels are cut to finished dimension after glue-up. Use the jointer or a sharp hand plane to smooth and square the edges of the panel stock to ensure tight, sound glue joints.

Lay out the position of joining plates 6 to 8 in. on center along the mating edges of the stock, then use a plate joiner to cut the slots (**Fig. 1**). Use a flat surface, such as the top of a table saw, as a registration surface when cutting the slots. Hold the stock and the plate joiner firmly to the table when cutting the plate slots.

Apply glue to the stock edges and plate slots (**Fig. 2**). Insert the joining plates and clamp the pieces together. Scrape off any glue squeeze-out after 15 or 20 minutes. When the glue is fully cured, scrape all panel surfaces smooth. Rip and crosscut the panels to finished size (**Fig. 3**).

The case sides have a false bottom rail fastened to them with glue and joining plates. This false rail is $1\frac{1}{8}$ in. thick, so it looks like standard rail and panel construction. However, its grain runs vertically (parallel to the side panel) so it will expand and contract with changing humidity at the same rate that the panel does. This greatly reduces the chances of a crack developing in the side panel due to moisture movement.

To make the false rail, rip, crosscut, and glue together a panel about 12 in. wide x $9\frac{1}{2}$ in. long. Clamp the panel to the bench and cut a $\frac{3}{16}$-in.-wide chamfer across its top and bottom edges (**Fig. 4**). Next, crosscut the workpiece to form two false rails. Cut the plate slots in each rail and the panel. Test fit the pieces before assembly (**Fig. 5**).

Materials List

Key	No.	Size and description (use)
A1	2	$\frac{3}{4}$ x $9\frac{1}{2}$ x $48\frac{7}{8}$" maple (side panel)
A2	2	$1\frac{1}{8}$ x 4 x $9\frac{1}{2}$" maple (side rail)
B1	2	2 x 2 x $58\frac{7}{8}$" maple (back leg)
B2	2	2 x 2 x $58\frac{7}{8}$" maple (front leg)
C	1	$\frac{3}{4}$ x 3 x $33\frac{1}{2}$" maple (back top rail)
D	1	$\frac{3}{4}$ x 4 x $33\frac{1}{2}$" maple (back bottom rail)
E	1	$\frac{3}{4}$ x 4 x $33\frac{1}{2}$" maple (front rail)
F	1	$1\frac{1}{8}$ x $12\frac{1}{2}$ x 32" maple (bottom shelf)
G	1	$\frac{3}{4}$ x 6 x $46\frac{7}{8}$" maple (back mullion)
H	1	$\frac{1}{2}$ x $13\frac{7}{8}$ x $46\frac{3}{4}$" maple (back panel)
I	1	$1\frac{1}{8}$ x $15\frac{1}{4}$ x $39\frac{1}{2}$" maple (case top)
J	4	$1\frac{1}{8}$ x $12\frac{1}{2}$ x $31\frac{7}{8}$" maple (shelf)
K	as reqd.	No. 20 joining plates

Misc.: 120-, 220-, and 320-grit sandpaper; transparent finish; 16 shelf pins; 4/0 steel wool.

Fig. 1 *Cut the joining plate slots in the strips that form the case sides. Use a benchtop or your table saw as a work surface.*

Fig. 2 *Apply glue to the slots and edges of the strips. Install the joining plates and clamp the pieces together.*

Fig. 3 *Use a sliding crosscut table on the table saw, or a circular saw and guide, to cut the case panels to finished length.*

Rip and crosscut the case legs to size from 10/4 stock. Lay out the curved taper on two sides of each leg as indicated in the plans. Use the band saw to cut the legs to shape, then clamp each leg to the workbench and remove the saw marks with a belt sander or a sharp hand plane (**Figs. 6 and 7**).

Lay out and cut the joining plate slots in the side panels and legs. Then apply glue to the joint between the leg and the panel, in the plate slots, and on the plates (**Fig. 8**). Assemble each side, and clamp the assembly together until the glue sets.

The panels that form the back rest in ½-in.-deep grooves in the side assembly. Cut the grooves with a ¼-in.-wide straight bit in the router, and use an edge guide. Note that there are mortises at both ends of the groove to house the tenons on the back rails. Adjust the router depth to ¹³⁄₁₆ in. to cut the mortises.

Move to the front of the side assembly, readjust the edge guide, and cut the ¹³⁄₁₆-in.-deep mortises for the front rail. Square the ends of all mortises with a chisel (**Fig. 9**).

Top, Shelves, and Back

Rip and crosscut stock to size for the front and back rails, and back center mullion. Also rip and crosscut the stock for the shelves, the top, and the back panels. All stock should be cut slightly oversize, then cut to finished dimension after glue-up. Scrape smooth both faces of each workpiece after it is cut to finished size.

Use the dado blades in the table saw to cut the tenons on the rail and mullion ends (**Fig. 10**). Since the dado blades leave small ridges on the surface of the tenon, it is good practice to cut the joints just a bit oversize and pare the tenons to fit with a sharp chisel. Also bear in mind that the tenons on the rails are ¾ in. long while those on the mullion are ½ in. long.

Lay out and cut the arched shape on the bottom edge of the front rail. Use the band saw to cut the shape, staying just to the waste side of the line. Then smooth the cut edge with

Fig. 4 *Glue up the stock that forms the false rail, and cut a ¹³⁄₁₆-in.-wide chamfer on its endgrain edges. Rip the panel in two.*

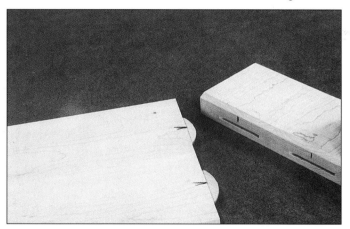

Fig. 5 *Cut joining plate slots in the side panel and false rail. Test fit the plates before gluing and clamping the two together.*

Fig. 6 *Use a band saw to cut the taper on the leg blanks. Always stay just to the waste side of the line and cut slowly.*

Fig. 7 *Clamp each leg to the workbench and use a belt sander or hand plane to remove saw marks and refine the curve.*

Fig. 8 *Cut matching joining plate slots in the legs and case sides. Apply glue as before then clamp the assembly together.*

Fig. 9 *Use a sharp chisel to square the ends of the mortises. Butt the chisel to the pencil line and chop down using a mallet.*

Fig. 10 *Use the dado blades in the table saw to cut the tenons on the rails and back center mullion. Cut the joints slightly oversize and pare to fit with a chisel.*

Fig. 11 *Use the band saw to cut the arch on the front rail. Smooth the saw marks with a scraper and spokeshave.*

a spokeshave and a scraper, working down to the line on several passes (**Fig. 11**).

Hold the mullion between bench dogs, and use the slotting cutter in the router to cut the ¼-in.-wide x ½-in.-deep groove in the edges of the mullion (**Fig. 12**). Repeat the procedure to cut the groove in the back rails.

Apply glue to the joints and assemble the mullion and back rails. Use a long bar clamp to pull the joints tight and check that the assembly is square by comparing opposite diagonal measurements. If the assembly is out of square, shift the clamps so they are closer to parallel with the longer diagonal measurement. Check the assembly for square, then let the glue set. Shave off any glue that squeezes from the joints.

Mark the location of the joining plate slots for the bottom shelf joint. Clamp a straightedge guide to the side to help position the plate joiner, and cut the slots by plunging the plate joiner downward (**Fig. 13**).

Mark and cut the slots for the joining plates that fasten the top to the rest of the cabinet. These slots are located along the top edge of the case sides and the top edge of the top rail. Also mark and cut the slots in the top edge of the front rail and on both ends and along the front edge of the bottom shelf.

Make a template for the shelf pinholes from a scrap piece of plywood or Masonite. Note that the pinholes are located 2½ in. from the edge of the case side and 3½ in. from the back edge of the case side. Clamp the template to the case side and bore the shelf pinholes (**Fig. 14**). Use a depth stop on the drill bit to ensure proper hole depth. You can wrap tape around the drill bit in case you don't own a commercially made stop collar, but be careful you don't push the tape back on the bit as you bore. Next, use a straight bit and edge guide to rout the rabbet around the edges of each back panel (**Fig. 15**).

The bottom edge of the rabbet should slide smoothly into the groove in the sides, mullion, and rails. Before cutting the

Fig. 12 *Secure the mullion to the workbench and use a slotting cutter to cut the groove that holds the back panels. Use the same procedure for the back rails.*

Fig. 13 *Clamp a straight piece of scrap across the case side. Butt the plate joiner to the straightedge and cut the plate slots.*

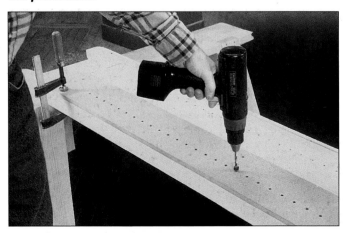

Fig. 14 *Make a template from sheet material and clamp it to the sides. Bore the shelf holes in the case sides with a portable drill.*

rabbet around each panel, set the router and make a test cut on a panel. Test the rabbet for correct fit using a grooved scrap block. The groove should be cut with the same slotting cutter used on the mullion, back rails, and sides.

If you find the test block does not slide on the edge, set the router to take a very fine shaving and make another pass along the rabbet. Slide the block along the perimeter of each panel after you are done cutting the rabbet to make sure they will fit the leg and rails, too.

Assembly and Finishing

Presand all case parts with 120- and 220-grit sandpaper, then wipe them down with a tack cloth.

To avoid a frantic rush during the case assembly, proceed in stages. You will glue and clamp together subassemblies that will then be assembled into the whole bookcase. First, apply glue and joining plates to the front rail. Set the bottom shelf in place and clamp the parts until the glue sets (**Fig. 16**).

Next, place one case side on a set of padded sawhorses and apply glue to the mortises for the top and bottom back rails. Spread glue on the matching rail tenons.

Next, position one of the back panels in the case side groove. Be careful not to get glue in either the groove or on the panel edge. Slide the rail-mullion assembly over the panel and into position in the case side. Use bar clamps to pull the joints tight.

In the same operation, apply glue to the joining plate slots that join the bottom shelf to the case side. Also apply glue to the mortise in the front edge of the case side (the mortise for the front rail). Spread glue on the matching front rail tenon. Slide the joining plates into their slots and assemble the bottom shelf and front rail to the side. Clamp the assembly, check it for square, and let the glue harden (**Fig. 17**).

After the glue has set, remove the clamps and slide the second back panel into position. Apply glue to the remaining joints and clamp the second side in the same manner.

Position the case facedown on sawhorses. Apply glue to the joining plate slots in the top edge of the case and the slots in the top. Install the case top with joining plates and use long bar clamps to pull the joints tight (**Fig. 18**). Use cauls to spread clamping pressure across the top.

Next, with a straight bit in the router table, cut the notches in the bottom of the shelves to engage the shelf pins (**Fig. 19**). Also cut the chamfers on the shelves (**Fig. 20**).

Sand the shelves with 120- and 220-grit sandpaper, then finish sand all parts with 320-grit paper. Dust the shelves off with a tack cloth.

Using a brush or clean rag, apply three coats of transparent finish to the bookcase. Leave a damp surface with each coat, wiping off the excess. Let each coat dry overnight, scuffing the finish lightly with 320-grit paper between coats. When the last coat has dried, rub the surface of the case with 4/0 steel wool, followed by a soft cloth.

Fig. 15 *Cut the rabbets in the back panels using a router, straight bit and edge guide. Move the router slowly over the panels.*

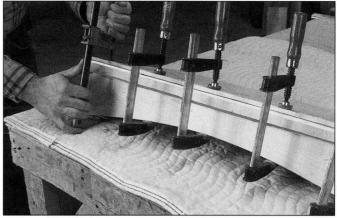

Fig. 16 *Assemble the bookshelf in stages. First, glue and clamp together the bottom shelf and the front rail until the glue sets.*

Fig. 17 *Glue and clamp the back rails and mullion. When the glue is dry, slide in a back panel. Clamp this to a side.*

Fig. 18 *When base assembly is complete, glue and clamp the top to the assembly. Cauls spread the clamping pressure.*

Fig. 19 *Use a small straight bit in the router table to cut the notches in the shelves. Clamp a stop to the table's fence.*

Fig. 20 *Hold each shelf to the workbench, then cut a chamfer on the top and bottom edge on the front of each shelf.*

Office Space

A comfortable and spacious work surface with full-size file drawers below.

One of the reasons that "home offices" are so popular these days is that the term can mean so many different things. We may call it a home office now, but it's not much different from the den, library, and study of days gone by. Though the name has changed, the essential function has remained the same: It's the place to go when you're serious about getting work done. And, as always, the heart of the room is the desk.

The one we've designed here has plenty of storage space—seven drawers in all—and plenty of surface area too, nearly 16 sq. ft. Its cool, clean lines suggest a seriousness that's good for any work environment.

*Key*POINTS

TIME
Prep Time	8 hours
Shop Time	20 hours
Assembly Time	20 hours

EFFORT
Skill Level	intermediate

COST / BENEFITS
Expense: **moderate**
- Our deep desk features **a lot of workspace—and storage space.**
- This workstation can stand alone or as **the centerpiece of a three-unit home office.**

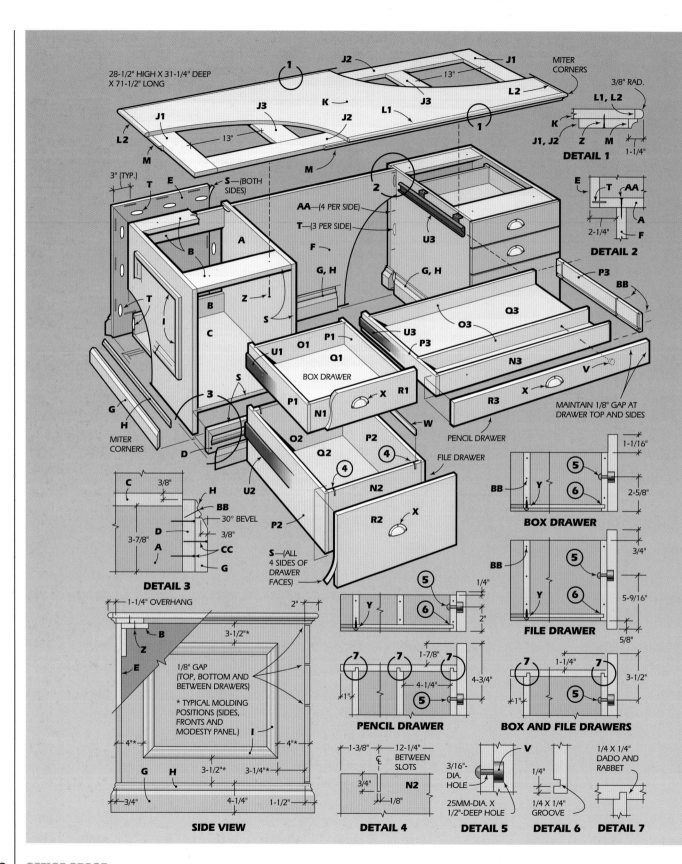

28-1/2" HIGH X 31-1/4" DEEP
X 71-1/2" LONG

MITER CORNERS

J1 J2 J3 13" L2 J1

K L1 J3 3/8" RAD.

L2 J1 J3 K J2 L1

M 13" M

DETAIL 1
L1, L2
K
J1, J2 Z M
1-1/4"

3" (TYP.) T E S—(BOTH SIDES)

DETAIL 2
E T AA
2-1/4" A
F

A B AA—(4 PER SIDE)
T—(3 PER SIDE) 2 U3

B F G, H G, H U3 P3 BB

T Z S Q3

B C O3 U3 P3 N3 V

T I S O1 P1 Q1 MAINTAIN 1/8" GAP AT DRAWER TOP AND SIDES

U1 BOX DRAWER

G S P1 N1 X R1 R3 X

H 3 D O2 P2 W

MITER CORNERS Q2 4 PENCIL DRAWER 1-1/16"
4 5
N2 FILE DRAWER BB Y 6 2-5/8"

DETAIL 3
C 3/8" H **BOX DRAWER**
BB 30° BEVEL U2 P2 3/4"
3-7/8" D 3/8" R2 X BB 5
A CC 5-9/16"
G Y 6
S—(ALL 4 SIDES OF DRAWER FACES) **FILE DRAWER** 5/8"
DETAIL 3

SIDE VIEW
1-1/4" OVERHANG 2"
B 3-1/2"*
Z 1/8" GAP (TOP, BOTTOM AND BETWEEN DRAWERS)
E * TYPICAL MOLDING POSITIONS (SIDES, FRONTS AND MODESTY PANEL)
I
4"* 4"*
G H 3-1/2"* 3-1/4"*
3/4" 4-1/4" 1-1/2"

5 7 7 7
Y 6 2" 1-7/8"
1" 4-1/4" 4-3/4"
5
PENCIL DRAWER 1" 5

7 7 7
1-1/4"
1" 5 3-1/2"
BOX AND FILE DRAWERS

1-3/8" 12-1/4" V
BETWEEN SLOTS 3/16"-DIA. HOLE 1/4"
3/4" N2 1/4 X 1/4" GROOVE
1/8" 25MM-DIA. X 1/2"-DEEP HOLE
1/4"
1/4 X 1/4" DADO AND RABBET

DETAIL 4 **DETAIL 5** **DETAIL 6** **DETAIL 7**

This desk is also the starting point for the credenza and wall-unit pieces that follow. All three are based on the same easy-to-build module. On the desk, each module has one file drawer and two utility drawers. On the credenza, each has two file drawers. And on the wall unit, you can choose drawers or doors. Here, we go into great detail about building the modules and the drawers. So be sure to review these instructions even if you plan only to build one of the other pieces.

Desk Pedestals

Begin construction by laying out your desk parts on sheets of 3/4-in. birch plywood. Cut them to rough size using a circular saw and a straightedge guide. Then use a table saw to rip and crosscut the parts to the finished size. The quickest and least expensive way to edge band the panels is to apply veneer edge tape, which has hot-melt adhesive on its back side. To bond the veneer to the edge, just clamp the panel in a vise, then use a household iron to press the tape onto the edge (**Fig. 1**). Once the veneer edging has cooled—which takes only a minute or two—use a sharp chisel to trim the tape flush to the panel's surface (**Fig. 2**).

Next, lay out the location of the joining-plate slots on the case bottom, back, and top rails. Use the plate joiner to cut the slots (**Fig. 3**). When it's necessary to cut the slots perpendicular to the edge of a panel—at the back of the case bottom, for example—clamp the panel to the table-saw rip fence and use the saw table as a registration surface (**Fig. 4**).

Fig. 1 ***Finish the plywood edges with iron-on veneer tape. Set the iron for high heat and press down to activate the hot-melt glue.***

Materials List

Key	No.	Size and description (use)
A	4	3/4 x 27 x 27 1/4" plywood (side)
B	8	3/4 x 4 x 16 1/2" plywood (rail)
C	2	3/4 x 16 1/2 x 27 1/4" plywood (bottom)
D	2	3/4 x 4 1/4 x 18" plywood (blocking)
E	2	3/4 x 18 x 27" plywood (panel)
F	1	3/4 x 27 x 33" plywood (modesty panel)
G	24 ft.	3/4 x 3 3/16" poplar (base molding)
H	24 ft.	3/8 x 1 1/16" pine (base trim)
I	50 ft.	11/16 x 1 5/8" pine (panel molding)
J1	2	3/4 x 4 x 28 3/4" plywood (support strip)
J2	2	3/4 x 4 x 61" plywood (support strip)
J3	2	3/4 x 4 x 20 3/4" plywood (support strip)
K	1	3/4 x 29 3/4 x 70" plywood (top)
L1	2	3/4 x 3/4 x 71 1/2" poplar (edge band)
L2	2	3/4 x 3/4 x 31 1/4" poplar (edge band)
M	18 ft.	3/4 x 3/4" pine (cove molding)
N1	4	1/2 x 4 1/2 x 15" plywood (drawer front)
N2	2	1/2 x 9 3/4 x 15" plywood (drawer front)
N3	1	1/2 x 3 x 28 1/2" plywood (drawer front)
O1	4	1/2 x 4 x 15" plywood (drawer back)
O2	2	1/2 x 9 1/4 x 15" plywood (drawer back)
O3	2	1/2 x 2 1/2 x 28 1/2" plywood (drawer back, partition)
P1	8	1/2 x 4 1/2 x 20" plywood (drawer side)
P2	4	1/2 x 9 3/4 x 26" plywood (drawer side)
P3	2	1/2 x 3 x 20" plywood (drawer side)
Q1	4	1/4 x 15 x 18 3/4" plywood (drawer bottom
Q2	2	1/4 x 15 x 24 3/4" plywood (drawer bottom)
Q3	1	1/4 x 18 3/4 x 28 1/2" plywood (drawer bottom)
R1	4	3/4 x 5 9/16 x 18" plywood (drawer face)
R2	2	3/4 x 11 1/8 x 18" plywood (drawer face)
R3	1	3/4 x 3 1/4 x 32 3/4" plywood (drawer face)
S	as reqd.	iron-on veneer tape
T	as reqd.	No. 20 joining plates
U1	4 pr.	drawer slides, 20" long
U2	2 pr.	drawer slides, 26" long
U3	1 pr.	drawer slides, 20" long
V	14	drawer face adjusters
W	4	1/8 x 3/4 x 19 1/4" aluminum flat stock (file hangers)
X	7	brass drawer pulls
Y	21	5/8" No. 5 rh screws
Z	24	1 1/4" No. 8 fh screws
AA	8	2" No. 8 fh screws
BB	as reqd.	1" brads
CC	as reqd.	4d finish nails

Misc.: 120- and 220-grit sandpaper; carpenter's glue; epoxy glue; wood filler; latex primer; latex paint.

Fig. 2 *Trim the edging tape flush to the panel with a sharp chisel. Cut with the grain direction, not against it, to prevent splitting.*

Fig. 3 *After cutting all the case parts to size and applying the edge tape, begin assembly by cutting plate slots in the back rails.*

Apply glue to slots and plates, then assemble the bottom-, top-, and back-rail joints.

Lay out and cut the plate slots for the joints between the case-bottom assembly and sides, and also between the top rails and sides. Assemble the pedestal box by gluing together the case sides, bottom assembly, and top rails (**Fig. 5**). Use clamps to pull the joints tight, then compare opposite diagonal measurements to be sure that the assembly is square (**Fig. 6**). If necessary, readjust the clamps, then let the glue set.

Because the desk pedestals are exposed on all sides, the back of the cases must be finished. Fabricate these backs by

applying solid wood edging to the two long edges of the plywood panels, as shown in the drawing. Then lay out and cut the joining-plate slots in the back panels and in the mating edges of the case sides. These plates are not absolutely necessary for structural integrity, but they do make positioning of the back panels automatic during assembly. Glue and clamp the parts in place. Then cut and edge band the top edge of the baseboard blocking. These blocks are used to bring out the surface of the baseboard beyond the front surface of the drawer faces. Install the blocks with glue and 4d finishing nails.

TECH *Tips*

Coat O' Paint
Most woodworkers are not too familiar with using paint to achieve a furniture-grade finish. If you've never used paint on a piece of furniture, there are a few things you should do to "brush up" on your skills before painting this project.

First, find a brush and roller that are up to the job. Most brushes and rollers are designed for applying architectural coatings, not those found on furniture. Finding the right equipment means using as fine a brush as possible or a foam roller. Apply some paint to a few pieces of scrap so you can develop a feel for how the tool flows the paint onto the surface and levels. Be especially mindful of corners as you work. And remember:

It's better to try and fail on a piece of scrap than on the furniture you just built. If you do blow it on the furniture itself don't worry. Wait until the paint is thoroughly hardened (this may take a few days), then sand out the blemish or remove the paint entirely using a stripper. Prime the surface again and start over.

It sounds basic, but beginners often overlook this fact: the higher the gloss, the more difficult it is to achieve a flawless finish. This is true with paint and clear finishes alike. If you're a beginner, choose a finish with reduced gloss like a satin or an eggshell. If you desire a gloss finish, it will require lots of practice and, eventually, resorting to spray equipment.

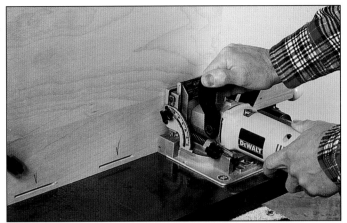

Fig. 4 *Cut the plate slots in the case bottom by clamping the panel to your table-saw fence and sliding the plate joiner across the table.*

Use clamps to temporarily hold the modesty panel in place against one of the pedestals. Mark the locations of the joining-plate slots, then do the same for the other pedestal. Cut the plate slots for these joints using a straightedge guide (**Fig. 7**). Then counterbore screw pilot holes from inside the pedestals to fasten the panel in place. These screws eliminate the need for awkward clamping.

Apply glue to slots and plates, then join the modesty panel to the pedestal. Drive 2-in. screws into the panel. Then do the same thing for the other pedestal (**Fig. 8**).

Cut the baseboard stock to size, then use a 30° chamfer bit in a router table to shape the top edge of the molding. Miter the ends and fasten them in place using glue and 4d finishing nails. Then cut and install the small panel molding around the top of the baseboard, using 1-in. brads (**Fig. 9**).

Mark the position of the large panel molding on the desk sides and front, as shown in the drawing. Again, attach the panel molding to the desk with 1-in. brads.

Desktop Construction

Cut the plywood panel to size for the desktop. Then cut the edging to size, miter the ends, and glue and clamp the edging to the top (**Fig. 10**). When the glue is dry, use a router with a ⅜-in.-rad. rounding-over bit to shape the top edge of the desk (**Fig. 11**). These bits have a ball-bearing pilot that rides against the edge of the work. So when it comes time to shape the underside of the top, the bearing no longer has a proper surface to ride against. Instead, use a router fence to guide the router for the bottom cut.

With the desktop upside down, cut and install the build-up strips 1¼ in. from the outside edges of the top. Fasten the strips with glue and screws. Next, cut and install the cove molding against the build-up strips (**Fig. 12**). To ensure proper fastening of the top to the pedestals—and to create a place to hang the pencil-drawer slides—install two cross strips, as shown.

Fig. 5 *Begin assembly with one side on the bench. Apply glue to plates, slots and edges, then push the second side in place.*

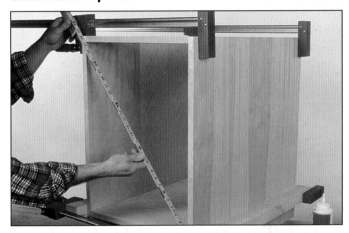

Fig. 6 *Draw all joints tight with clamps, then check the case for square by comparing opposite diagonal measurements.*

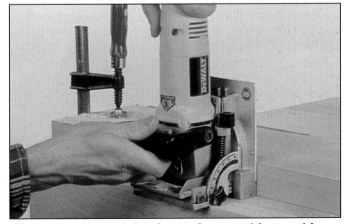

Fig. 7 *Clamp a straightedge to the case side to guide the joiner. Then, cut slots for the plates used to attach the modesty panel.*

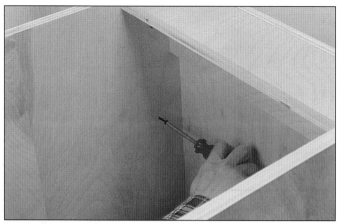

Fig. 8 *Apply glue to the modesty panel, plates, and slots and push them together. Bore pilot holes and drive screws to tighten the joint.*

Fig. 9 *Install the baseboard around the desk, then finish the profile by nailing panel molding above the baseboard.*

Fig. 10 *Begin the desktop by cutting the panel to size and cutting solid wood banding to fit the edges. Miter the corners of the banding.*

Fig. 11 *Glue and clamp the edge banding in place and, when the glue is dry, route the top edge with a ³⁄₈-in.-rad. rounding-over bit.*

Drawer Assembly

Begin by ripping and crosscutting the ½-in.-thick Baltic birch plywood to size for drawer sides, fronts, and backs. Cut the dadoes at the front edge of the drawer sides using dado blades in a table or radial-arm saw. Then cut the dadoes at the back edge of the sides. Follow this by cutting a rabbet at each end of the front and back panels, again using the dado blades. These rabbets form a tongue on the end of the drawer fronts and backs that fits neatly into the dadoes in the sides. Cut the same dado on the ends of the pencil-drawer partition. Finish the joinery cuts by making a groove in the sides and front to accept the drawer bottom.

The file drawers are designed to accept aluminum rails that support hanging file folders. These rails are cut from ⅛ x ¾-in. aluminum flat stock, available from your local hardware supplier. To cut the notches for these rails in the front and back panels, clamp a panel to a table-saw miter gauge in a

vertical position. Then set the saw blade to a ¾-in. height and make one pass over the blade. Repeat the procedure at the opposite end.

Cut the drawer bottoms from ¼-in.-thick birch plywood, taking care that these pieces are cut square. Next, sand all of the interior drawer parts with 120- and 220-grit sandpaper and dust off thoroughly.

Begin the assembly of each drawer by gluing together the front, back, and side panels (**Fig. 13**). Drive 1-in. wire nails through the sides and into the ends of the front and back panels. Finally, slide the bottom panel into the assembly (**Fig. 14**) and fasten it to the bottom edge of the drawer back with screws (**Fig. 15**).

When all drawers have been assembled, finish sand the drawer exteriors with 120- followed by 220-grit sandpaper. Make sure to ease the top edges of the drawer box to prevent cuts and splinters.

SKILL*Builder*

Down to the Finish

It may be a basic skill, but using finish nails to fasten trim is a skill nonetheless. The most important step when using finish nails to fasten hardwood trim is to predrill the nail hole. The pilot hole should be carefully matched to the nail diameter. The harder the wood, the more important this is. Red oak, for example, requires a very close match.

The drill bits that are used for finish nails tend to be small. Consequently, these are the kinds of bits that are easily loaded with a thin strip of wood shaving. To remedy the

situation, simply wipe the shaving from the bit with your thumb and index finger. If you don't, the bit is liable to cut slowly—so much so, that it may bend and break when you're drilling the next hole.

When you drive the finish nail, make sure its head is slightly above the surface, then countersink it with a nailset. A good rule of thumb is that the head rarely needs to be driven deeper than the head is high. Once the nail is driven and countersunk, the resulting depression above the nail is sufficiently deep for holding nail putty or filler consisting of sawdust and glue.

Fig. 12 *After the support strips have been installed on the bottom side of the top, miter and nail cove molding to the edges of the strips.*

Fig. 13 *Cut the drawer parts to size and finish sand them with 220-grit paper. Dust off, then apply glue to all joints and assemble the parts.*

Fig. 14 *Cut the drawer bottom to size and sand smooth with 220-grit paper. Then slide the bottom into the drawer assembly.*

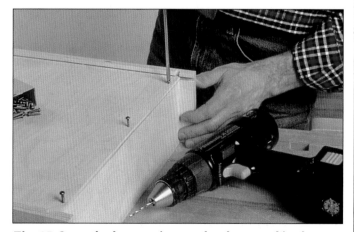

Fig. 15 *Once the bottom is completely seated in the drawer, bore pilot holes into the drawer back and install screws. Do not use glue.*

Fig. 16 *Attach slides to the pencil drawer and plane on the bottom side of the top. Drive mounting screws through the slotted holes.*

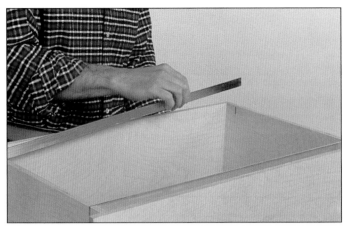

Fig. 17 *Cut aluminum bars for the hanging files to length. Then apply a dab of epoxy to the support slots and push the bars in place.*

Fig. 18 *Install the slides on the other drawer assemblies. Again, use the slotted holes so you can easily adjust the parts later.*

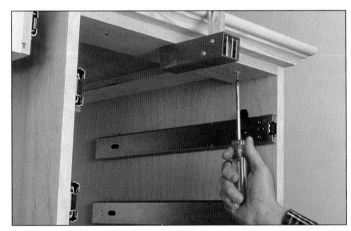

Fig. 19 *Place the top on the desk pedestals and clamp it in place. Bore pilot holes through the rails into the top and install screws.*

Fig. 20 *Bore holes in the back side of each drawer face for the adjusters. Then tap adjusters into the holes. No glue is needed.*

Fig. 21 *Attach the drawer faces to the drawer boxes by driving the screws through the drawer fronts and into the face adjusters.*

The pencil-drawer slides that we used have hanger brackets that mount to the bottom of the desktop. Fasten these brackets to the slide with the screws provided, so the flange points outward. Then pull the slides apart and attach the other section to the sides of the drawers. Use only the slotted vertical holes for attachment at this time to allow for adjustment of the drawer later. Push the slides together again and fasten the whole assembly to the desktop by driving screws through the slotted mounting holes (**Fig. 16**).

Before installing the drawer slides on the file drawers, make kerf cuts in the drawer front and back pieces to accommodate the aluminum bar stock that supports the hanging files. Then cut the bar stock to length and file the ends smooth. Next, place a drop of 5-minute epoxy in the kerfs and slide the bars into position (**Fig. 17**).

The drawer slides we used on the box and file drawers are different in design than the ones used for the pencil drawer. But the basic installation system is the same. Carefully read the instructions that accompany the slides, then lay out the locations of the screw centerlines on the drawer boxes. Fasten one side of each slide to the sides of the boxes, using the vertically slotted holes (**Fig. 18**). Bore pilot holes for the mounting screws, and hang the other side of each slide on the sides of the pedestals.

Once all the drawers are installed, make any necessary adjustments, then install the rest of the slide mounting screws. Remove the drawers from the cases and place the desktop in position over the pedestals. Use clamps to temporarily hold the top in place while you screw through the pedestal stretchers into the bottom side of the desktop (**Fig. 19**).

Next, cut and edge-band the drawer face panels. Since aligning these faces can be a slow and painstaking task, we used drawer face adjusters to join the faces and drawer fronts. These adjusters allow for ³⁄₁₆ in. of movement of the face in any direction, making alignment easy.

To mount the faces, first clamp them to the boxes in their desired position. Bore a ³⁄₁₆-in.-dia. hole for each adjuster through the drawer box front and just slightly into the back side of the face. This marks the location of the adjuster. Remove the face and use the drill press to bore a 25mm x ½-in.-deep recess for each adjuster, centered on the pilot holes. Then use a hammer to tap an adjuster into each recess (**Fig. 20**). Finally, attach the faces to the drawer boxes with the machine screws provided (**Fig. 21**).

Reinstall the drawers in the pedestals and make adjustments as necessary to achieve even margins between all drawers. Finally, lay out and bore pilot holes for the drawer pulls and set all nail heads. Fill any holes with a quality wood filler and, when it's dry, sand the entire desk with 220-grit sandpaper.

Apply one coat of acrylic latex primer and sand it lightly after it has dried. Then cover the piece with two more coats of quality latex paint. Once it's dry, install the drawers and the drawer hardware.

TOOL*Care*

Power to the Tools
Several things determine the life span of any tool, such as the severity of its use, the environment in which it's used, the number of hours that it's used, and the amount of maintenance that it sees. Put it all together, and a tool manufacturer could fill a chapter in a book about tool design and use. For now, though, we'll examine just one often-overlooked topic: power quality. Is the tool getting sufficient voltage and current?

If you're frequently stalling a corded power tool, you're either pressing it beyond its limits, or the tool is getting insufficient power. This may mean that you're running the tool on an extension cord of insufficient gauge—the cord may not be thick enough relative to the cord's length and the load that the cord is connected to.

For example, using a thin extension cord on a heavy-duty circular saw means the saw is getting insufficient voltage. To determine the correct size extension cord, look at the tool's amperage rating as stated on its motor plate, then buy a cord capable of delivering at least that voltage.

Is there a one-size-fits-all solution? Yes, as far as portable power tools are concerned, any cord capable of delivering 15 amps will do the trick. Thin and short cords may be capable of carrying 15 amps, but when you're talking about longer cords in the 50- to 100-ft. range, then you have to go with the heaviest gauge cords available. These will be designated as 12/3 or 10/3—that is 12 and 10 gauge, respectively, with three conductors (hot, neutral, and ground).

You can also make a heavy-duty extension cord from rubber-sheath and braided electrical cable and use heavy-duty fittings on each end. It's tempting to use inexpensive solid building wire to make a heavy-duty extension cord—and many people do—but it isn't good practice. Aside from being too stiff, the constant bending and unbending work hardens the solid conductors used in building wire. This can lead to a narrowed, weakened, or even broken conductor inside.

Computer Class

Here's plenty of room for all your electronic gear and a keyboard, too.

Once you have your office desk, you may think you're all set—until you put a computer, phone, fax machine, and pictures of the kids on that nice clean surface. Then you'll start to wonder where all the open space went and exactly where you're supposed to put any reference material.

This is where a credenza comes in. It provides that extra flat surface to hold all the necessary hardware, so your desk can be free for spreading out. Though you might think your credenza doesn't need full-size file drawers (like ours) or a design that matches your desk, these amenities can make your office life a lot easier.

*Key*POINTS

TIME
Prep Time .... **8 hours**
Shop Time .... **14 hours**
Assembly Time .... **20 hours**

EFFORT
Skill Level .... **intermediate**

COST / BENEFITS
Expense: **moderate**
• **This credenza boasts four letter-size file drawers, hanging-file hardware, full-extension slides, and a pullout keyboard platform.**

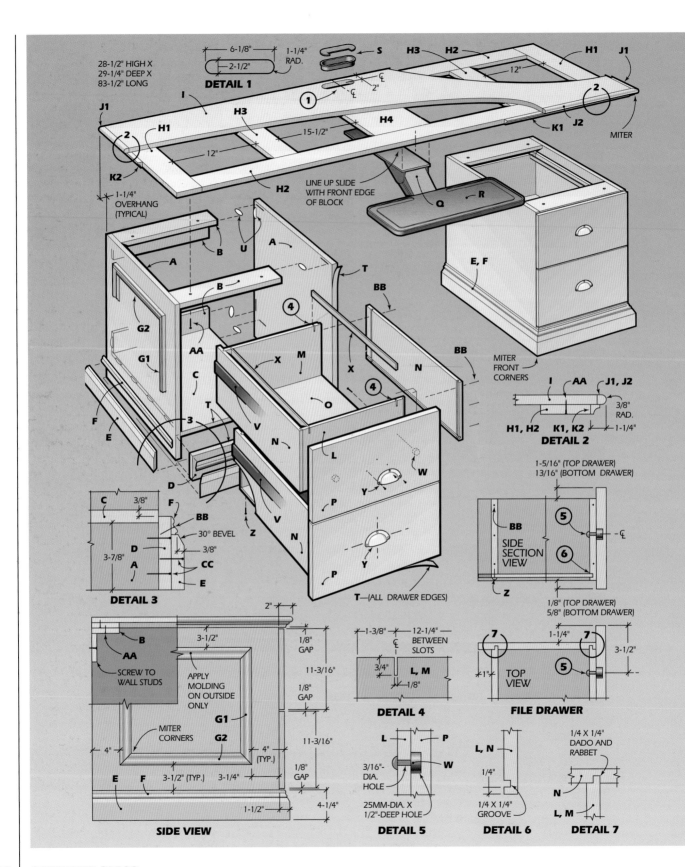

28-1/2" HIGH X
29-1/4" DEEP X
83-1/2" LONG

6-1/8"

1-1/4"
RAD.

2-1/2"

S

H3   H2   H1   J1

DETAIL 1

12"

2

MITER

I

J1

2

H1

H3

H4

15-1/2"

12"

K2

K1   J2

1-1/4"
OVERHANG
(TYPICAL)

H2

LINE UP SLIDE
WITH FRONT EDGE
OF BLOCK

Q   R

E, F

A

B   U   A

T

T

BB

BB

B

C

X   M

X

N

BB

MITER
FRONT
CORNERS

G2

4

4

G1

AA

C

O

I   AA   J1, J2

3/8"
RAD.

1-1/4"

H1, H2   K1, K2

DETAIL 2

T

F

E

V

N

L

W

3

D

Z

V

N

P

Y

1-5/16" (TOP DRAWER)
13/16" (BOTTOM DRAWER)

C

3/8"

F

BB   5

P

Y

BB

30° BEVEL

D   A

3/8"

CC

E

SIDE
SECTION
VIEW

5

6

3-7/8"

DETAIL 3

T—(ALL DRAWER EDGES)

Z

1/8" (TOP DRAWER)
5/8" (BOTTOM DRAWER)

2"

B

AA

SCREW TO
WALL STUDS

3-1/2"

1/8"
GAP

APPLY
MOLDING
ON OUTSIDE
ONLY

11-3/16"

1/8"
GAP

1-3/8"   12-1/4"

BETWEEN
SLOTS

3/4"

L, M

1/8"

7

1-1/4"

7

1"

TOP
VIEW

3-1/2"

5

FILE DRAWER

MITER
CORNERS

G1

G2

11-3/16"

DETAIL 4

4"

E   F

4"
(TYP.)

3-1/2" (TYP.)   3-1/4"

1/8"
GAP

L

P

3/16"-
DIA.
HOLE

W

L, N

1/4"

1/4 X 1/4"
DADO AND
RABBET

N

4-1/4"

1-1/2"

SIDE VIEW

25MM-DIA. X
1/2"-DEEP HOLE

DETAIL 5

1/4 X 1/4"
GROOVE

DETAIL 6

L, M

DETAIL 7

The pedestals are basically the same as the desk pedestals ("Office Space," page 178). All the details match, except this piece is designed to fit against a wall. Because of this, the back side of each pedestal is left open, and the back edge of the top has no molding. Since these file drawers are the same as those in the desk, we didn't repeat the procedures here. Review the desk story for complete drawer-making techniques.

Pedestal Assembly

Begin by cutting and edge banding the plywood parts for the pedestals. Then, lay out the joining-plate slots as shown in the drawing, and cut the slots with the plate joiner. Glue and clamp together the pedestal parts. Check for square and let the glue dry. Then install the blocking pieces—which fall behind the base molding—on both pedestals.

Since these units will be fastened to the wall, provisions must be made for returning the base molding to either the existing wall trim or to a new wainscoting, like we did. In both instances, it's easier to make the pedestal trim pieces fit the wall than it is to make the wall trim fit the pedestals.

Once the pedestals are complete, build the file drawers as shown in the drawing. Then lay out the position of the drawer slides in each pedestal. Since there are no backs on the cases, it helps to clamp a straightedge to the pedestal side to scribe the

centerline for the screw holes (**Fig. 1**). Then mark the locations of the screws and bore a pilot hole for each. Lay the pedestals on their sides—for working ease—and attach the cabinet slide members to the pedestals (**Fig. 2**).

Now you can mount the drawer sides of the slides to the drawer boxes, using the vertically slotted mounting holes. Install the drawers in the pedestal (**Fig. 3**), and make any adjustments needed to allow the drawers to operate smoothly. When satisfied, install the remaining mounting screws in the drawers and the pedestals. If no other adjustments are required, remove the drawers for the time being.

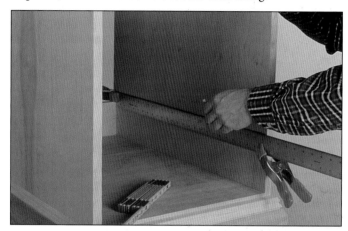

Fig. 1 *To simplify laying out the pedestal sides for the drawer slides, clamp a straightedge at the proper height and mark the side.*

Materials List

Key	No.	Size and description (use)
A	4	$3/4$ x 27 x $27^1/4$" plywood (side)
B	8	$3/4$ x 4 x $16^1/2$" plywood (rail)
C	2	$3/4$ x $16^1/2$ x $27^1/4$" plywood (bottom)
D	2	$3/4$ x $4^1/4$ x 18" plywood (blocking)
E	14 ft.	$3/4$ x $3^3/16$" poplar (base molding)
F	14 ft.	$3/8$ x $1^1/16$" poplar (base trim)
G1	4	$11/16$ x $1^5/8$ x $15^3/4$" pine (panel molding)
G2	4	$11/16$ x $1^5/8$ x 20" pine (panel molding)
H1	2	$3/4$ x 4 x 28" plywood (support strip)
H2	2	$3/4$ x 4 x 73" plywood (support strip)
H3	2	$3/4$ x 4 x 20" plywood (support strip)
H4	1	$3/4$ x 10 x 20" plywood (support strip)
I	1	$3/4$ x $28^1/2$ x 82" plywood (top)
J1	2	$3/4$ x $3/4$ x $29^1/4$" poplar (edge band)
J2	1	$3/4$ x $3/4$ x $83^1/2$" poplar (edge band)
K1	1	$3/4$ x $3/4$ x $82^1/2$" pine (cove molding)
K2	2	$3/4$ x $3/4$ x $28^3/4$" pine (cove molding)
L	4	$1/2$ x $9^3/4$ x 15" plywood (drawer front)
M	4	$1/2$ x $9^1/4$ x 15" plywood (drawer back)
N	8	$1/2$ x $9^3/4$ x 26" plywood (drawer side)
O	4	$1/4$ x 15 x $24^3/4$" plywood (drawer bottom)
P	4	$3/4$ x $11^3/16$ x 18" plywood (drawer face)
Q	1	keyboard slide
R	1	keyboard platform
S	1	cable grommet
T	as reqd.	iron-on veneer tape
U	as reqd.	No. 20 joining plates
V	4 pr.	drawer slides, 26" long
W	8	drawer face adjusters
X	8	$1/8$ x $3/4$ x 25" aluminum flat stock (file hangers)
Y	4	brass drawer pulls
Z	12	$5/8$" No. 5 rh screws
AA	27	$1^1/4$" No. 8 fh screws
BB	as reqd.	1" brads
CC	as reqd.	4d finish nails

Misc.: 120- and 220-grit sandpaper; carpenter's glue; epoxy glue; wood filler; latex primer; latex paint.

Fig. 2 *To attach the slides, lay the pedestal on its side, bore pilot holes, and drive the screws. Use only the slotted holes at first.*

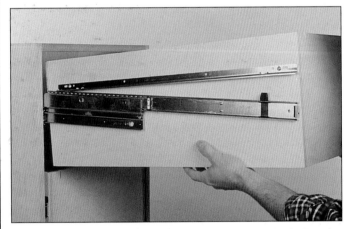

Fig. 3 *Attach the drawer side of the slide and lift drawer into place. Hook the slide components together at the back, then front.*

Fig. 4 *To attach the unit to the wall, plumb each pedestal in place and shim as required. Then drive screws into the wall studs.*

Lay out and install the panel molding on the sides of each pedestal. Use a miter box to cut the molding to length and 1-in. brads to attach the strips. Next, locate the pedestals against the wall where they will be installed and use a level to check for level and plumb (**Fig. 4**). If necessary, use shims under or behind the pedestals to achieve proper alignment.

Use a stud finder to locate the wall studs behind each pedestal, then drive screws through the back rails to fasten the units to the wall. Since the cases are 18 in. wide, it shouldn't be a problem to hit at least one stud within each pedestal. If you had to install shims, cut them off using a utility knife.

Top Construction and Finishing

Cut the plywood for the top to size, then cut and apply the solid wood edge banding on the front and two ends. Be sure to miter the corners at the joints. Use a ⅜-in.-rad. rounding-over bit in the router and an accessory fence to mold the edge of the top. Turn over the top and cut the support strips around the edges of the top to size. Attach these as shown in the drawing. Cut and attach the cove molding against the support strips, set the nail heads, and fill all holes with wood filler.

With the top still upside down, place the track for the keyboard slide in position and mark for the mounting screw holes (**Fig. 5**). Bore screw pilot holes and fasten the slide to the top. Then mark the screw locations for attaching the adjustable yoke to the keyboard tray. Bore these screw pilot holes and install the screws (**Fig. 6**). Then push the adjustable yoke onto the slide.

Because the credenza will hold computer, fax, and phone equipment, cable management is a consideration. To provide a space for routing these cables through the top, we chose a large grommet with a removable cap. To install this hardware, first remove the cap and place the grommet on top of the credenza, using the drawing as a guide to the proper location. Then trace around the outside of the grommet (**Fig. 7**) and bore a ½-in.-dia. access hole on the waste side of the line. Use a sabre saw to make the cut (**Fig. 8**), keeping just on the inside of the line to guarantee a snug fit and to keep the plywood surface from splintering. Press the grommet in place.

Next, put the top on the pedestals and adjust for an even reveal on both ends. Temporarily clamp the top to the pedestals and join the two by driving screws through the rails and into the underside of the top (**Fig. 9**). Cut, edge band, and install the drawer faces to the file drawers. Be sure to bore pilot holes at this time for the drawer pulls, but do not install them until after the painting is complete. Cut all the base molding and trim to finished length, and nail it in place. Then lay out and attach the panel molding on both pedestal sides.

Finish up by filling all nail holes and sanding all parts with 120-grit, followed by 220-grit sandpaper. Then prime the entire piece and, when it's dry, lightly sand with 220-grit paper. Remove the dust with a tack cloth, and apply two coats of high-quality latex paint.

Fig. 5 *Fabricate the top and turn it over. Then position the keyboard slide and mark the mounting screw locations. Bore pilot holes.*

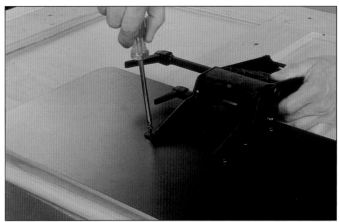

Fig. 6 *With the top still inverted, attach the keyboard tray to the slide and check for fit. Then remove the tray until the desk is painted.*

Fig. 7 *To install the cable grommet, clamp it to the surface of the top, as shown in the drawing, and trace the outside edge.*

Fig. 8 *Bore a blade entry hole on the waste side of the line. Cut a grommet hole using a sabre saw. Work slowly to avoid splintering.*

TECH *Tips*

Stud Alert
This project requires fastening the credenza pedestals to the wall. Of course, to do this, you'll need to locate the wall studs to fasten into. Here's a quick tip on using a stud finder. The most important thing to remember about these instruments is that they find the edge of the stud, not its center. Mark a line where the stud edge is detected and measure over ³⁄₄ in.—that marks the stud center.

Fig. 9 *Center the top on the pedestals and clamp it in place. Then bore pilot holes through the rails and attach the top with screws.*

Wall of Fame

One convenient place for reference material, mementos, and even a small stereo system.

Storage space is at a premium for most of us. We've filled up the basement and the attic, and it's been a few years since we parked a car in the garage. We know the time will come when we'll have to get things in order, but we also know that the time hasn't come yet.

But what works in our personal lives doesn't always work in our professional lives. The best example of this is a home office, where organization is one of the big keys to success. And one of the most important factors in good organization is having plenty of storage space that's close at hand and easy to use. That's why we created this multifunctional wall unit.

*Key*POINTS

TIME
Prep Time	8 hours
Shop Time	20 hours
Assembly Time	20 hours

EFFORT
Skill Level	intermediate

COST / BENEFITS
Expense: **moderate**
- This economical unit uses **minimal floor space** but provides **maximum storage**.
- **Deep, adjustable shelves** can hold books, oversize catalogs, and three-ring binders.

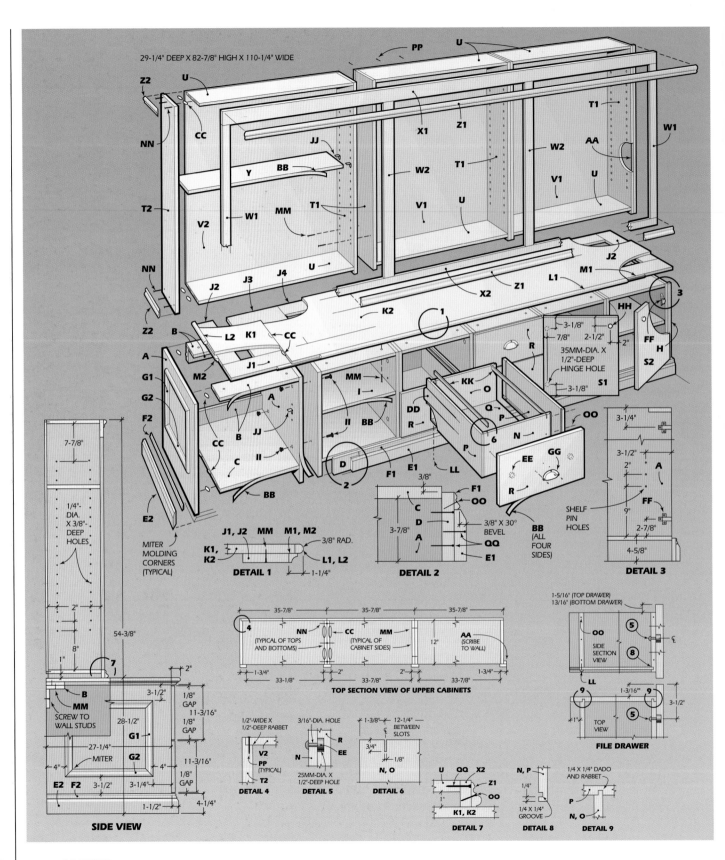

29-1/4" DEEP X 82-7/8" HIGH X 110-1/4" WIDE

DETAIL 1

J1, J2 MM M1, M2
K1,
K2
L1, L2
3/8" RAD.
1-1/4"

DETAIL 2

3/8"
C
D
A
3-7/8"
F1
OO
3/8" X 30°
BEVEL
QQ
E1

DETAIL 3

3-1/4"
3-1/2"
2"
A
9"
FF
SHELF
PIN
HOLES
2-7/8"
4-5/8"

SIDE VIEW

7-7/8"
1/4"-
DIA.
X 3/8".
DEEP
HOLES
2"
54-3/8"
8"
1"
7
B
MM
SCREW TO
WALL STUDS
28-1/2"
27-1/4"
4"
MITER
G1
G2
E2 F2
3-1/2"
1-1/2"
3-1/2"
1/8"
GAP
11-3/16"
1/8"
GAP
11-3/16"
1/8"
GAP
4-1/4"
2"
3-1/4"
4"

MITER
MOLDING
CORNERS
(TYPICAL)

TOP SECTION VIEW OF UPPER CABINETS

35-7/8"   35-7/8"   35-7/8"
4
NN   CC   MM
(TYPICAL OF TOPS
AND BOTTOMS)
(TYPICAL OF
CABINET SIDES)
12"
AA
(SCRIBE
TO WALL)
1-3/4"   1-3/4"
33-1/8"   33-7/8"   33-7/8"
2"   2"

DETAIL 4

1/2"-WIDE X
1/2"-DEEP RABBET
V2
PP
(TYPICAL)
T2

DETAIL 5

3/16"-DIA. HOLE
R
N
EE
25MM-DIA. X
1/2"-DEEP HOLE

DETAIL 6

1-3/8"   12-1/4"
BETWEEN
SLOTS
3/4"
1/8"
N, O

FILE DRAWER

1-5/16" (TOP DRAWER)
13/16" (BOTTOM DRAWER)
OO
5
8
SIDE
SECTION
VIEW
LL
1-3/16"
9   9
5
1"
TOP
VIEW
3-1/2"

DETAIL 7

U QQ X2
Z1
OO
K1, K2

DETAIL 8

N, P
1/4"
1/4 X 1/4"
GROOVE

DETAIL 9

1/4 X 1/4" DADO
AND RABBET
P
N, O

3-1/8"
7/8"   2-1/2"
2"
35MM-DIA. X
1/2"-DEEP
HINGE HOLE
3-1/8"
S1
HH
FF
H
S2

This economical unit occupies less than 24 sq. ft. of floor space. The lower part is based on the same 18-in.-wide module we used for our desk and credenza. In this case, six of these units are joined to form a combination of drawer and cabinet storage that supports a three-section bookshelf on top.

Construction

Begin by building six cabinet modules, following the assembly details used for the desk ("Office Space," page 178). Do not, however, cut or install the build-up blocking at the base of each cabinet. On this job, the blocking will be installed in one piece once the modules are moved into the office room.

Even though you'll have to resand portions of the casework, it's a good idea to sand the cabinet interiors at this point with 220- grit paper. In our layout, only one cabinet end is exposed, so it was necessary to apply the panel molding detail to only one cabinet side. Lay out the molding outline on the case side, then cut and attach the molding with glue

and 1-in. brads. Once all the modules are complete, clamp adjacent modules together. Then, bore clearance holes for the connector bolts that will join the cabinets together (**Fig. 1**).

Construct the file drawers using the techniques shown in the office desk story. Lay out the centerlines for the drawer-slide mounting screws, bore pilot holes for the screws, and install the slides in the case sides. Then, mount the slide members on the drawer boxes and install the drawers in the cases. Remember, when installing the slides, use only the slotted holes for mounting. Once you adjust the slides so the drawers operate properly, then you can install the remaining screws. Next, cut, edge band, and mount the drawer faces to

Materials List

Key	No.	Size and description (use)
A	12	$3/4$ x 27 x $27^1/4$" plywood (side)
B	24	$3/4$ x 4 x $16^1/2$" plywood (rail)
C	6	$3/4$ x $16^1/2$ x $27^1/4$" plywood (bottom)
D	1	$3/4$ x $4^1/4$ x 109" plywood (blocking strip)
E1	1	$3/4$ x $3^3/16$ x $109^3/4$" poplar (base molding)
E2	1	$3/4$ x $3^3/16$ x $28^3/4$" poplar (base molding)
F1	1	$3/8$ x $1^1/16$ x $109^3/8$" pine (base trim)
F2	1	$3/8$ x $1^1/16$ x $28^3/8$" pine (base trim)
G1	2	$11/16$ x $1^5/8$ x $15^3/4$" pine (panel molding)
G2	2	$11/16$ x $1^5/8$ x 20" pine (panel molding)
H	1	$3/4$ x 1 x $22^3/4$" poplar (spacer strip)
I	4	$3/4$ x $16^3/8$ x 27" poplar (adjustable shelf)
J1	1	$3/4$ x 4 x 109" plywood (support strip)
J2	2	$3/4$ x 4 x 24" plywood (support strip)
J3	1	$3/4$ x 12 x 24" plywood (support strip)
J4	1	$3/4$ x 4 x 90" plywood (support strip)
K1	1	$3/4$ x $13^1/2$ x $28^1/2$" plywood (top)
K2	1	$3/4$ x $28^1/2$ x 96" plywood (top)
L1	1	$3/4$ x $3/4$ x $110^1/4$" poplar (edge band)
L2	1	$3/4$ x $3/4$ x $29^1/4$" poplar (edge band)
M1	1	$3/4$ x $3/4$ x $109^3/4$" pine (cove molding)
M2	1	$3/4$ x $3/4$ x $28^3/4$" pine (cove molding)
N	4	$1/2$ x $9^3/4$ x 15" plywood (drawer front)
O	4	$1/2$ x $9^1/4$ x 15" plywood (drawer back)
P	8	$1/2$ x $9^3/4$ x 26" plywood (drawer side)
Q	4	$1/4$ x 15 x $24^3/4$" plywood (drawer bottom)
R	4	$3/4$ x $11^{13}/16$ x $17^7/8$" plywood (drawer face)
S1	2	$3/4$ x $17^7/8$ x $22^1/2$" plywood (door)
S2	2	$3/4$ x $17^{15}/..$ x $22^1/2$" plywood (door)
T1	5	$3/4$ x 12 x $54^3/8$" plywood (side)
T2	1	$3/4$ x $12^1/2$ x $54^3/8$" plywood (side)
U	6	$3/4$ x 12 x $34^3/8$" plywood (top, bottom)
V1	2	$1/2$ x $35^5/8$ x $53^3/8$" plywood (back)
V2	1	$1/2$ x $35^5/8$ x $53^3/8$" plywood (back)
W1	2	$3/4$ x $1^3/4$ x 49" poplar (stile)
W2	2	$3/4$ x 2 x 49" poplar (stile)
X1	1	$3/4$ x $3^5/8$ x $108^3/8$" poplar (rail)
X2	1	$3/4$ x $1^3/4$ x $108^3/8$" poplar (rail)
Y	9	$3/4$ x 12 x $34^1/4$" plywood (adjustable shelf)
Z1	2	$11/16$ x $1^5/8$ x $109^9/16$" pine (panel molding)
Z2	2	$11/16$ x $1^3/8$ x $131^5/16$" pine (panel molding)
AA	1	$3/4$ x $3/4$ x $54^3/8$" plywood (spacer)
BB	as reqd.	iron-on veneer tape
CC	as reqd.	No. 20 joining plates
DD	4 pr.	drawer slides, 26" long
EE	8	drawer face adjusters
FF	8	170° full overlay hinges
GG	4	brass drawer pulls (drawers)
HH	4	brass drawer pulls (cabinet doors)
II	20	joint connector bolts
JJ	52	brass shelf pins
KK	8	$1/8$ x $3/4$ x 25" aluminum flat stock
LL	12	$5/8$" No. 5 rh screws
MM	as reqd.	$1^1/4$" No. 8 fh screws
NN	as reqd.	2" No. 8 fh screws
OO	as reqd.	1" brads
PP	as reqd.	1" wire nails
QQ	as reqd.	4d finish nails

Misc.: 120- and 220-grit sandpaper; carpenter's glue; epoxy glue; wood filler; latex primer; latex paint.

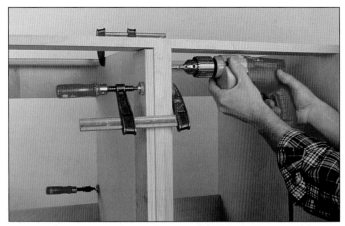

Fig. 1 *Clamp together adjacent base cabinets and bore clearance holes for the connector bolts. Test fit the bolts, then remove them.*

Fig. 2 *Lay out the proper position for all the door-hinge mounting plates. Then install the plates to the sides of the base cabinets.*

Fig. 3 *Cut the doors to size and lay out the proper positions for the hinges. Bore 35mm holes in the back sides using a drill press.*

Fig. 4 *Push the hinge into the hole and adjust until the hinge arm is perpendicular to the door edge. Fasten the hinge with screws.*

the file drawers, then bore pilot holes for the drawer pulls. Remove the drawers from the cases and set them aside until after the modules are installed in the room.

The cabinets on this unit have full overlay doors attached with fully concealed European-style hinges. This hinge system consists of two parts: a hinge arm that mounts to the door and a mounting plate that is screwed to the cabinet. The hinge arm is pushed onto the mounting plate and fastened with a screw. These units provide adjustments in three directions.

To begin assembly, cut and edge band the door panels, then lay out the hinge centerlines on the doors and the mounting-plate centerlines on the cabinet sides. Bore pilot holes for the screws, and attach the mounting plates to the cabinet sides (**Fig. 2**). Use the drill press to bore the hinge-cup recesses in the back side of the cabinet doors (**Fig. 3**), then press the cups into place and install the screws (**Fig. 4**). Bore pilot holes for the doorknobs and set the doors aside.

If one of your cabinets will be adjacent to a wall, install a 1-in.-wide scribe strip on the outside of the cabinet. This strip can be planed to account for irregularities in the wall surface, while providing clearance for a door or drawer to open.

To simplify installation of your cases, do as much prep work as possible while you are still in the workshop. To this end, fabricate a drilling template for the shelf-pin holes on the inside of the base cabinets. Use a piece of scrap plywood for the template, laying out the holes either according to our plan or to suit your own needs. Then clamp the template to the cabinet sides and bore the shelf-pin holes. Use a depth stop on the bit to keep the holes uniform (**Fig. 5**).

Installation

Bring the base cabinets to the office location and begin installation. Shim each cabinet as required to bring it level and plumb and join the cabinets with connector bolts. Use a stud finder to locate the wall studs, then screw each case to the wall through the back rail.

Cut and band the top edge of the blocking strip and install it along the bottom of the cabinets. Then cut, miter, and install the baseboard (**Fig. 6**). Cut and nail the small panel molding along the top of the baseboard.

Since the countertop for this unit is longer than the standard 8-ft. sheet of plywood, you have two construction options. You can special order a 10-ft.-long sheet of plywood, or you can join two pieces of plywood, as we did. If you opt for the latter, rip the stock to width, then cut and apply the end edge banding to one of the pieces before joining them together. It is much easier to clamp across a short panel than to one 9 ft. long.

Cut joining-plate slots in the mating edges of both pieces, then apply glue to the slots, plates, and edges and bring the pieces together (**Fig. 7**). Cut and attach a plywood cleat on the underside of the joint, using glue and screws (**Fig. 8**). Keep this cleat back from the front edge of the panel so the front support strip can pass by it.

Apply the front edge band to the countertop, then use the router and edge guide to round over the top edge. Cut and install the support strips to the bottom side of the countertop and fit the cove molding against the strips. Place the countertop over the base cabinets and check its fit against the walls. In most rooms, the wall corners are not square, so use a scriber to mark the top. Then trim to this marked line with a belt sander or a jigsaw (**Fig. 9**). Attach the top to the cabinets.

Next, hang and adjust the cabinet doors. To do this, first slide the hinge arms onto the mounting plates, then lock them in place with the large screw at the end of the hinge arm (**Fig. 10**). These screws also control the in-and-out adjustment of the hinges. To adjust the left-to-right alignment of the door, use the screws that are accessible through the small window in

Fig. 5 *Using a depth stop on the bit and a simple drill template as a guide, bore the shelf-pin holes in the sides of the cabinets.*

Fig. 6 *Place the base cabinets in proper position and join them together with connector bolts. Apply blocking and base trim along the bottom.*

Fig. 7 *Join the two top pieces that cover the base cabinets with joining plates and glue. Edge band the smaller piece first.*

Fig. 8 *Reinforce the top joint by attaching a 12-in.-wide cleat to the bottom side. Keep the cleat back so the front strip can span the joint.*

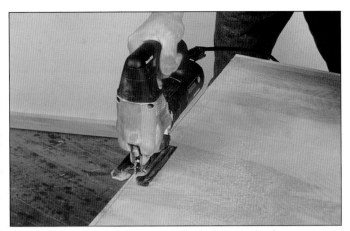

Fig. 9 *Once the top is complete, lay it on the base cabinets and scribe the end to the wall. Cut along the scribe line for a precise fit.*

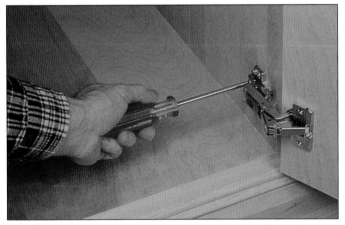

Fig. 10 *Lift the door—with the hinges already in place—into the door opening. Slide the hinges onto the plates and tighten.*

Fig. 11 *Cut the bookshelf side to size. Then cut a rabbet along its back edge for the back panel. Use a router with an edge guide.*

the hinge arm. The height adjustment is controlled by a screw on the mounting plate.

Reinstall the file drawers in their cases to complete the base installation. You'll probably have to readjust the door and drawer-face alignment once everything is in place.

Bookshelf Assembly and Finishing

The bookshelf portion of the storage unit is comprised of three nearly identical shelf bays. Because one side of the last bay is exposed, it is cut ½ in. wider than the rest of the sides to accommodate the back panel.

Rip and crosscut the plywood panels for the bookcase parts to finished size. Then use the router to cut the rabbet along the back edge of the outside case side (**Fig. 11**). Next, lay out the joining-plate locations on the case sides, tops, and bottoms. Use the plate joiner to cut the slots and clamp a straightedge in place to keep the slots aligned (**Fig. 12**). Create a drilling template from a strip of plywood for laying out the shelf-pin holes. Then clamp the template to each shelf side and bore the holes. Use a stop on the drill bit to guarantee holes of uniform depth.

Cut and glue the spacer strip to the outside surface of the case side that will butt against the wall. Then cut the plywood backs to size, and sand them and the other case parts with 220-grit paper.

To assemble a case section, apply glue to the plate slots and plates, then join the top and bottom shelves to the sides (**Fig. 13**). Since all sides but one are concealed, and the exposed side has moldings at its top and bottom, you can use screws to draw the joints tight, dispensing with the need for time-consuming clamps. Next, place each case on its face and apply glue to the back edges of the sides, top, and bottom. Then lower the back panel into place and fasten it to the case with 1-in. wire nails (**Fig. 14**).

Place the first case in position on the countertop and fasten it to the wall studs by screwing through the back of the case (**Fig. 15**). Use four screws per case, two at the top and two at the bottom, each driven into a wall stud.

Position the second case next to the first and clamp the two adjacent sides together, aligning the edges carefully, and screw together. Keep in mind that if you line up the screws with the row of shelf-pin holes, they will not be as noticeable later. Install the last case unit following the same procedure.

Cut the face-frame parts to size from poplar or pine stock. Use glue and 4d finish nails to install the frame. Begin with the bottom rail, then install the stiles (**Fig. 16**), and finish up by installing the top rail. Then cut and install the panel molding around the top and bottom of the bookcase unit (**Fig. 17**). Set and fill all nail holes.

Cut and edge band the shelves for the bookcase units and the base cabinets. Sand all case parts with 220-grit paper, then prime and paint with the color of your choice. When the piece is dry, install the door, drawer, and shelf hardware.

Fig. 12 *Cut plate slots in the bookshelf sides using a plate joiner. Clamp a straightedge to the side to keep the joiner aligned.*

Fig. 13 *Begin assembly of the shelf units by joining the bottom panels to the sides. Apply glue to the mating edges, slots, and plates.*

Fig. 14 *Once all the sides, tops, and bottoms are assembled, glue and nail the plywood backs to the shelf cases. Make sure each is square.*

Fig. 15 *Lift the corner shelf assembly into place and attach it to the wall studs with two screws near the top and two near the bottom.*

Fig. 16 *Cut the shelf stiles to size, then glue and nail them onto the case sides. Set the nail heads and cover them with wood filler.*

Fig. 17 *Miter the panel molding and nail the pieces onto the shelf assembly. Don't drive the nails completely until you're satisfied with the fit.*

Around the House

Return of a Classic

This traditional corner cabinet is a great solution for saving space in just about any room in your home.

For many of us, the quest for adequate storage space consumes quite a bit of our energy and time. It seems that our ability to accumulate objects just naturally exceeds our ability to find a proper place to keep them. One particularly nice solution to this problem is the corner cabinet. And because it's built to fit a corner, the cabinet uses its space efficiently. Another nice feature of this simple ash cabinet is that it complements many design schemes, and it's equally at home in your dining room, living room, or kitchen. Better still, you can tackle this easy-to-build project even if you don't have an elaborately equipped shop.

*Key*POINTS

TIME
Prep Time .... 6 hours
Shop Time .... 12 hours
Assembly Time .... 16 hours

EFFORT
Skill Level .... intermediate

COST / BENEFITS
Expense: moderate
• The corner cabinet offers lots of storage without sacrificing much wall space.
• You can change the scrolled headpiece for a more contemporary look.

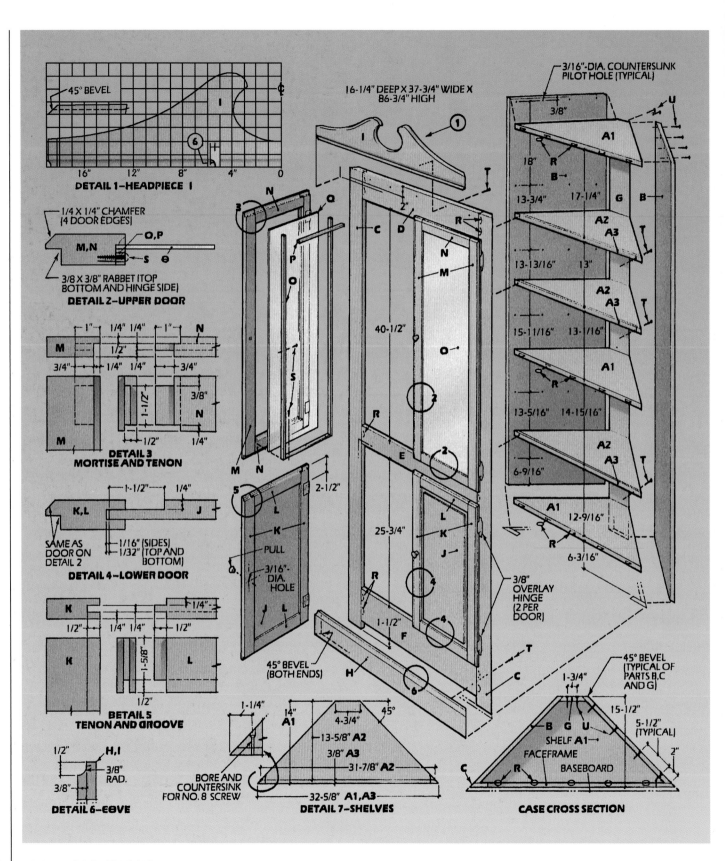

DETAIL 1—HEADPIECE I

45° BEVEL

I

6

16"   12"   8"   4"   0

1/4 X 1/4" CHAMFER
(4 DOOR EDGES)

O,P

M,N

S   θ

3/8 X 3/8" RABBET (TOP
BOTTOM AND HINGE SIDE)

DETAIL 2—UPPER DOOR

1"   1/4" 1/4"   1"   N

M

1/2"

3/4"   1/4" 1/4"   3/4"

1-1/2"   3/8"

N

M

1/2"   1/4"

DETAIL 3
MORTISE AND TENON

1-1/2"   1/4"

K,L   J

SAME AS
DOOR ON
DETAIL 2

1/16" (SIDES)
1/32" (TOP AND
BOTTOM)

DETAIL 4—LOWER DOOR

K

1/2"   1/4" 1/4"   1/2"

K   1/4"

1-5/8"

L

1/2"

DETAIL 5
TENON AND GROOVE

1/2"   H,I

3/8"
RAD.

3/8"

DETAIL 6—COVE

1-1/4"

A1

14"

4-3/4"   45°

13-5/8" A2

3/8" A3

31-7/8" A2

BORE AND
COUNTERSINK
FOR NO. 8 SCREW

32-5/8" A1, A3

DETAIL 7—SHELVES

16-1/4" DEEP X 37-3/4" WIDE X
86-3/4" HIGH   1

I

N

3

Q

C   D

P

O

S

M   N

40-1/2"

N

M

O

R

2

E

R   2

25-3/4"

L

K

L

J

R   4

F

4

2-1/2"

5

L

K

PULL

3/16"-
DIA.
HOLE

L

45° BEVEL
(BOTH ENDS)

H   C

2

6

1-1/2"

3/8"
OVERLAY
HINGE
(2 PER
DOOR)

T

3/16"-DIA. COUNTERSUNK
PILOT HOLE (TYPICAL)

U

3/8"

A1

18"   R

B

13-3/4"   17-1/4"   G   B

A2
A3

13-13/16"   13"

A2
A3

15-11/16"   13-1/16"

A1

R

13-5/16"   14-15/16"

A2
A3

6-9/16"

T

A1

R

12-9/16"

6-3/16"

T

45° BEVEL
(TYPICAL OF
PARTS B,C
AND G)

1-3/4"

15-1/2"

B   G   U

SHELF A1

FACEFRAME

BASEBOARD

5-1/2"
(TYPICAL)

2"

C   R

CASE CROSS SECTION

Although we used full-size shop machines for much of the work, you could use power and hand tools. A circular saw, router, hand plane, and an electric drill would do nicely. If you want to reduce the expense of the project, you might consider using poplar instead of ash. On the other hand, if money isn't a major issue, you might want to use the more traditional (and more expensive) walnut or cherry.

Making the Case Parts

Begin by ripping slightly overwidth pieces of ¾-in.-thick ash plywood for the cabinet shelves. Due to the triangular shape of the shelves, you can get the best yield from your materials by nesting the shelf cutouts along the length of the plywood panel. Lay out the shelves, leaving about 1 in. between each.

Next, cut strips for edge banding the exposed shelf edges and glue them to the front edge of the shelves (**Fig. 1**). When the glue has set, plane and sand the edge banding flush to the panel faces, then cut out the rough shape of each shelf.

The shelves will be cut to finished size with a template and a flush trimming bit in a router. Make the template from a piece of ¼-in. hardboard and screw it to the bottom of a shelf (**Fig. 2**). Next, clamp the shelf firmly to the worktable and cut around the shelf-blank template with a flush trimming bit in the router (**Fig. 3**).

Using the table saw, rip the panels for the case sides to rough width. Crosscut the pieces to finished length using a portable circular saw, guided by a straightedge clamped to the workpiece. Tilt the table saw blade to 45° and rip the long edges of the sides to finished dimension. Lay out the position

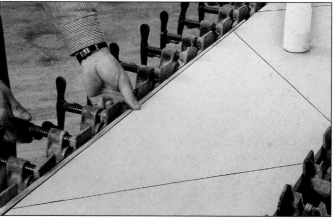

Fig. 1 *Lay out the shelves so they nest along the length of a piece of ash plywood. Then glue and clamp on the edge band.*

Fig. 2 *Cut out oversize shelf blanks. Make a ¼-in. hardboard template the shape of the shelf and screw it to the blank.*

Materials List

Key	No.	Size and description (use)
A1	3	¾ x 14 x 32⅝" ash plywood (shelf)
A2	3	¾ x 13⅝ x 31⅞" ash plywood (shelf)
A3	3	⅜ x ¾ x 32⅝" ash (edge band)
B	2	¾ x 20½ x 81½" ash plywood (side)
C	2	¾ x 3 x 81½" ash (stile)
D	1	¾ x 5 x 30¼" ash (top rail)
E	1	¾ x 3¼ x 30¼" ash (middle rail)
F	1	¾ x 5½ x 30¼" ash (bottom rail)
G	1	¾ x 4¾ x 75⁵⁄₁₆" ash (back)
H	1	¾ x 4 x 37¾" ash (baseboard)
I	1	¾ x 7¼ x 37¾" ash (headpiece)
J	2	½ x 12 x 22¹⁵⁄₁₆" ash (door panel)
K	4	¾ x 2⅛ x 26¼" ash (lower door stiles)
L	4	¾ x 2⅛ x 12⅛" ash (lower door rail)
M	4	¾ x 2⅛ x 41" ash (upper door stile)
N	4	¾ x 2⅛ x 13⅛" ash (upper door rail)
O	4	¼ x ⅜ x 37¼" ash (vertical stops)
P	4	¼ x ⅜ x 11⅛" ash (horizontal stops)
Q	2	⅛ x 11⅝ x 37¼" glass (panel)
R	22	joining plates/biscuits
S	32	⅝" No. 4 rh screws
T	11	1¼" No. 8 fh screws
U	36	2" No. 8 fh screws

Misc.: Tack cloth; satin polyurethane; mineral spirits; 120- and 220-grit sandpaper; steel wool; wood glue; 4 door pulls; 8 hinges (⅜-in. overlay).

Fig. 3 *Clamp the shelf-blank template to the worktable. Use a flush trimming bit in the router to cut the shelf blank to size.*

Fig. 4 *Lay out the position of the joining plates on face frame parts. The top and bottom rails have two plates per joint.*

Fig. 5 *Spread glue in the plate joint slot. Insert the plates and spread a little glue on the plates as well. Let the glue set before continuing.*

Fig. 6 *Clamp the face frame parts on a flat surface. Check diagonal measurements to be sure the face frame is square.*

of the shelves on each side, then bore pilot holes for attaching the sides to the shelves. Counterbore these holes on the outside surface of the sides.

Cut out the parts for the cabinet face frame from 4/4 ash. Note that the face frame is assembled using joining plates, though other methods, such as dowels or mortise-and-tenon construction, will work as well. If you use mortise-and-tenon construction, you'll need to increase the length of the rails to accommodate the tenons.

Lay out the face frame parts on an assembly table and mark the position of the joining plates at each stile-rail joint. Note that the wider rails at the top and bottom of the frame can accommodate two plates per joint. Use the plate joiner to cut the slots in stiles and rails for the plates. Hold the workpiece and plate joiner firmly on the work surface while cutting the slots (**Fig. 4**). Apply glue to the joining plate slots and plates, and assemble the face frame (**Fig. 5**). Use bar

clamps to bring the joints tight, then compare opposite diagonal measurements to check that the face frame is square (**Fig. 6**). If the frame is out of square, readjust the clamps to bring it into square.

Set the table saw blade to 45° and then rip the long edges of the face frame. The case top, bottom, and middle shelf are joined to the face frame with joining plates. Mark the position of these joining plates on the shelves and the face frame (**Fig. 7**). Cut the required slots with a straightedge clamped to the frame to position the plate joiner (**Fig. 8**).

Case Assembly

Cut the case back from solid 4/4 ash or ¾-in. ash plywood, and rip both edges at 45° on the table saw. Lay out the position of each shelf on the case back and use the drill press to bore and counterbore two pilot holes through the back for attaching each shelf.

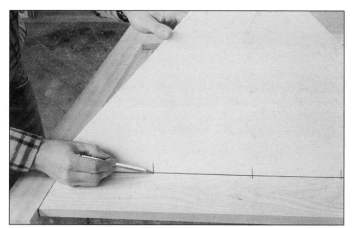

Fig. 7 *Use a pencil to mark the location of the joining plates on the face frame and on the top, middle, and bottom shelves.*

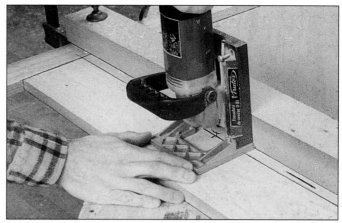

Fig. 8 *Cut joining plate slots on the back of the face frame using a straightedge clamped to the frame to guide the plate joiner.*

Fig. 9 *Use hot glue to attach small triangular clamping ears along the back edges of the top, middle, and bottom shelves.*

Cut small triangular blocks from scrap stock and attach them with hot glue to the back edges of the top, bottom, and middle shelves to act as clamping ears (**Fig. 9**). These ears make assembly easy. They are attached with just a dot of hot glue and are removed with a chisel after the shelves are joined to the cabinet face. Presand all interior cabinet parts with 120- and 220-grit sandpaper, dust off, and wipe with a tack cloth.

Apply glue to the joining plate slots and clamp the top, bottom, and middle shelves to the face frame (**Fig. 10**). Check that the shelves are square to the frame and let the glue set. While the glue sets, bore pilot holes through the edges of the remaining three shelves and attach them to the face frame with 1¼ in. No. 8 fh screws.

Position the case back and screw it to the backs of the shelves through the previously bored pilot holes (**Fig. 11**). Before driving the screws, remember to check that the shelves are perpendicular to the cabinet face.

TECH *Tips*

Flat as a Pancake
It would be a shame to go through all the trouble of cutting and fitting parts for a piece of furniture only to assemble it incorrectly. When you glue and clamp together an assembly or glue and clamp one subassembly to another, you have to do it on a reliably flat surface. This means either using the top of the workbench or building a small table—called an assembly table—that has a top that is only a couple of feet off the ground. Another method is to build a small but sturdy frame and panel and set it on a pair of sawhorses. Whatever method you use, just be sure that the surface on which the glued-together parts are placed is reliably flat and free of twist. If not, the assembly will take on the crookedness of the surface on which it was placed. One advantage to using a short table or other rigid surface is that, sometimes, you'll find it useful to clamp the assembly to the surface on which it is being assembled. That's often the case with large case pieces or other assemblies that have to be very carefully glued and clamped so that they are perfectly square and free of twist. A small error is multiplied over a long distance, which puts further emphasis on precision during the assembly sequence.

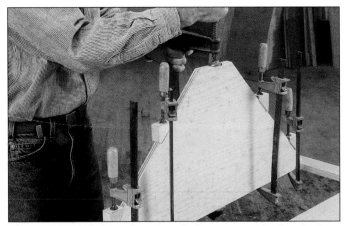

Fig. 10 *Use joining plates and glue to attach the shelves to the face frame. Remove clamping ears later with a sharp chisel.*

Fig. 11 *Position the case back, then drive screws—through prebored and counterbored holes—from the case back into the back of each shelf.*

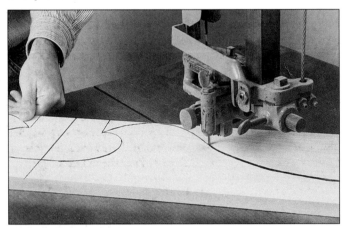

Fig. 12 *Cut a 45° angle on the ends of the headpiece. Trace the profile on the workpiece and cut it to shape, staying on the waste side of the line.*

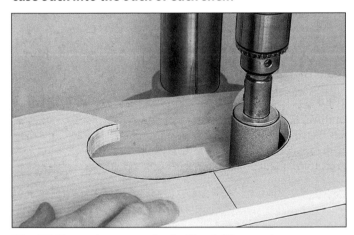

Fig. 13 *Use a drum sander in the drill press to remove saw marks and refine the profile of the cabinet's headpiece.*

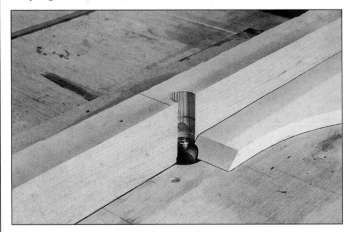

Fig. 14 *Use a cove molding bit in a router table to cut the cove on the top edge of the headpiece and on the bottom edge of the baseboard.*

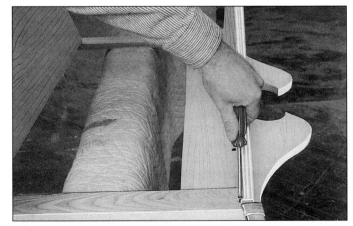

Fig. 15 *Hold the headpiece to the face frame with spring clamps. Bore pilot holes and screw the headpiece in place.*

Fig. 16 *Bore four evenly spaced pilot holes through the case sides, and attach the case sides by screwing them into the shelf edges.*

Fig. 17 *To support the plunge router while cutting a mortise in an upper door stile, clamp some scrap next to the stile.*

Remove the clamping ears from the shelf edges by prying gently under their edge with a sharp chisel. Cut the pieces for the baseboard trim and decorative headpiece to rough length and width. Then crosscut to finished dimension using the miter gauge on the table saw with the blade tipped to 45°.

Reset the blade to 90°, and rip the baseboard to finished width. Trace the outline of the headpiece on the blank, and cut out the piece on the band saw (**Fig. 12**). Stay on the waste side of the line as you cut. Then use a drum sander in the drill press to remove the saw marks (**Fig. 13**). If you don't have a

drill press, carefully remove the saw marks using files and rasps. Finish by sanding the edge smooth. Use a cove bit in the router table to shape the molding on the bottom edge of the headpiece and the top edge of the baseboard (**Fig. 14**).

Drill and countersink pilot holes through the back of the face frame for attaching the baseboard and headpiece. Attach both pieces using 1¼-in. No. 8 fh screws (**Fig. 15**).

Place one of the case sides in its proper position and attach it with 2-in. No. 8 fh screws. Bore a pilot hole for each screw and drive four evenly spaced screws along the length of each

MATERIAL *Matters*

Quarter Master
Woodworking is filled with odd nomenclature. Like any other skill or hobby, this craft is rife with words for techniques and equipment that just wouldn't make sense to the uninitiated.

Take the rabbet, a two-sided (right angle) notch. It comes from the Latin word *rabbeto*, meaning to "beat down." The edge of the wood is not beaten down, of course, but it is pared away by a plane, sawed away by a saw, or cut away by a spinning router bit.

A less-ancient oddity is used in describing lumber thickness. Dimension lumber used in construction is simply described as a 2x4 or something similar. But softwood and hardwood lumber uses the mysterious quarter-inch measurement. Typically, this is given as 4/4

for 1 in., 8/4 for 2 in., 12/4 for 3 in., and so on. Sometimes you see wood dimensioned as 5/4 or another odd number. Sawmills today are sufficiently accurate to produce wood of any dimension, from paper thin to 6 in. thick. So why has the quarter dimension method held on? Well, things change slowly in woodworking.

Still, it works well enough, and 1-in. increments are accurate enough at the initial stages of preparing lumber for a project. Woodworking is—or at least should be—a process that gains precision as the project moves closer to completion. When lumber is sawed to a given dimension, generally it's best to prepare the wood so that it is much thicker than actually needed. That way, it can be planed down so it is flat, straight, and square. It seems wasteful, but working with solid lumber, as opposed to engineered panels, will always be somewhat earthy, at least at the outset.

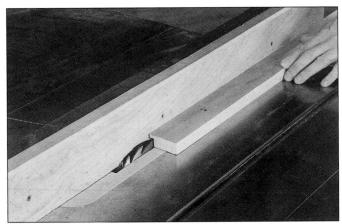

Fig. 18 *Use dado blades in the table saw to cut the rabbet on the inner edges of the upper door stiles and rails.*

Fig. 19 *Reset the blade height, then use the miter gauge and the rip fence to cut tenons on the upper door rails. Make the cheek cuts first.*

shelf (**Fig. 16**). This job can be completed quickly with a power screwdriver tip chucked in an electric drill. Follow the same procedure to attach the remaining side. When both sides are attached, stand the case up.

Door Construction

Rip and crosscut the door parts. Cut the mortises in the upper door stiles with a ¼-in.-dia. straight bit in a plunge router. Clamp some scrap pieces of the same width as the stile next to the stile to serve as a base for the router (**Fig. 17**). Use a sharp chisel to square the mortise ends. You can also bore out the bulk of the mortise on the drill press, then pare its sides and ends flat using a chisel.

Cut the rabbet on the upper door stiles and rails with dado blades in the table saw (**Fig. 18**). Readjust the dado blade

height and use the miter gauge in combination with the rip fence to cut the tenons on the upper door rails (**Figs. 19 and 20**). It's safe to use the miter gauge and rip fence together in this operation, where normally it is not. In this case, cutting the tenon does not produce a scrap piece that can get wedged between the miter gauge and the fence.

Readjust the saw fence to cut the tenons on the lower door rails. Change the dado blades to cut the groove in the lower door stiles and rails. Next, rip, crosscut, and joint the stock for the lower door panels. Glue and clamp together two panels. After the glue has set, scrape and plane the panels smooth. Cut the panels to finished size. Then, using a straight bit in the router table, cut the wide rabbet around each panel.

Next, seal the lower door panels with a coat of finish, thinned 50 percent with its proper solvent. Let the finish dry,

TECH *Tips*

Now Ear This

A "clamping ear" is an odd name to give to a woodworking procedure, but that's the way it is. A clamping ear is a small triangular projection that is temporarily attached to an angular or curved surface to provide clamping pressure. The head of the clamp is placed on the ear, and clamping pressure is applied in a straight line.

On this project, we show a clamping ear fastened with a dot of hot glue. In other cases, it's just as easy to use a screw or two. The clamping ear is usually attached to a surface that is covered later

in the assembly process, so a mark or two on it is really no big deal.

A larger lesson remains to be learned here, though. And that is, don't be afraid to be inventive and make your own assembly devices and methods. The important thing is to end up with an assembly or subassembly that is flat, square, and free of twist. Clamping force has to be applied in a straight line in most cases, and it has to be applied evenly and not excessively. Use whatever trick or device gets you there. Call it an ear, a nose, or a throat. It really doesn't matter.

Fig. 20 *Tip the rails on edge, butt them against the fence, and then cut the shoulder on each upper door rail tenon.*

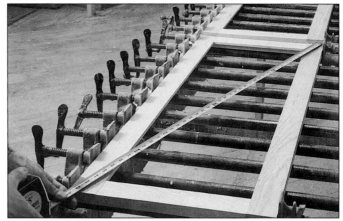

Fig. 21 *Glue and clamp the upper doors. Check the assembly for square by comparing diagonal measurements.*

Fig. 22 *Slide the panel into the stile-rail assembly on a lower door. Then clamp the assembly with the remaining stile.*

Fig. 23 *Clamp a straight board to the front of the cabinet to support the doors as you screw their hinges to the face frame.*

and sand the panels lightly with 220-grit sandpaper before installing them.

Apply glue to the mortises and tenons on the upper door and clamp the parts. Check the assembly for square and let the glue dry (**Fig. 21**).

Glue and press together three pieces of each lower door, and slide the panel in place (**Fig. 22**). Glue and press the stile in place, then clamp the door until the glue is dry. Cut the rabbet on three sides of each door on the router table.

Use a chamfer bit in the router table to cut the molded edge around the face of each door.

Mount the hinges to the back of each door. Next, clamp a board across the cabinet to support the doors during installation. Bore the pilot holes in the face frame and screw the door hinges in place (**Fig. 23**).

Bore holes for the door pulls, but do not install them. Remove the doors from the cabinet. Fit the glass panels in the upper doors and cut the stops to hold them. Bore pilot holes for screws, then install the stops to test their fit. Remove the stops and glass, then finish sand the case and doors. Dust off thoroughly, then wipe the case with a tack cloth before applying the finish.

Apply a coat of satin polyurethane to the cabinet, thinned 20 percent with mineral spirits, and let it dry overnight. Then sand the cabinet lightly with 220-grit sandpaper. Dust off the workpiece again and apply the next coat—this time without any thinner. Let it dry overnight, sand it lightly with 220-grit paper, and apply the final coat. After it's dry, rub it out with 4/0 steel wool.

Install the glass in the upper doors, and reinstall the hinges and door pulls. Rehang the doors, and the cabinet is done. For the neatest fit, remove and miter the baseboard along the walls where you will install the cabinet. Screw through the case sides into a stud to install the cabinet.

Neatness Counts

Keep your magazines in perfect order with this simple but elegant rack.

Two or three evenings spent puttering around the workshop is all it takes to build this magazine rack—and it's a great way to relax. It also produces a means of keeping magazines off your living room coffee table or the nightstand in your bedroom. The piece consists of a pair of identical three-piece frames that are joined together with a self-locking half-lap. Practically any wood can be used for this piece, but we chose yellow poplar. It works easily and, when finished with a clear topcoat, it takes on a cream color tinged with green. Poplar is widely available, and it is more reasonably priced than other cabinet-grade woods.

*Key*POINTS

TIME
Prep Time .... 1 hour
Shop Time .... 3 hours
Assembly Time .... 3 hours

EFFORT
Skill Level .... basic

COST / BENEFITS
Expense: low
• An **easy, relaxing project** that yields a useful piece of furniture.
• This **simple design** works in any room.

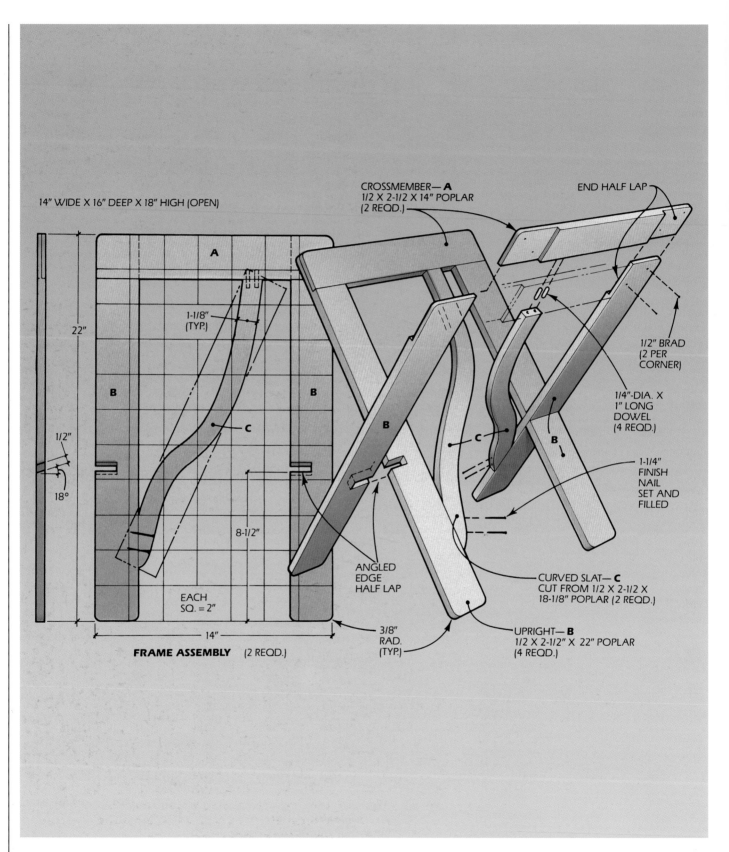

14" WIDE X 16" DEEP X 18" HIGH (OPEN)

CROSSMEMBER— **A**
1/2 X 2-1/2 X 14" POPLAR
(2 REQD.)

END HALF LAP

22"

1-1/8"
(TYP.)

B   **B**

C

1/2"

18°

8-1/2"

EACH
SQ. = 2"

14"

FRAME ASSEMBLY (2 REQD.)

3/8"
RAD.
(TYP.)

ANGLED
EDGE
HALF LAP

B

C   **B**

1/2" BRAD
(2 PER
CORNER)

1/4"-DIA. X
1" LONG
DOWEL
(4 REQD.)

1-1/4"
FINISH
NAIL
SET AND
FILLED

CURVED SLAT— **C**
CUT FROM 1/2 X 2-1/2 X
18-1/8" POPLAR (2 REQD.)

UPRIGHT— **B**
1/2 X 2-1/2 X 22" POPLAR
(4 REQD.)

Getting Started

Begin by ripping and crosscutting the ½-in. stock for the pair of uprights and the crossmember for each three-piece frame. Then mark the ends for the half-laps (**Fig. 1**)

Each half-lap is made with two cuts on the table saw. Use a tenoning jig to hold the workpiece vertically. If you don't have a commercial tenoning jig, you can make one (**Figs. 2 and 3**). A homemade tenoning jig simply consists of a saddle-like device that rides on the fence. The saddle's center equals the fence's thickness.

After you complete the end cuts, lower the blade and use the miter gauge to make the shoulder cuts that drop out the waste. Use a guide block clamped to the miter gauge fence when cutting the shoulders to ensure consistency from cut to cut (**Fig. 4**).

Cut the angled-edge half-laps next. Raise the saw blade so it projects a hair over half the width of the stock. Set the miter fence for an 18° miter, then make several passes to form the notch. Clamp a stop block to the miter gauge fence, and butt the workpiece to it (**Fig. 5**). Keep in mind that it's easy to get confused when cutting an angled half-lap joint. Remember to refer to the drawing often, and carefully mark out each notch before sawing it.

Before assembling the frames, check the fit of the edge notches (**Fig. 6**). You'll want to avoid a snug fit so that you can allow for a slight buildup of finish. Apply glue to the half-laps, and drive two ½-in.-long brads to hold the pieces in alignment, then clamp the pieces together.

Making the Crossbraces

While the glue is drying, rip and crosscut the crossbraces. Cut them to size and shape, then use a doweling jig to bore a pair of holes for ¼-in. dowel pins in the top ends only (**Fig. 7**).

Insert a pair of dowel centers in the holes to transfer the hole centers to the frame crossmember. To do this, press the lower edge of the crossbrace against the frame edge, then slide the slat against the horizontal frame member to make the marks (**Fig. 8**). Draw cross lines through the indents, and use the doweling jig to bore the holes.

Materials List

Key	No.	Size and description (use)
A	2	½ x 2½ x 14" poplar (crossmembers)
B	4	½ x 2½ x 22" poplar (uprights)
C	2	½ x 2½ x 18⅛" poplar (curved slats)
D	as reqd.	½" brads
E	4	¼"-dia x 1" dowels
F	as reqd.	1¼" finish nails

Misc.: Glue; 120- and 220-grit sandpaper; clear satin finish.

Fig. 1 *Rip and crosscut the frame members to size, then hold them in place to mark the guidelines for the half-lap joints.*

Fig. 2 *Use a tenoning jig to make the cheek cut in the frame members. Position the strip behind the workpiece to prevent tearout.*

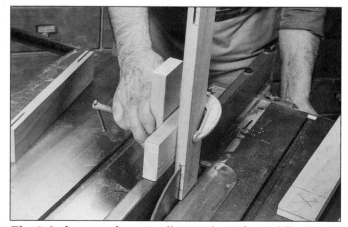

Fig. 3 *A shop-made tenon jig consists of a saddle that slides along the fence. The workpiece is clamped to it and moved over the blade.*

Push dowels into the ends of the crossmembers using a little glue. Also apply a little glue at the bottom of the crossmember. Then push the dowels into the holes in the frame. Fasten the frame with 1¼-in.-long finish nails at the bottom after the upper end is seated (**Fig. 9**).

Finishing Up

Ease all the corners on the magazine rack by sanding them with a padded block. Then smooth the surfaces with 120-grit sandpaper. Follow this with 220-grit paper. Wipe off any sanding dust with a tack cloth.

We finished our rack with three coats of clear satin finish. For proper use, follow the manufacturer's instructions, and allow each coat to dry before applying the next.

After you have finished all of the pieces, push the two sides of the frame together (**Fig. 10**). The joint is self-locking, so you won't need to use glue.

SKILL*Builder*

Take a Lap
The half-lap joint used in this project is one of the easiest to make if you have a table saw, but it can be surprisingly difficult to make if all you have are hand tools. If you have to make the joint with hand tools, here's how to go about it.

First, mark the joint's shape using a square, a marking gauge, and a marking knife. Remove the bulk of the waste from the joint by sawing. Depending on how skilled you are using a saw, you should cut anywhere from 1/16 in. away from the line left by the marking gauge or marking knife to just touching the line.

After the waste is cut away, pare down to the line using a razor-sharp chisel, a cabinetmaker's tool known as a shoulder plane, or the stubby version of this tool, the bullnose shoulder plane.

The shoulder plane has a cutter that's the full width of the body and sides that are perpendicular to the sole. This enables the tool to work into the corners of the half-lap. True, with practice, you can do a nice, neat, and fast job simply by paring with a sharp chisel. But a shoulder plane makes short work of this, and it's far more precise. If you intend to do much work with hand tools, you'll need to buy a shoulder plane at some point.

You know you have planed far enough when you split the line left by the marking gauge or marking knife.

Fig. 4 *Use a miter gauge to make the shoulder cuts. Clamp a guide block to the fence to ensure identical repeat cuts.*

Fig. 5 *Tilt the miter gauge to 18° to make the half-lap joints. Clamp a stop block on the fence to make consistent cuts.*

Fig. 6 *Check the half-lap for proper fit. The joint should be slightly loose to allow for a couple of coats of finish on both sides.*

MATERIAL*Matters*

Popular Poplar

This magazine rack is built out of a beautiful American wood, the yellow poplar or tulip tree, so named for its lily-like flowers. In the forest, these trees are tall and majestic with beautiful straight trunks that can reach 50 to 100 ft. before the first branch appears.

Old poplars may have trunks 5 to 6 ft. in diameter, and on rare occasions, larger ones are found. Poplar is easily worked with hand tools or machine tools and once worked, it tends to remain very stable. The fact that it stays put so nicely makes it ideal for use as the principle wood in a project—and it's also great for drawer frames or back panel assemblies. Poplar takes finish well, so it can be stained or painted with equally good results.

These qualities have made the poplar sought after for many years. It was widely used in country furniture, especially in the Appalachian mountains. (The poplar's range covers almost the entire eastern third of the U.S., from southern New York to northern Florida.) For a moderately priced hardwood, poplar may be your best bet.

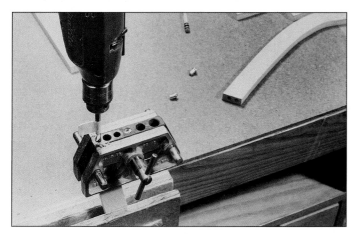

Fig. 7 *Use a doweling jig to bore holes in the slat's small end. Seat the jig so the holes will be perpendicular to the slat's face.*

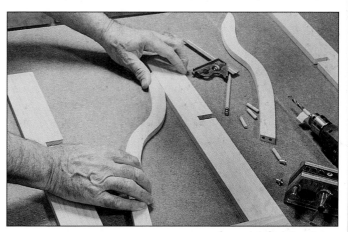

Fig. 8 *Use dowel centers to mark matching hole centers in the frame. Press firmly on slat's lower edge while sliding it forward.*

Fig. 9 *Secure the slat with glue and two dowel pins at the top and two nails at the bottom. Drive the nails after the upper end is seated.*

Fig. 10 *Push the two sections together without glue—the joint is self-locking. Apply finish to each section before assembly.*

Bread Winner

Mobilize your kitchen with this rollaway pine baking cart with Corian top.

Back in the days when baking was a daily chore in many households, it wasn't unusual for the kitchen to feature a specific area for preparing, kneading, and rolling out the dough. Today, homemakers all over the country have rediscovered the art of baking as a way to produce high-quality breads and pastries.

Our baking cart provides the extra work and storage space that baking requires, and is designed as an independent rollaway unit that fits neatly into any kitchen layout. The attractive Corian top is durable and easy to clean, and the shelves below can hold mixing bowls, baking sheets, and other baking necessities.

*Key*POINTS

TIME
Prep Time . . . . 8 hours
Shop Time . . . . 12 hours
Assembly Time . . . . 20 hours

EFFORT
Skill Level . . . . intermediate

COST / BENEFITS
Expense: moderate
• Featuring **classic detailing in an updated format**, our baking cart is compatible with both contemporary and traditional kitchens.

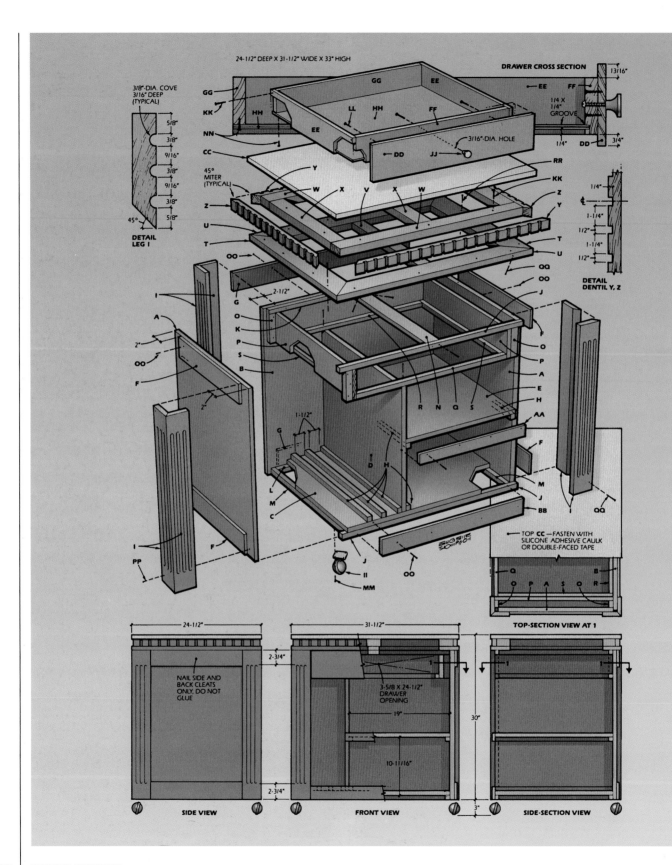

24-1/2" DEEP X 31-1/2" WIDE X 33" HIGH

DRAWER CROSS SECTION

13/16"

3/8"-DIA. COVE
3/16" DEEP
(TYPICAL)

5/8"
3/8"
9/16"
3/8"
9/16"
3/8"
5/8"

45°

DETAIL
LEG I

45° MITER
(TYPICAL)

GG

KK

NN

CC

EE

LL

HH

HH

FF

EE

FF

1/4 X 1/4"
GROOVE

3/16"-DIA. HOLE

JJ

DD

DD

1/4"

3/4"

RR

KK

Z

Y

T

U

QQ

OO

1/4"

1-1/4"

1/2"

1-1/4"

1/2"

DETAIL
DENTIL Y, Z

Y

W

X

V

X

W

Z

U

T

OO

G

O

K

P

S

B

I

A

2"

OO

F

2"

1-1/2"

G

L

M

C

D

H

J

II

MM

OO

2-1/2"

J

O

F

O

P

A

E

H

AA

F

M

J

BB

I

QQ

F

I

PP

R

N

Q

S

TOP CC —FASTEN WITH
SILICONE ADHESIVE CAULK
OR DOUBLE-FACED TAPE

Q

O

P

A

S

O

R

B

R

TOP-SECTION VIEW AT 1

24-1/2"

NAIL SIDE AND
BACK CLEATS
ONLY, DO NOT
GLUE

SIDE VIEW

31-1/2"

2-3/4"

3-5/8 X 24-1/2"
DRAWER
OPENING

19"

10-11/16"

30"

2-3/4"

3"

FRONT VIEW

SIDE-SECTION VIEW

The No. 2 common pine construction of our baking cart means you won't have to search far afield for material. The simplified joinery only requires the most common power and hand tools, pipe clamps, and a table saw.

Making the Panels

The sides, back, bottom, shelf, and partition are all made by gluing 1x4 stock edge to edge. Crosscut the stock for each panel slightly oversize. Apply glue and use pipe clamps above and below the panel to help distribute the pressure evenly (**Fig. 1**). Make sure the panel is flat when clamped up. After the glue has cured, scrape off any excess and glue up the remaining panels in the same way.

Use a belt sander to smooth the panel surfaces (**Fig. 2**). Secure each piece to your workbench with clamps or between bench dogs for this operation. You can also toenail the panels to your worktable. Use small finishing nails placed at the panel ends and set below the surface. Keep the sander moving at all times to avoid gouging the panel, and use minimal pressure.

Next, mark the finished panel dimensions on each piece and lay out the cutting lines. Double check that the layouts are square and to exact size. Clamp a straightedge to the panels for guiding your circular saw (**Fig. 3**).

Rip 1x4 stock to ½ in. thick x 3 in. wide for the side and back cleats. Crosscut to length and secure to the panels with 3d finishing nails (**Fig. 4**). To avoid humidity changes possibly cracking or warping the panels, don't use glue.

The Fluted Legs

Crosscut the 1x4 leg stock to exact length. Then construct a jig to hold the pieces for routing the flutes. Cut a piece of ¾-in.-thick stock to 8 in. wide x 34 in. long for the jig base. Secure a piece of scrap stock cut to the same length as the legs to one side of the jig base (**Fig. 5**). Then attach two end blocks to the base so the leg stock will be supported on three sides. Fasten stop blocks to the end pieces for limiting the travel of your router. These are positioned so the flutes begin 2¾ in. in from each end. The spacing of the stop blocks is determined by the size of your router base.

Install a ⅜-in.-dia. corebox bit in your router and adjust the depth of cut to 3/16 in. Adjust the router edge guide attachment to cut the center flute. After this flute has been cut on each leg piece, adjust the guide to cut an outer flute. When you have completed this cut on all pieces, simply reverse the stock for the third flute.

Materials List

Key	No.	Size and description (use)
A	2	¾ x 21½ x 27¼" pine (sides)
B	1	¾ x 27¼ x 29½" pine (back)
C	1	¾ x 22¼ x 28½" pine (bottom)
D	1	¾ x 22¼ x 20⅝" pine (partition)
E	1	¾ x 19 x 22¼" pine (shelf)
F	4	½ x 3 x 17½" pine (side cleat)
G	2	½ x 3 x 24½" pine (back cleat)
H	6	¾ x ¾ x 22¼" pine (support strip)
I	8	¾ x 3½ x 27¼" pine (leg)
J	2	¾ x ¾ x 30" pine (front strip)
K	1	¾ x ¾ x 28½" pine (top back strip)
L	1	¾ x ¾ x 27" pine (back strip)
M	2	¾ x ¾ x 21½" pine (side strip)
N	1	¾ x 2 x 20¾" pine (spreader)
O	4	¾ x 1¼ x 4⅜" pine (block)
P	2	¾ x 4⅜ x 22¼" pine (side guide)
Q	1	¾ x ¾ x 24½" pine (drawer support)
R	1	¾ x ¾ x 23" pine (drawer support)
S	2	¾ x ¾ x 21½" pine (drawer support)
T	2	¾ x 3½ x 24½" pine (short cap)
U	2	¾ x 3½ x 31½" pine (long cap)
V	1	¾ x 3½ x 17½" pine (cap filler)
W	2	1¼ x 2½ x 29½" pine (blocking)
X	3	1¼ x 2½ x 17½" pine (blocking)
Y	2	¾ x 1¼ x 31" pine (long dentil)
Z	2	¾ x 1¼ x 24" pine (short dentil)
AA	1	½ x 1½ x 17¾" pine (trim)
BB	1	½ x 2¼ x 14½" pine (trim)
CC	1	¾ x 14½ x 34½" Corian (top)
DD	1	½ x 5 1/16 x 24⅜" pine (drawer face)
EE	2	¾ x 3½ x 22¼" pine (drawer side)
FF	1	¾ x 3½ x 22⅞" pine (drawer front)
GG	1	¾ x 3 x 22⅞" pine (drawer back)
HH	1	¼ x 21¾ x 23⅜" plywood (bottom)
II	4	2¼-in. resilient tread casters
JJ	1	drawer pull
KK	20	2" No. 8 fh screws
LL	4	1" No. 10 fh screws
MM	16	1¼" No. 8 fh screws
NN	4	⅝" No. 3 rh screws
OO	as reqd.	1" wire brads
PP	as reqd.	3d finish nails
QQ	as reqd.	4d finish nails
RR	as reqd.	6d finish nails

Misc.: 120- and 220-grit sandpaper; glue; 4/0 steel wool; polyurethane varnish; mineral spirits; silicone adhesive caulk.

Fig. 1 *Edge-glue 1x4 boards for the panels. Alternate clamps above and below. Be sure the panels lie flat when the clamps are tightened.*

Fig. 2 *After glue has cured, scrape off excess and belt-sand the panels smooth. Keep the sander moving with even pressure.*

Fig. 3 *Mark the panels to exact size for cutting. Clamp each panel to the worktable and use a straight board to guide the saw.*

Fig. 4 *Select the best face of the side and back panels and nail the cleats in place. To avoid cracking or warping of the panel, don't use glue.*

Fig. 5 *The leg fluting jig holds the leg pieces in place and limits router travel. Use a ³⁄₈-in.-dia. corebox bit and router edge guide.*

Fig. 6 *After ripping a 45° bevel on one edge of each leg piece, apply glue and nail pairs together with 4d finishing nails.*

Rip a 45° bevel along one edge of each leg piece. Assemble the legs by first placing one piece in your vise with the inner edge of the bevel in line with the benchtop. Partially drive several 4d finishing nails in the beveled edge of the adjoining piece so their points poke through. Apply glue and press the second piece in place on the first (**Fig. 6**). Drive the nails, set the leg aside to dry, and complete the remaining legs in the same manner.

Assembling the Case

Attach two legs to the back with glue and 3d finishing nails. Attach the front legs to the sides in the same manner and then join the sides to the rear legs (**Fig. 7**). Tie the cart front together by attaching the ¾-in.-sq. strips across the front at the top and bottom (**Fig. 8**). Then install the ledger strips around the inside bottom edges of the case for supporting the bottom and attach the strip at the top edge of the back (**Fig. 9**). Toenail the spreader to the rear top strip and secure it at the front by nailing through the front strip.

Next, install the bottom to the bottom ledger strips with glue and 3d finishing nails. Cut and install the corner blocks and attach the drawer side guides to the blocks with glue and 4d finishing nails (**Fig. 10**). Attach the drawer support strips to the drawer side guides. Then install the front and rear drawer supports.

The ¾-in.-sq. strips on the cart bottom serve as dividers for tray storage and for holding the partition. After attaching these strips, slide the partition in place (**Figs. 11 and 12**). Secure it by nailing through the cart bottom and through the drawer support strips. Then, install the shelf cleats and shelf.

Constructing the Top

Use a miter box to cut the 1x4 stock for the cap to exact length and secure the pieces to the cart with 6d finishing nails (**Fig. 13**). Use glue on the miter joints and nail through each joint to ensure a tight fit. Then cut and install the cap spacer over the center spreader as shown in the drawing.

Rip 2x3 stock to 1¼ in. thick x 2½ in. wide for the top blocking. Cut each piece to length and clamp in place on the cart (**Fig. 14**). Secure the blocking to the assembly with 2-in. No. 8 fh screws.

To make the dentil molding, first crosscut a length of 1x12 stock to at least 36 in. long. Install a ½-in.-dia. straight bit in your router and cut ¼-in.-deep dadoes across the face of the board leaving a 1¼-in. space between each dado (**Fig. 15**). Make sure that the workpiece is clamped firmly to the bench and use a straightedge clamped to the stock to guide your router. All four lengths of dentil molding are ripped from this board. Cut at least 17 dadoes across the 1x12 stock to accommodate the long front and rear pieces.

Rip the dentil molding to 1¼ in. wide (**Fig. 16**). Use a miter box to cut each piece to length and attach to the top blocking with 4d finishing nails and glue.

Fig. 7 *Use glue and 4d finishing nails to secure the legs to the back. Attach one leg to each side, then glue and nail the sides to the rear legs.*

Fig. 8 *After nailing ¾-in.-sq. strips across the cart front, nail strips around the bottom edge of the sides and back to support the bottom panel.*

Fig. 9 *Glue and nail the ¾-in.-sq. strip to the upper back edge. Then secure the corner blocks with 3d finishing nails and glue.*

Fig. 10 *Cut the drawer guides to size and attach them to the corner blocks. Then install the drawer support strips to the sides, back, and front.*

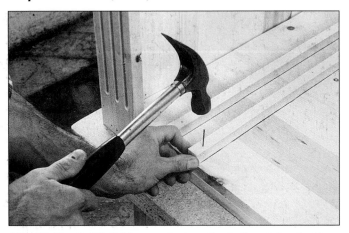

Fig. 11 *Use 3d finishing nails to attach the strips to the cart bottom. These act as spacers for holding trays and the case partition.*

Fig. 12 *Slide the partition in and nail up through bottom. Secure the top edge by nailing through the front and rear drawer supports.*

Cut and apply the trim strips as shown in the drawing. Turn the cart upside down, then mark and bore pilot holes for screwing the casters in place. Install the casters with 1¼-in. No. 8 fh screws.

Making the Drawer

Cut all parts for the drawer to finished dimension. Use a dado blade mounted in the table saw to cut the grooves in the drawer sides and front that contain the drawer bottom (**Fig. 17**). Join the sides, front, and back with 2-in. No. 8 fh screws. Slide the bottom in place, check that the drawer is square, and screw the bottom to the drawer back with ⅝-in. No. 3 rh screws (**Fig. 18**).

Cut the drawer face to size and attach it to the drawer front with 1-in. No. 10 fh screws. Bore the hole for the drawer pull and install.

Finishing the Cart

Set all nails and fill. Then sand the entire cart with 120- and then 220-grit sandpaper. For a durable natural finish, apply three coats of polyurethane varnish, thinning the first coat 20 percent with mineral spirits. Sand lightly and dust off between coats. After the final coat has dried, rub the cart with 4/0 steel wool for a satin finish.

We topped off our baking cart with a ¾-in.-thick piece of Corian for attractiveness and durability. This material is available at building suppliers and through kitchen and bathroom cabinet showrooms. You can usually get it cut to size; otherwise you will need to use a router with a straight bit to cut it to finished size. Attach the Corian to the cart top with silicone adhesive caulk for a permanent installation. For a top that can be removed at a later date, use double-sided tape.

Other options for the top include plastic laminate glued to a particleboard or plywood panel, or a slab of marble or granite for that authentic pastry-rolling surface.

MATERIAL*Matters*

Easy as Pie
Although this is a book about woodworking, we can't resist imparting a little kitchen wisdom. For this project, we suggest a Corian top for rolling pastry. But before you spend the money, you might try a cheaper option: the humble pastry cloth, which you can find anywhere kitchen supplies are sold. Simply place the cloth on your cart or countertop, dust its surface with flour, and roll out your pie crust. You'll probably be pleasantly surprised with how well it works.

Fig. 13 *After cutting the 1x4 cap pieces to length, nail them in place on the cart. Use glue and nail through each joint with finishing nails.*

Fig. 14 *Cut the 1³/₄-in.-thick spacer blocking to length and clamp it in place. Secure it to the cap assembly with 2-in. No. 8 fh screws.*

Fig. 15 *Begin the dentil molding by routing ¹/₂-in.-wide dadoes across 1x12 stock. The board clamped to the work guides the router.*

Fig. 16 *Set the table saw fence to rip 1¹/₄-in.-wide strips of dentil molding. Miter the pieces and install them with finishing nails and glue.*

Fig. 17 *After cutting the drawer components to size, cut a ¹/₄ x ¹/₄-in. groove in the sides and front with a dado blade mounted in the table saw.*

Fig. 18 *Screw the sides, front, and back together and slide the bottom in. Secure the bottom to the back with ⁵/₈-in. No. 3 rh screws.*

Vanity Fair

Solid cabinetwork and attention to detail place this vanity head and shoulders above the rest.

When it comes to fine home woodworking, the bathroom is probably the last place in your house you think of. However, there's no reason to ignore it. With a few free weekends, you can produce cabinetry that's better than just about anything you can buy in stores.

Our bathroom vanity features solid oak and oak-veneer plywood construction, louvered doors, and an easy-to-install plastic laminate countertop. The simple but sturdy drawers are mounted on readily available drawer tracks, and the handsome louvered doors are made with a router jig that we'll show you how to build.

*Key*POINTS

TIME
Prep Time .... **10 hours**
Shop Time .... **20 hours**
Assembly Time .... **24 hours**

EFFORT
Skill Level .... **intermediate**

COST / BENEFITS
Expense: **moderate**
• You don't have to settle for what's commercially available—the basic construction details are **easily modified** to suit your family's needs.

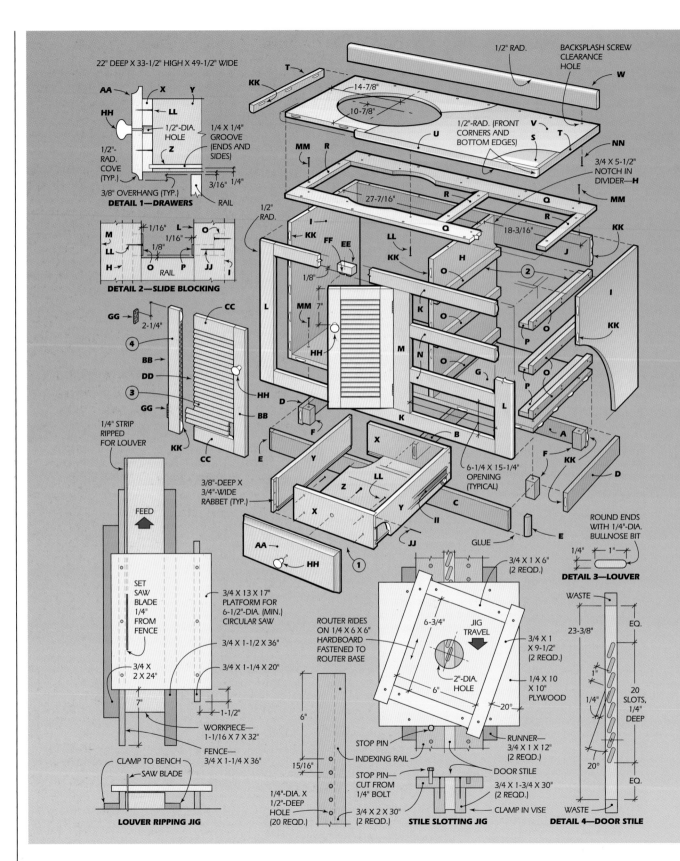

22" DEEP X 33-1/2" HIGH X 49-1/2" WIDE

AA
X
Y
HH
LL
1/2"-DIA. HOLE
1/4 X 1/4" GROOVE (ENDS AND SIDES)
1/2"-RAD. COVE (TYP.)
Z
3/16" 1/4"
3/8" OVERHANG (TYP.)
RAIL

DETAIL 1—DRAWERS

1/16"
L
M
LL
1/16"
1/8"
O
H
O
RAIL
P
JJ
I

DETAIL 2—SLIDE BLOCKING

GG
2-1/4"
CC
4
BB
DD
3
GG
HH
BB
KK
CC
E
D

1/4" STRIP RIPPED FOR LOUVER

3/8"-DEEP X 3/4"-WIDE RABBET (TYP.)

FEED

SET SAW BLADE 1/4" FROM FENCE

3/4 X 2 X 24"

3/4 X 13 X 17" PLATFORM FOR 6-1/2"-DIA. (MIN.) CIRCULAR SAW

3/4 X 1-1/2 X 36"

3/4 X 1-1/4 X 20"

7"

1-1/2"

WORKPIECE— 1-1/16 X 7 X 32"

FENCE— 3/4 X 1-1/4 X 36"

CLAMP TO BENCH
SAW BLADE

LOUVER RIPPING JIG

T
KK
14-7/8"
10-7/8"
1/2" RAD.
BACKSPLASH SCREW CLEARANCE HOLE
W
1/2"-RAD. (FRONT CORNERS AND BOTTOM EDGES)
U
V
S
T
NN
3/4 X 5-1/2" NOTCH IN DIVIDER—H
MM

R
I
KK
FF
EE
LL
KK
H
O
27-7/16"
R
Q
R
18-3/16"
J
KK
2

1/2" RAD.
MM
L
MM
7"
HH
K
O
M
N
O
G
K
L
B
A
F
KK
D

I
KK
O
P
O
P

6-1/4 X 15-1/4" OPENING (TYPICAL)

F
E
GLUE

X
Y
LL
Z
X
Y
C
II
AA
HH
JJ
1

ROUND ENDS WITH 1/4"-DIA. BULLNOSE BIT
1/4" 1"

DETAIL 3—LOUVER

3/4 X 1 X 6" (2 REQD.)

ROUTER RIDES ON 1/4 X 6 X 6" HARDBOARD FASTENED TO ROUTER BASE

6-3/4"
JIG TRAVEL
2"-DIA. HOLE
6"
20°

3/4 X 1 X 9-1/2" (2 REQD.)

1/4 X 10 X 10" PLYWOOD

RUNNER— 3/4 X 1 X 12" (2 REQD.)

6"
15/16"

STOP PIN

INDEXING RAIL

STOP PIN CUT FROM 1/4" BOLT

DOOR STILE

3/4 X 1-3/4 X 30" (2 REQD.)

CLAMP IN VISE

1/4"-DIA. X 1/2"-DEEP HOLE (20 REQD.)

3/4 X 2 X 30" (2 REQD.)

STILE SLOTTING JIG

WASTE
23-3/8"
1"
1/4"
20°
WASTE

EQ.
20 SLOTS, 1/4" DEEP
EQ.

DETAIL 4—DOOR STILE

Case Construction

Begin by marking the cutting lines for the case sides, divider, floor, and base pieces on the back face of an oak plywood panel. Install a smooth-cutting plywood blade in your circular saw and tack a wooden straightedge in place to act as a guide.

Switch to a combination blade to cut the solid stock to size for the face frames, door frames, and drawer fronts. Note that the door stiles are cut 6 in. longer than the finished length. Use a T square cutting guide to ensure square crosscuts. When ripping the relatively narrow rails and stiles, tape the workpiece to a plywood panel, edge to edge. Then clamp a straightedge ripping guide to the plywood and make the cut. Rip the oak pieces slightly oversize, and smooth the edges with a hand plane. When the oak case pieces are done, cut the pine rear ledger to size. Code each panel and board to indicate adjoining members so you won't get the parts mixed up. Then

Fig. 1 *Place both the joiner and the work on a flat surface. Use a plate joiner to cut the plate slots for joining the case pieces.*

Fig. 2 *To cut centered slots in the face frame pieces, place the oak components in a jig that also holds the joiner in position.*

Materials List

Key	No.	Size and description (use)
A	1	$^3/_4$ x $3^1/_2$ x $44^7/_8$" pine (rear base)
B	1	$^3/_4$ x $3^1/_2$ x $17^3/_4$" pine (center base)
C	1	$^3/_4$ x $3^1/_2$ x $44^7/_8$" plywood (front base)
D	2	$^3/_4$ x $3^1/_2$ x $18^1/_2$" plywood (side base)
E	2	$^3/_4$ x $^3/_4$ x $3^1/_2$" oak (corner)
F	4	$1^1/_2$ x $1^1/_2$ x $3^1/_2$" pine (corner cleat)
G	1	$^3/_4$ x $20^1/_2$ x $46^3/_8$" plywood (bottom)
H	1	$^3/_4$ x $20^1/_2$ x $27^3/_4$" plywood (divider)
I	2	$^3/_4$ x $20^1/_2$ x $28^1/_2$" plywood (side)
J	1	$^3/_4$ x $5^1/_2$ x $46^3/_8$" pine (ledger)
K	2	$^3/_4$ x $2^1/_2$ x $41^7/_8$" oak (cabinet rail)
L	2	$^3/_4$ x 3 x $28^1/_2$" oak (cabinet stile)
M	1	$^3/_4$ x 3 x $23^1/_2$" oak (divider stile)
N	2	$^3/_4$ x $2^3/_8$ x $15^1/_4$" oak (drawer rail)
O	6	$^3/_4$ x $1^1/_2$ x $20^1/_2$" pine (track blocking)
P	3	$^3/_4$ x $1^9/_{16}$ x $20^1/_2$" pine (track blocking)
Q	2	$^3/_4$ x $3^1/_2$ x $47^7/_8$" pine (cleat)
R	3	$^3/_4$ x $1^1/_2$ x $14^1/_4$" pine (cleat)
S	1	$^3/_4$ x $21^5/_{16}$ x 48" particleboard (countertop)
T	2	$^3/_4$ x $1^1/_2$ x $21^5/_{16}$" oak (trim)
U	1	$^3/_4$ x $1^1/_2$ x $49^1/_2$" oak (trim)
V	1	$^3/_4$ x $22^1/_{16}$ x $49^1/_2$" laminate (surface)

Key	No.	Size and description (use)
W	1	$^3/_4$ x $3^1/_2$ x $49^1/_2$" oak (backsplash)
X	6	$^3/_4$ x $5^1/_2$ x $13^3/_8$" pine (drawer end)
Y	6	$^3/_4$ x $5^1/_2$ x 20" pine (drawer side)
Z	3	$^1/_4$ x $13^1/_8$ x 19" plywood (bottom)
AA	3	$^3/_4$ x 7 x 16" oak (drawer front)
BB*	4	$^3/_4$ x $2^1/_4$ x $23^3/_8$" oak (door stile)
CC	4	$^3/_4$ x $2^1/_4$ x $7^3/_{16}$" oak (door rail)
DD	40	$^1/_4$ x 1 x $7^9/_{16}$" oak (louver)
EE	1	$1^1/_2$ x $1^1/_2$ x $4^1/_2$" pine (stop block)
FF	2	magnetic catches
GG	2 pr.	hinges
HH	5	drawer/door pulls
II	3	20" side-mount drawer track sets
JJ	as reqd.	$1^1/_2$" finish nails
KK	as reqd.	No. 0 plates
LL	as reqd.	$1^1/_4$" No. 8 fh screws
MM	as reqd.	$1^1/_2$" No. 8 fh screws
NN	as reqd.	2" No. 8 fh screws

Misc.: Glue; sandpaper; colonial maple stain; clear semigloss polycrylic polyurethane finish.

* Finished size shown, cut 6" oversize in length.

Fig. 3 *After marking for frame-to-case plates, lay the frame on the bench to cut the slots. Use a guide strip to locate the divider-stile slots.*

Fig. 4 *Cut the notch for the rear ledger on the rear upper corner of the divider. Then, apply glue and secure the divider to the floor.*

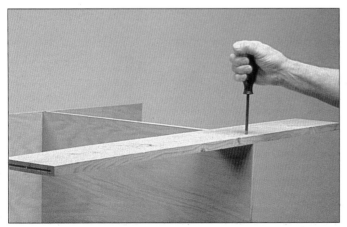

Fig. 5 *After the floor and divider have been joined with plates, glue and screw the pine rear ledger to the cabinet divider.*

butt adjacent members and mark the joining plate locations on each pair of pieces. On face frame pieces and adjoining plywood parts, mark the plate locations on the two end stiles only—you will mark the floor and divider plate slots after the frame and case have been assembled.

To cut the slots, place the workpiece and plate joiner on a flat surface. Be sure to place all workpieces finish-side down to avoid misalignment due to stock thickness variations (**Fig. 1**).

To cut the slots in the ends of the face frame members, construct a jig to center the joiner relative to the work. Place a 1x2 on each edge of the workpiece. Center your plate joiner across the ends of the three pieces, and mark the joiner base width on the 1x2s. Then notch the ends of the 1x2s at the marks, return them to the workpiece, and tack a small piece of ¼-in. plywood to the 1x2s that straddle the work (**Fig. 2**).

The face frame is assembled in two stages. First, apply glue to the plate slots in the divider stile, drawer rails, right end stile, and the corresponding slots in the top and bottom long rails. Don't apply glue to join the left stile to the top and bottom rails. Then install plates in all the slots and assemble the frame. Clamp the top and bottom rails to the divider stile. Follow this by clamping across to tighten the right end stile joints and the drawer rail joints. Double check that the frame is aligned properly. When the glue has dried, join the left stile to the top and bottom rails with glue and clamps.

To locate the plate slots for joining the face frame to the cabinet, first insert dry plates in the four cabinet panels and temporarily assemble the sides, floor, and divider. Align the face frame over the case panels and mark the centerlines for all the slots. To cut the divider-stile slots, clamp a strip to the stile's rear face to provide a guide for the joiner (**Fig. 3**).

Before assembling the case, use a sabre saw to cut the notch in the divider for the rear ledger (**Fig. 4**). Then apply glue to the divider and floor slots and draw the pieces together with screws. Attach the rear ledger with screws and glue (**Fig. 5**).

Apply glue to the slots for joining the case sides to the floor, and assemble. Insert dry plates into the face frame slots and temporarily add the frame to keep the assembly square. After the glue has dried, glue the face frame to the case (**Fig. 6**).

Then, sand the entire assembly—a random-orbit sander is best for the face frame—and round the case corners with a router and ½-in.-rad. rounding-over bit (**Fig. 7**).

Doors and Drawers

To build the door-stile slotting jig, first make the indexing rails, as shown in the drawing. Use a doweling jig to bore ¼-in.-dia. holes, ½ in. deep and spaced ¹⁵/₁₆ in. apart along the centerline of each ¾ x 2 x 30-in. strip (**Fig. 8**).

Next, build the router carriage. Because the two door stiles are mirror images of the other two, you'll need to rebuild the carriage to angle the cuts in the opposite way after the first two stiles are slotted. At the center of the 10-in.-sq. carriage base, draw centerlines angled at 20° and cut the 2-in.-dia. hole. Add

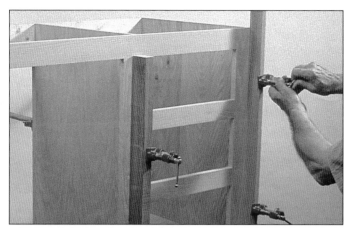

Fig. 6 *After the glue has dried on the case assembly, glue the face frame in place and clamp. Use cauls to distribute pressure.*

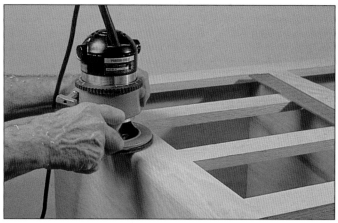

Fig. 7 *Use a router and ¹⁄₂-in.-rad. rounding-over bit to trim the case corners. Sand the entire case and frame smooth.*

Fig. 8 *Begin the door-stile slotting jig by making the indexing rails. Bore ¹⁄₄-in. holes spaced ¹⁵⁄₁₆ in. apart along the centerlines.*

Fig. 9 *Clamp the work between the rails and butt the jig against the stop pin. Move the pin after each slot. Reverse the jig after two stiles have been cut.*

the guide frame pieces centered around the 20° centerlines. Attach the runners, spacing them so a stile with an indexing rail on each side will be centered beneath the carriage.

Center and attach a 6 x 6-in. hardboard base to your router. On the first stile, mark the approximate position of the first slot. Clamp the stile between the indexing rails, and place the carriage over it so the carriage is centered at the slot mark. Insert a ¹⁄₄-in.-bolt stop pin in the nearest hole on the indexing rail, and butt the carriage against the pin. To ensure that the jig won't slip, tack a small nail into the indexing rail at the opposite end of the carriage.

With a ¹⁄₄-in. straight bit installed, place the router in the carriage frame, tilt it so the bit doesn't contact the work, and turn on the router. Lower the bit and guide the router in the frame to make the slot. Then move the stop pin and repeat the process. After 20 slots have been cut in two of the stiles, reverse the guide frame and complete the other stiles (**Fig. 9**).

Fig. 10 *Align the rails with the louver slots on the stiles. After marking the work, cut the stiles to length and cut joining plate slots.*

Cut all stiles to length so that the slots are aligned, and cut the slots for the door plate joints (**Fig. 10**).

It's best to rip the louvers on a table saw. If you don't have one, you can use a circular saw. First, build the louver ripping jig shown in the drawing. Mount this to a piece of hardboard, and secure it to your bench with clamps (**Fig. 11**). To use this jig, have a helper stand at the out-feed side of the saw. When most of the cut is made, have your helper draw the workpiece through. Then smooth the louver faces with a cabinet scraper.

Mount a ⅛-in.-rad. half-round bit in a router table, and adjust the fence so that when both edges are rounded, the louver width is 1 in. (**Fig. 12**). Make test cuts on scrap first. Next, round the edges of the oak stock.

Stain and finish the louvers. Then glue two rails to one stile of each door. When the glue is dry, apply slow-setting hide glue to the remaining plate joints of one door and install the louvers in a stile. As you bring the frame together, shift each

louver so it rests in slots on both sides (**Fig. 13**). Then, clamp and repeat the process on the other door.

Cut 1x6 pine to size for the drawer sides and ends. Rout the end rabbets on the sides and the groove for the drawer bottom. Assemble the drawers with glue and finishing nails.

Use a ¾-in.-rad. cove bit to trim the drawer fronts (**Fig. 14**). Install the drawer blocking and tracks. To align the fronts, first drive screws from inside each drawer so the points just protrude. Then use cleats clamped below each front to hold them in place. Press the fronts toward the drawer to transfer the screw locations (**Fig. 15**). Finally, install the doors (**Fig. 16**).

Final Steps

Cut the oak backsplash and particleboard countertop to size. Trace the sink pattern on the top panel, and use a sabre saw to make the cutout (**Fig. 17**). Cut the oak trim pieces to size, join them to the panel with plates, and round their edges with a ½-in.-rad. bit. Attach the countertop cleats and spacers to the cabinet. Place the top in position and bore the screw pilot holes from underneath. Remove the top, and bore the pilot holes for attaching the backsplash. Round the backsplash, as shown.

Cut the laminate oversize, and apply contact cement to it and the top panel. Place spacer strips on the countertop, and position the laminate on the strips. Pull out the strips one at a time as you press the laminate in place. Use a router and flush-trimming bit to trim the excess laminate and the sink cutout (**Fig. 18**). Slightly bevel the outside edges with a bevel-trimming bit or a flat smooth mill file.

To build the cabinet base, attach the oak plywood members to the corner cleats. Then add the quarter-round oak corners.

We finished the exterior, base, and backsplash with colonial maple stain followed by three coats of clear semigloss polycrylic finish. Protect the interior panels with one coat of finish. Before installing the backsplash and sink, apply a bead of silicone caulk to the mating surfaces (**Fig. 19**).

Fig. 11 *If you don't have a table saw, mount a circular saw on the jig and pass the work underneath. Have a helper at the out-feed side.*

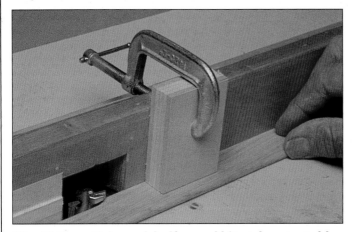

Fig. 12 *Use a ⅛-in.-rad. half-round bit and router table to cut the louver edges. Set the fence to produce a finished 1-in. louver width.*

Fig. 13 *Assemble the frame with louvers installed in one side. Draw the stiles together and lift the louvers into opposite slots.*

Fig. 14 *Use a router and ¾-in.-rad. cove bit to trim the drawer fronts. Scrap pieces clamped to the edges will prevent splitting.*

Fig. 15 *Clamp a strip below each drawer opening to help position the drawer fronts. Use partially driven screws to mark the pilot holes.*

Fig. 16 *Position the louvered doors and mark the screw pilot holes for the hinges. Then install the doors and check for a good fit.*

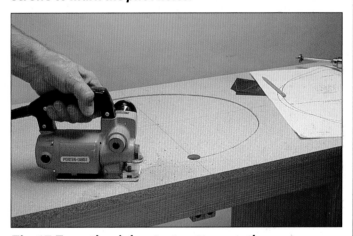

Fig. 17 *Trace the sink cutout pattern on the particleboard top panel. Then follow the outline with a sabre saw to make the cut.*

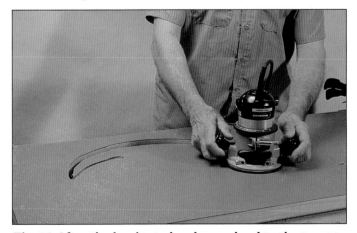

Fig. 18 *After the laminate has been glued to the top, bore a starter hole and rout the cutout with a flush-trimming bit.*

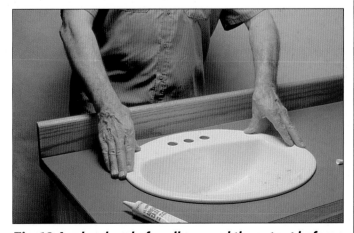

Fig. 19 *Apply a bead of caulk around the cutout before installing the sink. Also apply caulk under the oak backsplash before securing.*

Top Gun

Proudly display your long arms and pistols in this well-crafted cherry cabinet.

Many firearms are either laid flat under a bed, stood in a closet, or buried in a drawer. Others are simply laid across bland-looking racks. It doesn't have to be that way. Firearms should be stored in a convenient and secure place that allows us to admire and handle them or easily remove them for hunting or target practice. We think this gun cabinet succeeds on all counts. Long arms are stood in the upper case, pistols displayed in the lower case. Supplies and ammunition may be stored in the two drawers below. With security in mind, the upper and lower doors are equipped with locks, as are the drawers.

*Key*POINTS

TIME
Prep Time	8 hours
Shop Time	20 hours
Assembly Time	20 hours

EFFORT
Skill Level	expert

COST / BENEFITS
Expense: **expensive**
- The moldings, hardware, and proportions suggest **refinement, not merely storage.**
- **Low-voltage halogen lamps** shine the spotlight on your most prized firearms.

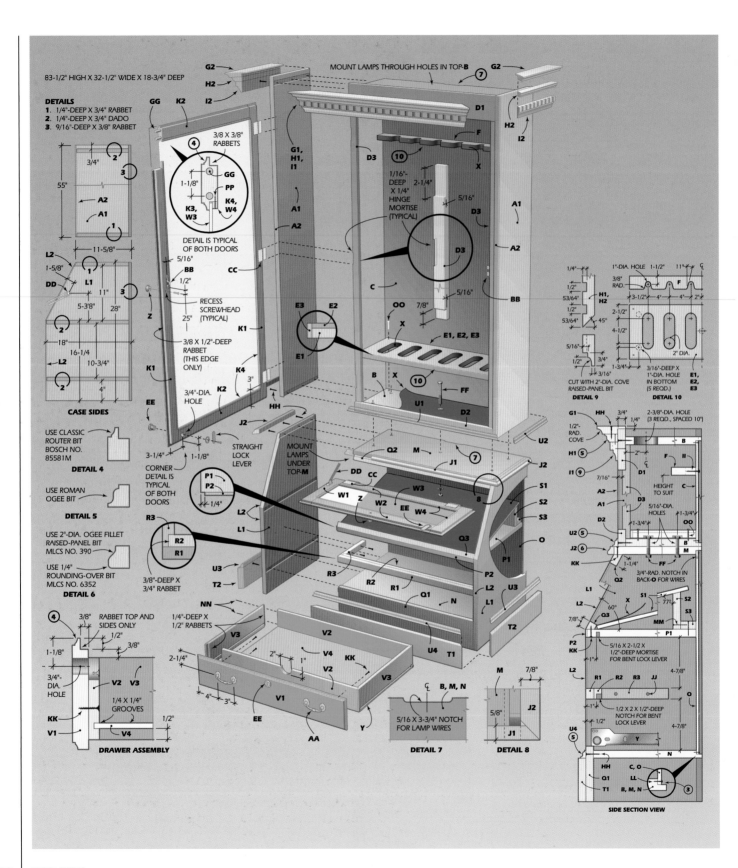

83-1/2" HIGH X 32-1/2" WIDE X 18-3/4" DEEP

MOUNT LAMPS THROUGH HOLES IN TOP-**B**

DETAILS
1. 1/4"-DEEP X 3/4" RABBET
2. 1/4"-DEEP X 3/4" DADO
3. 9/16"-DEEP X 3/8" RABBET

3/8 X 3/8" RABBETS

1-1/8"

DETAIL IS TYPICAL OF BOTH DOORS

5/16"

1/2"

RECESS SCREWHEAD (TYPICAL)

3/8 X 1/2"-DEEP RABBET (THIS EDGE ONLY)

3/4"-DIA. HOLE

CASE SIDES

55"

11-5/8"

1-5/8"

11"

5-3/8"   28"

18"

16-1/4

10-3/4"

4"

USE CLASSIC ROUTER BIT BOSCH NO. 85581M

DETAIL 4

USE ROMAN OGEE BIT

DETAIL 5

USE 2"-DIA. OGEE FILLET RAISED-PANEL BIT MLCS NO. 390

USE 1/4" ROUNDING-OVER BIT MLCS NO. 6352

DETAIL 6

3/8 X 3/4 RABBET TOP AND SIDES ONLY

1/2"

3/8"

1-1/8"

3/4"-DIA. HOLE

1/4 X 1/4" GROOVES

1/2"

DRAWER ASSEMBLY

CORNER DETAIL IS TYPICAL OF BOTH DOORS

3-1/4"   1-1/8"

STRAIGHT LOCK LEVER

1/4"

3/8"-DEEP X 3/4" RABBET

MOUNT LAMPS UNDER TOP-**M**

NN

1/4"-DEEP X 1/2" RABBETS

2-1/4"

2"

1"

4"   3"

1/16"-DEEP X 1/4" HINGE MORTISE (TYPICAL)

2-1/4"

5/16"

7/8"

HEIGHT TO SUIT

5/16 X 3-3/4" NOTCH FOR LAMP WIRES

DETAIL 7

M   7/8"

5/8"

DETAIL 8

1/4"

1/2"

53/64"

1/2"

53/64"

45°

5/16"

1/2"   3/4"

CUT WITH 2"-DIA. COVE RAISED-PANEL BIT

DETAIL 9

1"-DIA. HOLE   1-1/2"   11°

3/8" RAD.

3-1/2"   4"   4"   2"

2-1/2"

4-1/2"

2" DIA.

1-3/4"

3/16"-DEEP X 1"-DIA. HOLE IN BOTTOM (5 REQD.)

DETAIL 10

1/2"-RAD. COVE

3/4"

2-3/8"-DIA. HOLE (3 REQD., SPACED 10")

2"

7/16"

1-3/4"

5/16"-DIA. HOLES

1-3/4"

1-1/4"

3/4"-RAD. NOTCH IN BACK-**O** FOR WIRES

60°

77°

5/16 X 2-1/2 X 1/2"-DEEP MORTISE FOR BENT LOCK LEVER

1"

1"

1/2 X 2 X 1/2"-DEEP NOTCH FOR BENT LOCK LEVER

4-7/8"

4-7/8"

1/2"

SIDE SECTION VIEW

A gun cabinet can be an eye-catching piece of furniture, and we've designed this piece to be as elegant as anything else you would want to build. It's constructed of cherry plywood and solid cherry, and the glazing is impact-resistant acrylic sheet.

As projects go, this gun cabinet requires rather advanced skills. If you've already built a cabinet of one type or another, then it should be well within your capability. If you've never built a cabinet, study the plans and materials list carefully before beginning the project.

Case Construction

The gun cabinet is really two separate cases built from cherry plywood. To make each case look like it is built from solid lumber, edge bands are glued to the front edge of each case panel. The drawer fronts and door frames are solid cherry.

Materials List

Key	No.	Size and description (use)
A1	2	3/4 x 11 7/16 x 55" cherry plywood (side)
A2	2	3/16 x 3/4 x 55" cherry (edge band)
B	2	3/4 x 10 7/8 x 27 1/2" cherry plywood (top/bottom)
C	1	1/4 x 27 3/4 x 53 1/2" cherry plywood (back)
D1	1	3/4 x 3 3/8 x 27" cherry (rail)
D2	1	3/4 x 1 5/8 x 27" cherry (rail)
D3	2	3/4 x 1 x 52 3/4" cherry (stiffener)
E1	1	1/2 x 9 7/16 x 27" plywood (butt rest)
E2	1	1/4 x 9 7/16 x 27" plywood (butt rest)
E3	1	3/16 x 3/4 x 27" cherry (edge band)
F	1	3/4 x 2 1/2 x 27" cherry (barrel rest)
G1	1	3/4 x 2 3/4 x 32 1/2" cherry (molding)
G2	2	3/4 x 2 3/4 x 13 5/8" cherry (molding)
H1	1	3/4 x 1 1/4 x 31" cherry (molding)
H2	2	3/4 x 1 1/4 x 12 7/8" cherry (molding)
I1	1	3/4 x 1 3/4 x 30" cherry (molding)
I2	2	3/4 x 1 3/4 x 12 3/8" cherry (molding)
J1	1	5/8 x 3/4 x 30 1/4" cherry (molding)
J2	2	3/4 x 7/8 x 12 5/8" cherry (molding)
K1	2	3/4 x 2 3/8 x 50 1/8" cherry (stile)
K2	2	3/4 x 2 3/8 x 22 7/8" cherry (rail)
K3	1	1/8 x 23 1/2 x 46" acrylic sheet
K4	1	1/4 x 5/16 x 144" cherry (retainer)
L1	2	3/4 x 17 13/16 x 28" cherry plywood (side)
L2	1	3/16 x 3/4 x 120" cherry (edge band)
M	1	3/4 x 12 x 27" cherry plywood (top)
N	1	3/4 x 17 1/4 x 27 1/2" cherry plywood (bottom)
O	1	1/4 x 23 1/4 x 27 3/4" cherry plywood (back)
P1	1	3/4 x 17 7/16 x 27 1/2" plywood (shelf)
P2	1	3/16 x 3/4 x 27" cherry (edge band)
Q1	1	3/4 x 5 1/8 x 27" cherry (rail)
Q2	1	3/4 x 1/4 x 27" cherry (rail)
Q3	1	3/4 x 7/8 x 27" cherry (rail)
R1	1	3/4 x 1 x 27" cherry (divider)
R2	1	3/4 x 1 x 26 1/4" cherry (divider)
R3	2	3/4 x 1 x 7 1/4" cherry (divider)
S1	1	3/8 x 16 x 26 7/8" plywood (platform)
S2	1	3/4 x 3 5/8 x 26 7/8" cherry (support)
S3	1	3/4 x 1 1/2 x 26 7/8" cherry (cleat)
T1	1	3/4 x 4 x 30" cherry (molding)
T2	2	3/4 x 4 x 18 3/4" cherry (molding)
U1	1	1/2 x 3/4 x 29 1/2" cherry (molding)
U2	1	1/2 x 3/4 x 12 1/8" cherry (molding)
U3	2	1/2 x 3/4 x 18 1/2" cherry (molding)
U4	1	1/2 x 3/4 x 29 1/2" cherry (molding)
V1	2	3/4 x 5 x 27 5/8" cherry (drawer face)
V2	4	1/2 x 3 3/4 x 25 1/2" plywood (drawer front/back)
V3	4	1/2 x 3 3/4 x 16" plywood (drawer side)
V4	2	1/4 x 15 1/2 x 25 1/2" plywood (drawer bottom)
W1	2	3/4 x 2 3/8 x 11 1/4" cherry (stile)
W2	2	3/4 x 2 3/8 x 22 7/8" cherry (rail)
W3	2	1/8 x 7 1/8 x 23 1/2" acrylic sheet
W4	1	1/4 x 5/16 x 72" cherry (retainer)
X	as reqd.	self-adhesive green felt
Y	2	drawer slides
Z	2	doorknobs
AA	2 pr.	drawer pulls
BB	1	twin-ball catch
CC	3 pr.	hinges
DD	1	lid support
EE	4	locks
FF	5	5/16" carriage bolts
GG	16	5/16 x 2" dowels
HH	3	1 1/2" No. 8 fh screws
II	3	1 1/4" No. 8 rh screws
JJ	4	1 1/4" No. 6 fh screws
KK	10	1" No. 6 drywall screws
LL	46	1/2" No. 6 panhead screws
MM	10	1 1/2" finish nails
NN	40	1" finish nails
OO	4	1" 18-ga. brass escutcheon pins
PP	63	5/8" 19-ga. nails

Misc.: Danish oil finish; semigloss polyurethane; sandpaper; wood glue; masking tape; two 3-light, 20-watt halogen Combilight kits.

Fig. 1 *Use a strip of wood and a pair of blocks to position the guide strip on the case side. Nail the strip to the panel.*

Fig. 2 *To cut the angle on each side panel, slide the guide strip in the miter gauge groove and push the panel through the blade.*

Fig. 3 *Use a router with a straight bit and a parallel fence jig to cut the rabbets and dadoes in the case sides. The jig ensures a precise cut.*

The first step in case construction is to rough cut the plywood into smaller panels that you then cut to finished size on a table saw. The rough cut is made with a circular saw. Be sure to position the plywood so that the surface that will become the outside is facing down.

The finished cuts are made on the table saw. To make the angled cuts on the lower case pieces, take each rough-cut panel and nail a ⅜ x ¾ x 24-in.-long tack strip to it as a guide. The tack strip rides in the saw's miter gauge slot. To position the tack strip accurately, nail a positioning strip to the panel and then butt spacer blocks to it. Butt the tack strip to the blocks and nail it in place (**Fig. 1**). Slide the tack strip into the miter gauge slot, and feed the panel through the blade (**Fig. 2**).

The next step is to cut the dadoes and rabbets in the case panels with a router and straight bit. When cutting the dadoes for the horizontal panels, be sure to use a ²³⁄₃₂-in. straight bit because this is the actual thickness of ¾-in. plywood.

Mark the position of the dadoes on each side panel and make a dado jig to guide the router. Note that the jig uses a pair of guide rails that are spaced apart by a distance equal to the router's width. The guide rails are fastened with crossrails at either end, which are positioned so the panel slides snugly between them. Use the router and the panel to position the rails. To cut the dadoes, clamp the jig in place and run the router through the crossrails at either end (**Fig. 3**). This ensures a clean cut and a dado of the exact width needed.

Next, use a smooth-cutting blade to rip the edge strips. Cut them to finished length, apply glue to them and the panel edges, and then hold them in place with masking tape (**Fig. 4**). Drive a tiny ½-in. 20-ga. brad near the end of each strip to help hold it in place. When the glue has dried, carefully plane the strips flush to the panel's surface, and use a chisel to cut the strip away at the top corner of the lower case (**Fig. 5**).

Before assembling the case, remember to bore holes for the low-voltage lighting in the horizontal panels of the upper

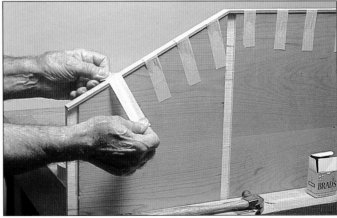

Fig. 4 *The edge banding is glued, and held in place using masking tape. A pair of brads in each band keeps it from slipping.*

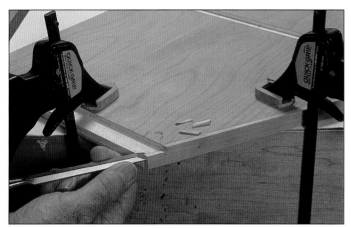

Fig. 5 *The edge banding blocks the rabbet at the top of the lower case. Use a chisel to pare away the edge band at this point.*

case. Also, make the crossrails for the upper case. The upper case sides, crossrails, and horizontal panels are glued and clamped together. Drive screws through the case sides and into the horizontal panels. Do the same with the lower case—in both instances the screws will be hidden by the moldings. Mark, cut, and install the stiffeners in the upper case. Note that the stiffeners are notched behind the top rail and the left one is mortised to clear the hinge leaf. Cut and temporarily install the back panel, and then cut the shallow wiring recess in the top horizontal panel.

Glue, clamp, and screw the lower case sides to the horizontal panels (**Fig. 6**). Attach the beveled upper and lower middle rails with glue and screws. Note that the drawer divider is not permanently installed in the lower case until after the drawers are mounted and the locks are installed in the drawer fronts.

Moldings

The cabinet's dentil molding is made with a router and a ½-in.-dia. straight bit. Bolt a fence to the router's base $\frac{53}{64}$ in. from the bit. Rip the molding stock and joint its edges so they are parallel and the ends square. Make the first dado cut, move the fence into the groove, make the second cut, and continue on in this fashion until the molding is complete (**Fig. 7**). Make several passes on the outer table to cut the thumbnail molding on the dentil's lower edge (**Fig. 8**). Cut the rest of the moldings for the cabinet on the router table, then rip them off on the table saw (**Fig. 9**).

Attach the moldings to the case, beginning with the dentil. Clamp it in place, and make its miters. Bore pilot holes in it for alignment nails. Glue and clamp the molding and drive the nails through it. Attach the side dentil moldings in the same sequence.

To apply the ogee molding above the dentil, follow the same sequence, but don't nail the molding to the case. Attach it to the dentil molding with nails from above (**Fig. 10**).

Fig. 6 *Glue and clamp the lower case sides' other horizontal panels and drive screws into its upper and lower panels.*

Fig. 7 *The dentil molding is cut using a router with a guide strip screwed to its base. The strip rides in the previously cut dado.*

Fig. 8 *Cut the thumbnail molding on the lower edge of the dentil molding using a router table and a cove raised-panel bit.*

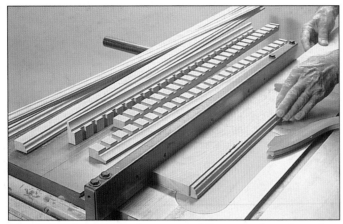

Fig. 9 *Cut the cabinet's ogee moldings on the edge of a wide board, then rip the molding off the board on the table saw.*

Fig. 10 *The ogee molding above the dentil is held in place with glue and nails that are driven into the molding below.*

Supports, Doors, Drawers, and Lighting

Make the butt-rest panel, then bore 2-in.-dia. holes in it, and saw out the waste between them. Trim the cutouts using a router and flush-trimming bit. Run the router against a plywood fence clamped to the panel (**Fig. 11**).

Cut out the barrel rest, bore a series of 1-in.-dia. holes in it, and make a series of cuts tangent to the holes using a sabre saw. Make the pistol platform, cover it with felt, and leave it aside to be installed after the cabinet is finished.

Next, tip and crosscut the door rails and stiles. Mark the centerlines on the pieces, and use a dowel jig to bore holes in either the rails or the stiles. Insert dowel centers in the holes and align the parts using a framing square. Press the parts together (**Fig. 12**), and use a dowel jig to bore holes on the marks (**Fig. 13**). Insert dowels in the holes, then glue and clamp the assembly. Sand the doors using a random-orbit oscillating sander (**Fig. 14**).

Cut the glazing rabbets inside the doors, and cut the molded edges on them. Cut the door's glazing strips, and round the strip ends to fit the rabbets. Buy acrylic glazing cut to size, then sand the glazing's corners to fit the rabbets. Install the glazing after the case is finished.

Now, lay the upper and lower cases on their backs, and temporarily install the door hinges. Lay each door in place over the hinge. Press down on the door so that a small dimple on the hinge marks the hinge's position on the door (**Fig. 15**). Remove the door and lay it on the workbench. Position a hinge on the dents and use the hinge as a template to bore the screw holes.

Rip, crosscut, and joint the drawer parts, then cut the rabbets and grooves in the parts. Also cut a half circle in each drawer box for lock clearance. Glue and clamp the drawer boxes. Make the drawer fronts and bore a lock hole in each.

Install the drawer slides in the case per the manufacturer's directions. Mount each drawer box in its slides and drive four

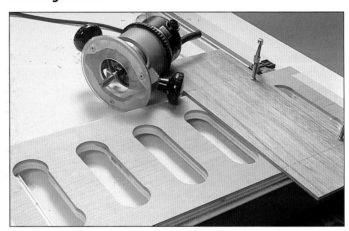

Fig. 11 *Smooth the slots in the butt rest using a flush-trimming bit and a router. Run the router along a fence clamped in place.*

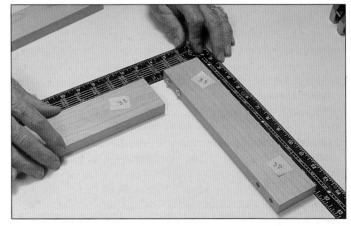

Fig. 12 *With dowel centers inserted in the holes, press the door parts together while aligning them with a framing square.*

Fig. 13 *Position the dowel jig using the marks created by the dowel centers. Then bore the remaining dowel holes with your drill.*

Fig. 14 *Sanding door rails and stiles can often be tricky. Avoid crossgrain sanding by using a random-orbit oscillating sander.*

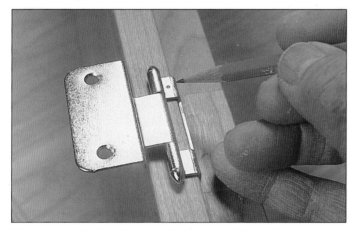

Fig. 15 *Small dimples on the hinges will mark the location of the screw holes when the door is pressed on top of them.*

Fig. 16 *Press each drawer face onto its drawer box. Four screws driven through the box make registration marks on the drawer face.*

drywall screws through each drawer front. Hold the drawer front in front of the drawer boxes and press the drawer front against the drywall screws to mark the drawer front location on the box (**Fig. 16**). Bore pilot holes on the marks, mount the locks on the drawer fronts, and install the drawer fronts.

Mark the location of the lock cam levers on the drawer divider and on the bottom of the pistol compartment shelf. Remove the divider and shelf, and then cut the mortises to accommodate the lock cam lever. Reinstall the divider.

Now stack the cases, clamp them together, and bore holes for the connecting bolts. Bolt the two cases together and carefully finish sand. We applied two coats of cherry danish oil finish, followed by two coats of semigloss polyurethane. The finish was applied on the doors, drawers, and case assembly separately.

Install these components after you are through applying finish on them. The pistol compartment shelf, the glazing in the doors, the gun supports, and the plywood back panels are installed after finishing. The final touch is to install two 3-light, 20-watt halogen Combilight kits, sold at home centers and lighting showrooms.

MATERIAL *Matters*

Faux Cherry
Our project calls for cherry plywood, but you can also get nice results with birch plywood, which is more widely available and usually less expensive. Pick through the stock of birch plywood at the lumberyard, and you're liable to uncover panels with very attractive grain patterns.

The Case For Quality

Show off your skills—and give your tools the home they deserve.

I f you're a mechanic, finding a toolbox is no problem—there are dozens on the market, from huge roll-around shop cases to small metal boxes. Framers, plumbers, and electricians are well served, too, with everything from pickup-truck storage to tool bags and belts.

But if you're a shop-bound woodworker, the picture changes. There's simply little out there that suits the range and variety of hand tools most woodworkers like to have around the shop. For those who refuse to make do with second best there's only one acceptable solution—build your own wooden toolbox designed expressly for a woodworking shop.

*Key*POINTS

TIME
Prep Time . . . . **4 hours**
Shop Time . . . . **10 hours**
Assembly Time . . . . **12 hours**

EFFORT
Skill Level . . . . **intermediate**

COST / BENEFITS
Expense: **moderate**
• Solid cherry frame-and-panel construction, wooden drawer slides, and dovetailed drawers combine to make this piece **a standout in any shop.**

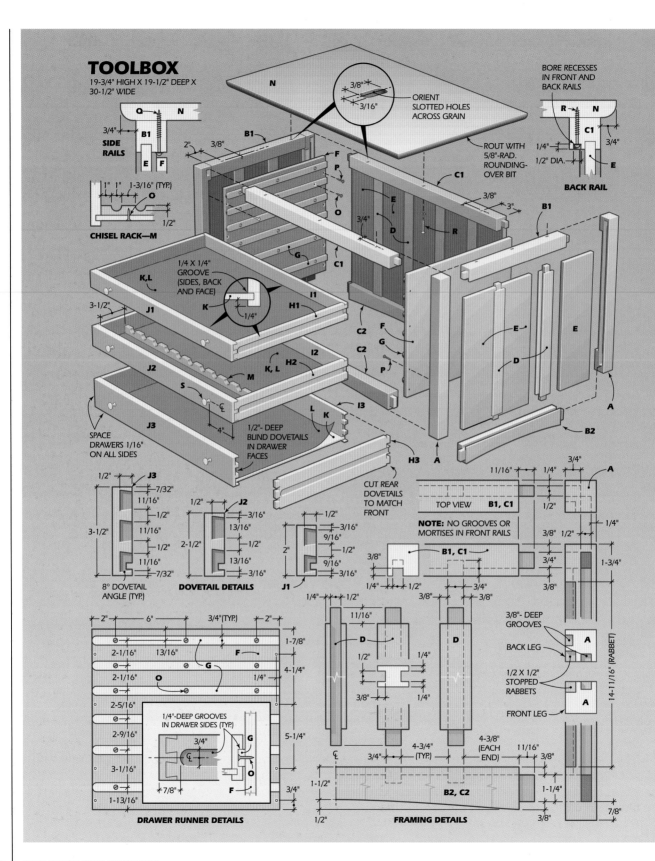

TOOLBOX

19-3/4" HIGH X 19-1/2" DEEP X
30-1/2" WIDE

BORE RECESSES
IN FRONT AND
BACK RAILS

ORIENT
SLOTTED HOLES
ACROSS GRAIN

3/8"
3/16"

3/4"

SIDE
RAILS

B1

E   F

Q   N

1" 1" 1-3/16" (TYP.)

O

1/2"

CHISEL RACK—M

B1

2"   3/8"

B1

F

P

O

G

C1

1/4 X 1/4"
GROOVE
(SIDES, BACK
AND FACE)

K,L

3-1/2"

J1

K

1/4"

H1

I1

J2

K, L   H2

M

I2

S

C

J3

4"

SPACE
DRAWERS 1/16"
ON ALL SIDES

1/2"- DEEP
BLIND DOVETAILS
IN DRAWER
FACES

L   K

I3

H3   A

ROUT WITH
5/8"-RAD.
ROUNDING-
OVER BIT

C1

E

D

R

3/4"

3/8"   3"

C2

F
G
P

C2

C2

B1

R   N
C1
E

1/4"
1/2" DIA.

3/4"

BACK RAIL

B1

E

E

D

A

B2

A

1/2"   J3

7/32"
11/16"
1/2"
11/16"
1/2"
11/16"
7/32"

3-1/2"

8° DOVETAIL
ANGLE (TYP.)

1/2"   J2

3/16"
13/16"
1/2"
13/16"
3/16"

2-1/2"

DOVETAIL DETAILS

1/2"

2"

J1

3/16"
9/16"
1/2"
9/16"
3/16"

1/4"   1/2"

11/16"   1/4"   3/4"   A

TOP VIEW   B1, C1   1/2"   1/4"

NOTE: NO GROOVES OR
MORTISES IN FRONT RAILS

3/8"   1/2"

3/8"

B1, C1   3/4"

1/4"   1/2"   3/4"   3/8"

1-3/4"

CUT REAR
DOVETAILS
TO MATCH
FRONT

2"   6"   3/4"(TYP.)   2"

2-1/16"   13/16"

F

G

O

2-1/16"

2-5/16"

2-9/16"

3-1/16"

1-13/16"

1/4"-DEEP GROOVES
IN DRAWER SIDES (TYP.)

3/4"

G

C

O

F

7/8"

DRAWER RUNNER DETAILS

1-7/8"

4-1/4"

1/4"

5-1/4"

3/4"

11/16"

D

1/2"

3/8"

1/4"

1/4"

D

4-3/4"
(TYP.)

4-3/8"
(EACH
END)

3/4"

C

1-1/2"

1/2"

B2, C2

FRAMING DETAILS

3/8"   3/4"

3/8"- DEEP
GROOVES

BACK LEG

1/2 X 1/2"
STOPPED
RABBETS

FRONT LEG

A

A

A

11/16"   3/8"

1-1/4"

7/8"

14-11/16" (RABBET)

Of course, building a case for your hand tools is more than a practical solution to a storage problem. It's an opportunity to fine-tune and show off your woodworking skills. Our design is based on an early 20th century Arts & Crafts theme and features traditional frame-and-panel construction and hand-dovetailed drawers.

Building the Case

Joint and rip the leg blanks from 1½-in.-thick cherry stock. Then crosscut each piece several inches longer than the finished dimension. Next, cut the rail and mullion blanks in the same way. Cut ½-in.-thick cherry stock to size for the toolbox panels.

Lay out the mortises in the leg blanks so that there's extra waste stock extended beyond them at the ends. To ensure uniform positioning, clamp the pieces together and use a square to mark across them. Then lay out the mullion mortises in the rails.

Set up a plunge router with a ½-in.-dia. spiral up-cutting bit and edge guide, and rout most of the waste from each mortise (**Fig. 1**). Note that the extra length at the ends of each blank supports the router base for these cuts. Then rout the mortises in the top and bottom rails. After routing, the mortises will have round ends. Square all mortise ends with a sharp chisel (**Fig. 2**). Readjust the router bit depth and cut the panel grooves in the legs, rails, and mullions (**Fig. 3**). Then lay out and rout the stopped rabbets for the plywood inner sides, and square the rabbet ends.

Using a dado blade in the table saw, cut the tenons on the rail and mullion ends. First, set the blade height to cut both sides of the centered mullion tenons and the outside faces of the off-center rail tenons. Then adjust the blade height to cut the inside of the rail tenons (**Fig. 4**). Finally, adjust the blade height once more to cut the shoulders as shown in the drawing.

Lay out the arched profile on each bottom rail and use a band saw or sabre saw to make the curved cuts. Keep the saw kerf on the waste side of the layout line. When the rails are cut to shape, smooth the rough-sawn surfaces with a spokeshave, scraper, and sandpaper.

Bore holes through the top rails for securing the toolbox top. Note that each hole is elongated to allow the top to expand and contract with the change in seasons. Bore two holes side by side for each screw. Then use a ⅛-in. chisel to connect the holes. Counterbore the holes in the front and

Fig. 1 *Use a plunge router with an edge guide to cut the mortises. Extra length at each end of the workpiece supports the router.*

Materials List

Key	No.	Size and description (use)
A	4	1½ x 1½ x 18¹⁵⁄₁₆" cherry (leg)
B1	2	1½ x 1½ x 16³⁄₈" cherry (top side rail)
B2	2	1½ x 2 x 16³⁄₈" cherry (bottom side rail)
C1	2	1½ x 1½ x 27³⁄₈" cherry (top rear rail)
C2	2	1½ x 2 x 27³⁄₈" cherry (bottom rear rail)
D	8	1 x 1½ x 16⁵⁄₁₆" cherry (mullion)
E	11	½ x 4⅝ x 15¹¹⁄₁₆" cherry (panel)
F	2	½ x 14¹¹⁄₁₆ x 16" plywood (inner side)
G	12	⁵⁄₁₆ x ¾ x 16" cherry (runner)
H1	6	½ x 2 x 16⁹⁄₁₆" maple (drawer side)
H2	4	½ x 2½ x 16⁹⁄₁₆" maple (drawer side)
H3	2	½ x 3½ x 16⁹⁄₁₆" maple (drawer side)
I1	3	½ x 2 x 25⅞" maple (drawer back)
I2	2	½ x 2½ x 25⅞" maple (drawer back)
I3	1	½ x 3½ x 25⅞" maple (drawer back)
J1	3	¹³⁄₁₆ x 2 x 25⅞" cherry (drawer front)
J2	2	¹³⁄₁₆ x 2½ x 25⅞" cherry (drawer front)
J3	1	¹³⁄₁₆ x 3½ x 25⅞" cherry (drawer front)
K	6	¼ x 16¹⁄₁₆ x 25⅜" plywood (drawer bottom)
L	6	15⁹⁄₁₆ x 24⅞" felt (liner)
M	1	½ x ⅞ x 24⅞" maple (rack)
N	1	¹³⁄₁₆ x 19½ x 30½" cherry (top)
O	39	¾" No. 6 fh wood screws
P	16	1" No. 6 fh wood screws
Q	6	2" No. 8 rh wood screws and washers
R	6	1¾" No. 8 rh wood screws and washers
S	12	drawer pulls

Misc.: Sandpaper; glue; paste wax; Waterlox Original Sealer/Finish.

Fig. 2 *After removing most of the waste with the router, use a sharp chisel to square the ends of the mortises in both legs and rails.*

Fig. 3 *Reset the router cutting depth for the panel grooves in the legs and rails. Use the same setup for the grooves along the mullion edges.*

TOOL*Care*

Keep the Edge

Storing hand tools is different than storing power tools. For one thing, hand tools have cutting edges. A plane is stored with the cutter in place, but a drill is rarely stored with the bit installed. With that in mind, decide what method works best for storing your hand tools. But no matter what, remember that the tool's cutting edge has to be protected so that it isn't dulled when you place the tool in the box or remove it.

Fig. 4 *Cut the tenons on the rail ends using a dado blade in the table saw. Note that the rail tenons are not centered.*

Fig. 5 *Join the mullions to the lower back rail. Spread glue on the mortise-and-tenon joints and install the panels. Then add the top rail and clamp.*

Fig. 6 *After installing the inner case sides, lay out the drawer guide locations and install the guides with ³⁄₄-in. No. 6 screws.*

back rails so the screw heads won't interfere with the operation of the top drawer.

Sand the panels before assembling the sides and back. Apply glue to the mortise-and-tenon joints of the back assembly, taking care not to get glue in the panel grooves.

Install the panels and mullions in the lower rail (**Fig. 5**), and then position the top rail and use clamps to pull the joints tight. After assembling the sides in the same way, join the legs to the side-rail ends. When the glue has set, join the side assemblies to the front and back rails.

Cut the plywood inner sides to size, bore and countersink screw holes, and screw the inner sides to the legs. Lay out the locations of the drawer guide strips, and cut the strips to size. We found the easiest way to make these strips is to first rout a bull-nose profile along the end of a wide board. Then rip the strips from the board, cut them to length, and screw them in place (**Fig. 6**).

Drawer Construction

Cut the ½-in.-thick maple drawer sides and backs to finished size and use ¹³⁄₁₆-in. cherry for the faces. Note that blind dovetails join the sides to the face and through dovetails join the sides to the back. The tail patterns, though, are the same at the front and the back. Lay out the dovetails on the drawer sides with an adjustable bevel and marking gauge. Use a sharp knife to scribe the lines.

To cut the tails, first make the crossgrain cuts at the top and bottom edges of the side. Keep the saw kerf about ¹⁄₃₂ in. on the waste side of the line. Then hold the piece upright in your vise and saw the sides of each dovetail (**Fig. 7**).

With the tails defined by saw cuts, remove the waste between them by alternating vertical and horizontal cuts with a chisel (**Fig. 8**). Stay about ¹⁄₃₂ in. from the bottom dovetail line until the waste is removed. Cut precisely along the layout lines, taking care to keep the cuts square to the board's face.

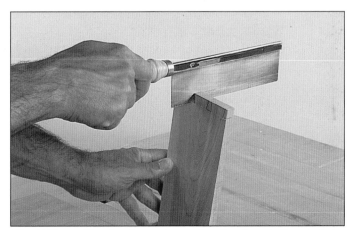

Fig. 7 *Use a fine backsaw to make the dovetail cuts in the ends of the drawer sides. Stay about* ¹⁄₃₂ *in. on the waste side of the line.*

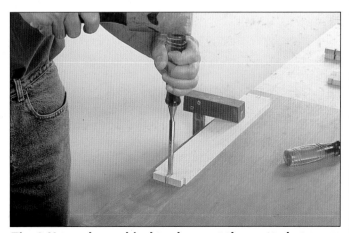

Fig. 8 *Use a sharp chisel to chop out the waste between the tails. Cut halfway through, then turn the piece over to finish the job.*

To lay out the pins, first mark the mating pieces so they won't get mixed up during assembly. Use a marking gauge to scribe guide lines across the ends and inside faces of the drawer fronts (**Fig. 9**) and along both inside and outside faces of the drawer backs. With a drawer front held vertically, position the mating side over it and use a sharp knife to scribe the outline of the tails (**Fig. 10**). Follow the same technique for each joint.

To cut the pins on the drawer backs, use the same cutting techniques used for the tails.

However, you'll want to use a different technique for the drawer fronts. First, begin by making sharply angled cuts to define the blind pins (**Fig. 11**). Then alternate vertical and horizontal chisel cuts to chop out the waste (**Fig. 12**). Once again, you'll want to keep about ½ in. from the lines. Finish by carefully paring, making sure to check the fit of the joint as you go along.

Use a dado blade to cut the ¼-in. groove in the drawer parts that house each drawer bottom (**Fig. 13**).

Cut the bottom panels to size and sand the inside surfaces of the drawer parts. Be sure to avoid sanding the dovetail joint surfaces.

Use a small brush to spread glue on each dovetail joint for one drawer. Join the back and front to one side, then slide the bottom panel into its groove. Position the opposite side, clamp, and check that the drawer is square.

When the glue has set on all drawers, plane or sand the outer surfaces until smooth. Use a ¾-in.-dia. straight bit in the router table to cut grooves in the drawer sides for the guide strips (**Fig. 14**).

Test the fit of each drawer in the case. If a drawer is too tight, sand the guides until it slides smoothly. If the drawer is too loose, shim the guide strips with paper or veneer to tighten the fit.

Fig. 9 *Use a marking gauge to scribe guide lines across the drawer-front ends. The lines indicate the ends of the drawer-side dovetails.*

Fig. 10 *Position the drawer side to trace the outline of the dovetails on the end of the drawer front. Use a sharp knife to trace the profile.*

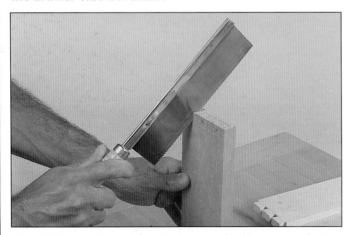

Fig. 11 *To start blind front pins, angle the saw so that the cut extends diagonally across the joint. Stay about ¹/₃₂ in. to waste side of line.*

Fig. 12 *Alternate horizontal and vertical cuts to remove the waste in the drawer-front pins. Test the fit often to achieve a tight joint.*

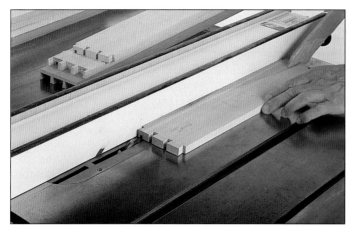

Fig. 13 *Use a dado blade in the table saw to cut ¼-in. grooves on the inside of the drawer parts for the drawer-bottom panels.*

Fig. 14 *Use a straight bit in the router table to cut the guide-strip grooves in the drawer sides. A stop block limits the cut.*

Glue up stock to form the toolbox top panel, and cut it to size. Use a ⅜-in.-rad. rounding-over bit for the profile along the bottom edge. To attach the top, first invert it on a padded surface. Then temporarily remove the inner case sides and position the case on the top. Bore pilot holes into the top and install the screws.

Finishing Touches

After sanding, we applied three coats of Waterlox Original Sealer/Finish. To promote easy sliding, apply paste wax to the drawer guide strips and the grooves in the drawer sides.

We also lined the drawers with heavy pool-table felt. Use a utility knife to cut the felt to size and then simply lay each piece in a drawer bottom. To make a chisel rack, bore a series of 1-in. holes in a ½-in.-thick strip of maple. Rip the strip through the center of the holes (**Fig. 15**) and cut it to fit inside one of the drawers.

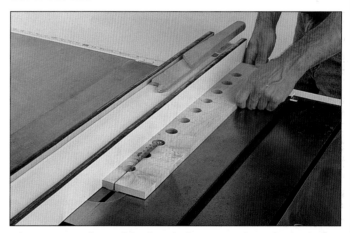

Fig. 15 *To make a chisel rack, bore a series of 1-in. holes in ½-in. maple. Then rip the strip in half and secure it to the drawer bottom.*

SKILL*Builder*

The Ultimate Edge
Ever wonder how experienced woodworkers manage to produce a razor-sharp edge on their chisels and hand plane cutters? There are lots of little tricks to sharpening, and lots of different ways to do it properly. Of course, no one single way is correct, so we offer a few suggestions.

Sharpening actually removes a tiny layer of steel. The last little bit that comes off the chisel or plane cutter is shaped like a piece of wire. In fact, it's called the wire edge. To remove it properly, you must pull it off the edge. On a sharpening stone, that means the last stroke is one in which you pull the tool toward you. With chisels and plane irons, place the back against the stone and pull the tool across the edge of the stone.

To do this on a buffing wheel, place the tool so the wheel is turning away from the tool's edge. That is, hold the tool so its edge is near the bottom of the wheel and the cutting edge is facing the back of the wheel. If you hold the tool with the wheel turning into the cutting edge, you'll dull the tool and ruin the buffing wheel.

Picture Credits

LINCOLN'S CHEST (Pg. 10):
Lead Photo: William Lasky;
Illustration: Eugene Thompson;
Step Photos: William Lasky.

CHERRY JUBILEE (Pg. 16):
Lead Photo: Rosario Capotosto;
Illustration: Eugene Thompson;
Step Photos: Rosario Capotosto.

VIEWING HABITS (Pg. 22):
Lead Photo: J.R. Rost;
Illustration: Eugene Thompson;
Step Photos: Rosario Capotosto.

FIELD OF DREAMS (Pg. 32):
Lead Photo: Neal Barrett;
Illustration: Eugene Thompson;
Step Photos: Neal Barrett.

CLEAN ROOM (Pg. 40):
Lead Photo: Neal Barrett;
Illustration: Eugene Thompson;
Step Photos: Neal Barrett.

STAY TUNED (Pg. 46):
Lead Photo: Neal Barrett;
Illustration: Eugene Thompson;
Step Photos: Neal Barrett.

TOP DRAWER (Pg. 54):
Lead Photo: Neal Barrett;
Illustration: Eugene Thompson;
Step Photos: Neal Barrett.

CHILD'S PLAY (Pg. 62):
Lead Photo: J.R. Rost;
Illustration: Eugene Thompson;
Step Photos: Rosario Capotosto.

WARMING TREND (Pg. 68):
Lead Photo: J.R. Rost;
Illustration: Eugene Thompson;
Step Photos: Neal Barrett.

DRESSED UP (Pg. 76):
Lead Photo: Neal Barrett;
Illustration: Eugene Thompson;
Step Photos: Neal Barrett.

GENTLEMAN'S WARDROBE (Pg. 84):
Lead Photo: J.R. Rost;
Illustration: Eugene Thompson;
Step Photos: Neal Barrett.

A PLACE FOR EVERYTHING (Pg. 92):
Lead Photo: J.R. Rost;
Illustration: Eugene Thompson;
Step Photos: Neal Barrett.

CLOSET CONTROL (Pg. 100):
Lead Photo: J.R. Rost;
Illustration: Eugene Thompson;
Step Photos: Neal Barrett.

BOOK KEEPER (Pg. 110):
Lead Photo: J.R. Rost;
Illustration: Eugene Thompson;
Step Photos: Neal Barrett.

CYBER SECRETARY (Pg. 118):
Lead Photo: Neal Barrett;
Illustration: Eugene Thompson;
Step Photos: Neal Barrett.

OPEN FOR VIEWING (Pg. 128):
Lead Photo: Neal Barrett;
Illustration: Eugene Thompson;
Step Photos: Neal Barrett.

BOOKWORM'S BOOKCASE (Pg. 136):
Lead Photo: John Griebsch;
Illustration: Eugene Thompson;
Step Photos: Neal Barrett.

GRAND DISPLAY (Pg. 144):
Lead Photo: Neal Barrett;
Illustration: Eugene Thompson;
Step Photos: Neal Barrett.

DESK OF DISTINCTION (Pg. 152):
Lead Photo: Neal Barrett;
Illustration: Eugene Thompson;
Step Photos: Neal Barrett.

SURROUND SOUND (Pg. 162):
Lead Photo: Neal Barrett;
Illustration: Eugene Thompson;
Step Photos: Neal Barrett.

SHELF LIFE (Pg. 170):
Lead Photo: John Griebsch;
Illustration: Eugene Thompson;
Step Photos: Neal Barrett.

OFFICE SPACE (Pg. 178):
Lead Photo: John Griebsch;
Illustration: Eugene Thompson;
Step Photos: Neal Barrett.

COMPUTER CLASS (Pg. 188):
Lead Photo: John Griebsch;
Illustration: Eugene Thompson;
Step Photos: Neal Barrett.

WALL OF FAME (Pg. 194):
Lead Photo: John Griebsch;
Illustration: Eugene Thompson;
Step Photos: Neal Barrett.

RETURN OF A CLASSIC (Pg. 204):
Lead Photo: J.R. Rost;
Illustration: Eugene Thompson;
Step Photos: Neal Barrett.

NEATNESS COUNTS (Pg. 214):
Lead Photo: J.R. Rost;
Illustration: Eugene Thompson;
Step Photos: Rosario Capotosto.

BREAD WINNER (Pg. 220):
Lead Photo: J.R. Rost;
Illustration: Eugene Thompson;
Step Photos: Neal Barrett.

VANITY FAIR (Pg. 228):
Lead Photo: Rosario Capotosto;
Illustration: Eugene Thompson;
Step Photos: Rosario Capotosto.

TOP GUN (Pg. 236):
Lead Photo: Brian Kosoff;
Illustration: Eugene Thompson;
Step Photos: Rosario Capotosto.

THE CASE FOR QUALITY (Pg. 244):
Lead Photo: Neal Barrett;
Illustration: Eugene Thompson;
Step Photos: Neal Barrett.

Conversion Chart

US STANDARD TO METRIC

US Standard = Metric

Inches x 2.54	=	centimeters
Feet x 30.48	=	centimeters
Yards x .9144	=	meters
Sq. in. x 6.452	=	square cm
Sq. ft. x 929	=	square cm
Sq. yd. x 8361	=	square cm
Ounce x 28.35	=	gram
Pound x .45	=	kilogram

Common Approx. Conversions

$^3/_8$ in.	=	1 cm
1 in.	=	2.5 cm
2 in.	=	5 cm
$2^1/_2$ in.	=	6.5 cm
1 ft.	=	30 cm

Metric Conversion Tables

Metric Measurement	Imperial Equivalent	Imperial Measurement	Metric Equivalent
1mm	$^1/_{32}$ in.	$^1/_8$ in.	3.2mm
2mm	$^1/_{16}$ in.	$^1/_4$ in.	6.4mm
3mm	$^1/_8$ in.	$^3/_8$ in.	9.5mm
6mm	$^1/_4$ in.	$^1/_2$ in.	13mm
7mm	$^9/_{32}$ in. ($^1/_4$")	$^5/_8$ in.	16mm
10mm	$^{13}/_{32}$ in. ($^3/_8$")	$^3/_4$ in.	19mm
2cm (20mm)	$^3/_4$ in.	$^7/_8$ in.	2.2cm
3cm	$1^3/_{16}$ in.	1 in.	2.5cm
4cm	$1^9/_{16}$ in.	$1^1/_4$ in.	3.2cm
5cm	2 in.	$1^1/_2$ in.	3.8cm
6cm	$2^3/_8$ in.	$1^3/_4$ in.	4.4cm
7cm	$2^3/_4$ in.	2 in.	5.1cm
8cm	$3^1/_8$ in.	$2^1/_4$ in.	5.7cm
9cm	$3^1/_2$ in.	$2^1/_2$ in.	6.4cm
10cm	$3^{15}/_{16}$ in. (4")	$2^3/_4$ in.	7.0cm
15cm	$5^7/_8$ in.	3 in.	7.6cm
20cm	$7^7/_8$ in.	$3^1/_4$ in.	8.3cm
25cm	$9^{13}/_{16}$ in.	$3^1/_2$ in.	8.9cm
30cm	$11^{13}/_{16}$ in.	$3^3/_4$ in.	9.5cm
35cm	$13^3/_4$ in.	4 in.	10.2cm
40cm	$15^3/_4$ in.	$4^1/_2$ in.	11.4cm
42cm	$16^1/_2$ in.	5 in.	12.7cm

Index